PHOTOGRAPHING
IN THE STUDIO

PHOTOGRAPHING
IN THE STUDIO

Gary Kolb
Southern Illinois University

Photographic Illustrations by Daniel Overturf
Southern Illinois University

WCB Brown & Benchmark
P U B L I S H E R S

Madison, Wisconsin•Dubuque, Iowa•Indianapolis, Indiana
Melbourne, Australia•Oxford, England

Book Team

Editor *Kathleen Nietzke Wolkoff*
Developmental Editor *Sue Pulvermacher-Alt/Susan J. McCormick*
Photo Editor *Judi L. David*
Visuals/Design Developmental Consultant *Marilyn A. Phelps*
Visuals/Design Freelance Specialist *Mary L. Christianson*
Publishing Services Specialist *Sherry Padden*
Marketing Manager *Steven Yetter*
Advertising Manager *Jodi Rymer*

Brown & Benchmark

A Division of Wm. C. Brown Communications, Inc.

Vice President and General Manager *Thomas E. Doran*
Editor in Chief *Edgar J. Laube*
Executive Editor *Ed Bartell*
Executive Editor *Stan Stoga*
National Sales Manager *Eric Ziegler*
Director of CourseResource *Kathy Law Laube*
Director of CourseSystems *Chris Rogers*
Director of Marketing *Sue Simon*
Director of Production *Vickie Putman Caughron*
Imaging Group Manager *Chuck Carpenter*
Manager of Visuals and Design *Faye M. Schilling*
Design Manager *Jac Tilton*
Art Manager *Janice Roerig*
Permissions/Records Manager *Connie Allendorf*

Wm. C. Brown Communications, Inc.

President and Chief Executive Officer *G. Franklin Lewis*
Corporate Vice President, President of WCB Manufacturing *Roger Meyer*
Vice President and Chief Financial Officer *Robert Chesterman*

Cover photo *Environmental Altarpiece*, © Jim White Photography–
Chicago

Illustrations by *Gary Kolb*

Interior and cover design by *Sailer & Cook Creative Services*

A Times Mirror Company

Library of Congress Catalog Card Number: 92–70317

ISBN 0-697-13189-0

Printed in the United States of America by Wm. C. Brown Communications, Inc.,
2460 Kerper Boulevard, Dubuque, IA 52001

10 9 8 7 6 5 4 3 2 1

For
Georgia Wessel and Annie Clark
Illumination and Innocence

CONTENTS

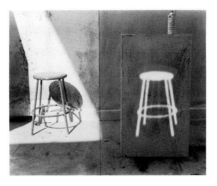

[part]

②

LIGHTING IN PRACTICE

[part]

③

THE STUDIO ENVIRONMENT

[part]

④

EXTENSIONS
TOOLS, TECHNIQUES, AND TECHNOLOGIES

PREFACE

The diversity of contemporary photographic practice provides many possibilities and few limitations. For the purposes of this text I would begin with the word "control" and then add "construction." These words are not exclusive to photographic techniques but also refer to meaning. Both image and meaning are crafted. One unique aspect of most studio photography is that in the studio the photographer builds an image from a knowledge of potentials rather than edits it from a world of infinite possibilities. In the world, photographers edit from a reality of continuous space and time; in the studio, photographers contrive both space and time. Starting with an emptiness, the studio photographer constructs a controlled picture embodying many possibilities for both visualization and meaning.

The need for a comprehensive book dealing with photographing in the studio environment became clear to me while searching for a text for my class, Introduction to the Studio, taught in the Department of Cinema and Photography at Southern Illinois University at Carbondale. I discovered many books dealing with parts of the course content, but none were broad enough for my application. As the course was refined and solidified, the structure detailed in extensive notes, and the topical areas integrated to form a comprehensive whole, I developed a uniquely broad perspective on the education of studio photographers.

I have brought this perspective to bear in this work. It is a text designed to be comprehensive and accessible. It is an instructional text and a reference text. It deals not only with "how to" but also with the more important question of "why to". The book explores basic visual and technical tools used in studio photography and forays into the realms of creativity, ideas, and expressive communication. The scope of the book is intentionally broad. I have a penchant for comprehensive views. We can only make truly creative decisions if we understand systems rather than individual components. This is as true of photography as it is of life: specific knowledge is a stepping stone to general principles. The ability of the mind to create a synthesis of diverse ideas and shape a new whole is the hallmark of creative activity.

There is an integrated approach carried throughout this work. It is founded on the belief that all visual images share certain traits and are based in material realities with physical limits and potentials. As important, is an awareness of the culturally established symbolic content that we can use creatively to communicate with our images. Questions relating to form, intent, authorship, and context are critical in establishing the range of possible meanings of an image; and, after all, meaning is important.

This book provides the reader with some important basic tools and techniques for constructing meaning. Like vocabulary, these tools can be used in a mundane or a creative manner; they can be used responsibly or with little regard for the effect of their communicative power to shape our world. I never question the validity of my students' images, but I do force them to accept responsibility for the statements their work contains. This book is about exercising control over statement—visually, technically, and meaningfully. Images don't just happen, they are made. Make them with thought and integrity.

Acknowledgments

I would like to thank a number of people whose time, energy, and patience have contributed significantly to the completion of this book. First, and foremost, to my family—Georgia Wessel and Annie Clark—thank you for bearing with my obsession! Your support has meant a great deal to me throughout this endeavor. To all of the photographers and others who have generously contributed their images for use in the text, I offer a heartfelt thank you. Your belief in the value of education and your willingness to share your work and observations will be an invaluable contribution to the future of our medium. It is in the students that that future lies, and I would especially like to thank my current and former students who have given me more than they will ever know. Your energy, your hard work, your pursuit of excellence, and your eagerness to challenge yourselves make teaching worthwhile. I would like to give a very special thanks to Daniel Overturf who produced the instructional photographic illustrations for the text. You came into the project at a pivotal point and your diligence, skill, and many hours of work made the completion of the illustrations a reality. Without you, Dan, the book would still be in production! Also contributing to the production of the illustrations through the donation of materials and the loan of equipment were the Polaroid Corporation, Paul C. Buff, Inc. (White Lightning), Tekno, Inc. (Balcar), Victor Hasselblad, Inc., and B & L Photo. Thank you for your critical support. Lastly I would like to thank the editorial staff at Brown & Benchmark—especially Sue Alt and Marc Morehouse—for their belief in the project and their patience in seeing it through with me.

Reviewers

C. L. Terry Gips
University of Maryland

Michael Peven
University of Arkansas

John Rocco
Lansing Community College

Contributing Photographers

Gary Abatelli
Ruth Bernhard
Laura Bogue
Martin Brief
Bruce Charlesworth
Cedric Chatterley
Ken Coplan
Keith Cotton
Eileen Cowin
Robert Cumming
Michael Datoli
John Divola
Paul Elledge
Bob Forrest
Al Francekevich
Susan Friedman
Greg Gillis
George Grigus
Todd Haiman
Marc Hauser
Christopher Hawker
David Haxton
Guy Hurka
Aaron Jones
Dave Jordano
Barbara Karant
Barbara Kasten
Gary Kolb
Nick Koudis
William Larson
David Levinthal
Giorgio Majno
Paul Marshall
Raymond Meier
Neil Molinaro
Kevin Mooney
R. J. Muna
Patrick Nagatani
Steve Nozicka
Scott Olsen
Daniel Overturf
Leasha Overturf
Olivia Parker
Cheryl Pendleton
Ray Perkins
Ken Perrin
Thomas Porett
Charles Purvis
Scott Raffe
John Reuter
Uldis Saule
Rob Shields
Charles Shotwell
Sandy Skoglund
Kip Swehla
Joyce Tenneson
Carl Toth
Andree Tracey
Janis Tracy
Arthur Tress
Joe Vitone
Jeff Wall
James Welling
Glen Wexler
Jim White
James Wojcik
Joe Ziolkowski

Organizations Contributing Photographs

The Backdrop Solution—Sy Sajid
Jayne H. Baum Gallery
Calumet Photographic
Denny Mfg. Co.
Duggal Color Projects
Laurence Miller Gallery

PHOTOGRAPHING
IN THE STUDIO

Jim White Photography, Chicago

VISUAL PERCEPTION AND PHOTOGRAPHS

Where does the photographic image originate? The obvious answer might be "in the world." This is not a trick question, but rather a fundamental concern for both image makers and image viewers. The answer to this question is multifaceted, complex in nature, and worth exploration. The principles that one discovers in this search are definitive of the nature of photographic communication. The lessons one learns can be directly applied to crafting powerful photographs. Finally, the search itself can lead one to a new understanding of the possibilities and the limitations of photography. The search must focus both outward and inward. The origin of the photographic image lies as much within the inner world of the photographer as it does in the outer world of physical reality.

Photography is a complex system for producing two-dimensional representations of subjects in the outer world. This is, of course, not a complete definition of the medium;

however, it provides a working platform for beginning a search into the nature of photography as an image-forming system. The larger goal of this search is to discover the complex relationship between two-dimensional representational images, visual perception, and the communication of meaning.

One must begin somewhere. The study of the structure and functioning of the human visual system provides a base which leads one into related areas that, taken together, comprise the search to understanding visual perception and how it relates to photography. Indeed, it is the visual system that provides the link between the photographic image and its meaning. The visual system apprehends, decodes, and restructures two-dimensional images and thus begins the construction of meaning. This is a physical and psychological process that is complex in nature. It has been the focus of scientific, philosophical, and artistic dialogue for hundreds of years, yet

it is still not completely understood. This chapter will begin with a summary of related concepts from diverse fields regarding the visual process. It will then move toward developing a working system for constructing and decoding visual imagery.

The Visual System

The human visual system, like photographic systems, is structured to respond to incoming energy. This energy enters the system in the form of visible light—either radiant light from a direct source or reflected light from surfaces in the environment. Most photographic systems are also designed to respond to visible light. Light enters the visual system through the optical structures of the eye and normally enters photographic systems through the optical structures of a camera. In the eye, light is focused upon the retina where the stimulation of cells forms nerve impulses that are transmitted to the brain. In the camera, light is focused upon film where a latent image is formed for later development. There would seem to be a striking correspondence between the visual system and photographic systems, but the analogy breaks down rather rapidly when subjected to critical scrutiny.

The visual process could be summarized as follows: light from a source travels through a medium and either enters the eye directly or falls upon a surface in the world; surfaces reflect light to the eye; that light is focused upon the retina where various cells respond by forming nerve impulses that are transmitted along the optic nerve to the brain; the brain processes these impulses and synthesizes the data into potentially meaningful structures; identification, integration, meaning, and response follow. This complex of processes forms what is commonly known as visual perception.

The photographic process could likewise be summarized as follows: light from a source travels through a medium and either enters the lens directly or falls upon a surface in the world; surfaces reflect light to the lens; that light is then focused upon film where a latent image is formed through the absorption of energy by the film emulsion; this latent image is later developed and processed into a photographic print or transparency; identification, integration, meaning, and response are not part of the photographic system. The photograph is essentially coded data, a representation of the world that obeys specific physical and optical rules. By itself it is meaningless—only the act of perception can lend meaning to the photograph. This act of perception constitutes the basic

and fundamental difference between photography and visual perception.

The other differences are myriad and specific to the manner in which each system functions. Film accumulates light in either multiple or extended exposures; the retina does not. The camera can freeze motion; the eye cannot. The photograph can be rendered in shades of gray; the eye sees in color. Photography is a process of selection and separation; it is inherently interruptive of the continuity of experience. Vision is a process of ongoing integration; it is inherently connected with and reinforces the continuity of experience. Photographs consist of only visual information. The visual system is constantly supplemented and influenced by information from the other senses. Finally, cameras never learn. They have fixed capabilities. The visual system is linked directly to the brain and is constantly in a state of flux, expansion, and learning. The list could continue for many pages.

The visual system does have limitations. The eye, like film, has threshold levels that must be attained before a stimulus is apprehended; thus, light levels that are too low will not support the visual process. The level of detail that can be resolved by the eye is limited. Also, the ability of the brain to maintain accurate memory images of color is quite poor. During the past century many experiments within the fields of physiology and psychology have attempted to identify the capabilities, limitations, and specific functions of the visual system. The results of these experiments form a body of discourse in which contemporary theories of the visual process are rooted.

Gestalt Psychology

The previous discussion summarized the physical process that underlies visual perception. Now attention will turn to the psychological process that helps construct visual images. Much of the research that has been conducted into visual perception has taken place in the field of Gestalt psychology. By definition, Gestalt is not derived from or comprised of component parts; it is rather a complete and unanalyzable wholeness. Gestalt is experience in all of its integrated complexity. Gestalt psychologists have investigated the identification of visual stimuli and the foundation of perceptual knowledge.

Gestalt psychology deals primarily with the organization of information into meaningful wholes. Its basic principle is stated simply in what has become a modern cliché, "The whole is greater than the sum of its parts." The principles of Gestalt psychology can be applied to all five senses as well as to complex mental processes. Since its introduction, Gestalt psychology has generated a great deal of research in the area of visual perception. A set of guiding principles has been developed from Gestalt psychology that seems to apply to human visual perception on a cross-cultural level. Given the same physical base, perceptual capacities of human beings seem to follow predictable tendencies. Though some evidence suggests that visual perception is influenced by cultural and environmental factors, it is widely held that basic eye/brain perceptual principles govern the visual process. These principles are discoverable and measurable, and they can be used in constructing visual images or environments to facilitate or confuse coherent visual experience.

The base processes of perception are rooted in the act of discrimination. The comparing and contrasting of various discrete elements form the sensory textures that are necessary for perception to function. When the senses are exposed to a totally homogeneous visual field, tactile surface, sound, taste, or scent, they are unable to detect differences and cease to provide meaningful input. The constant stimulation of the same sensory cells with a continuous level of input fatigues the cells and results in their ceasing to produce nerve impulses. The senses cease to exist in any meaningful way. Sensory deprivation has long been used as a means of shutting off the outer, physical world in order to explore the inner world. Examples of this range from the control of the body and senses through meditation by Hindu Yogis to physio/psychological experiments with isolation tanks done by Dr. John C. Lilly and other twentieth century scientists.

At first this necessity for differentiation may seem antithetical to the basic synthesis of wholes postulated by Gestalt psychology. However, it is the existence of discrete elements and the ability to identify, order, and group them that make the synthesis of larger, meaningful wholes possible. Individual stimuli and the comparative nature of the senses provide building blocks that are processed and linked to form higher concepts and structures just as words are linked to form sentences, paragraphs, and books. The individual perceived elements are meaningful, but they are subordinate to the higher concepts communicated by the whole. When we read a novel, it is primarily the story we remember, not the individual words. Only upon close study and examination is the novel dissected to its component words—each element analyzed individually. The same can be said about human sense perceptions. Humans can direct them into a detailed deconstruction of experience, but they normally function to synthesize not analyze.

Figure and Ground

In *Perception and Photography* Richard Zakia states, "The first step in perception is distinguishing figure from ground." Figure is the object of attention; ground is everything else in the perceptual field. As mentioned previously, this statement applies to all of the senses. It may denote a simple one-to-one relationship or a complex system of interrelated sensations. A lone, small, black square on a large, white canvas would provide a simple visual figure-ground relationship. Braille is an example of a high-level tactile figure-ground system for communication of complex ideas. An orchestra can become the ground for the auditory figure of a solo instrument. The figure-ground relationship can take many forms.

Visual figure-ground relationships have been the focus of much research. The perception of figure against ground is a basic building block of visual imagery. A strong figure-ground relationship is one in which the figure is easily separated from the ground; it is perceived among its surroundings. This strong relationship strengthens the discriminatory abilities of the perceptual system and encourages clear communication. A weak figure-ground relationship will confuse perception and hinder communication.

Two basic strategies in the construction of two-dimensional visual imagery are identifiable: figure-ground strategies and field strategies. Though these strategies can overlap, they are each characterized by distinct organizational qualities. A figure-ground image is one in which certain objects, points, or spaces in the image are of greater importance than, and are distinguishable from, the rest of the image. The rest of the image serves as a supporting fabric. The viewer perceives a separate figure within the ground of the image (figure 1.1). A field image is the opposite in that each part of the image is as important as every other part. No one object, point, or space in the image dominates the viewer's perception. The viewer must perceive the image as a whole (figure 1.2). In a field image, the entire image could be taken as a figure against the ground of its surrounding environment.

Zakia points out five important aspects of figure-ground relationships in two-dimensional images. Four of these are directly applicable to this discussion: figure often appears nearer in space than ground; figure and ground cannot be seen simultaneously; figure usually occupies a smaller area than does ground; and, figure is seen as having contour while ground is not. A fifth observation, often overlooked, is that figure and ground cannot exist independently.

[figure 1.1]

Chris Hawker's use of a plain background, simple subject, and direct light creates a strong figure-ground relationship in this photograph. Our attention is directed at the dark figure surrounded by the light ground.

Photograph by Christopher Hawker

[figure 1.2]

In a field image, our attention is equally drawn to every area of the photograph. The image is balanced in its dynamic compositional forces. No one figure asserts itself.

The concept of figure makes no sense without ground just as the concept of light makes no sense without darkness. They are mutually interdependent. Figure and ground must be given equal weight in the construction of an image. One must remember that the viewer perceives and receives information from both elements in a photograph—each element communicating equally.

Four Gestalt Principles

Gestalt proposes that visual stimuli that are easily grouped to form a whole will be more likely seen as a complete, single figure than as discrete, individual pieces. Zakia believes four Gestalt principles—proximity, similarity, continuity, and closure—that facilitate the grouping of visual stimuli into wholes, are directly applicable to photography.

Proximity dictates that the closer two or more visual elements are to each other, the greater the probability that they will be seen as a single element, a group, or a pattern. An interesting aspect of proximity in photographs is the compression of the three-dimensional space of the physical world to the two-dimensional space of the photographic image. Objects that were not in proximity to each other in three-dimensional space can be brought into proximity in unexpected ways in two-dimensional translations (figure 1.3). Proximity can also be used creatively and intentionally to force relationships on the viewer as in constructions, collages, and montages where objects and/or images are placed on or near each other in the contained space of a frame (figure 1.4). Additionally, the proximity of edges is one of the primary clues used to identify discrete shapes and bounded areas that are read as figures in visual imagery.

Proximity can be extended to play a role in the sequencing of photographs where the placement of images next to each other, in a particular order, affects the manner in which the viewer "reads" the images.

Similarity holds that visual elements similar in shape, tone, color, texture, size, and/or position tend to be grouped or related. Similarity can be a stronger force than proximity in the grouping of visual elements (figure 1.5). Symmetry is a special case of similarity in which one half of an object or image contains all of the information necessary to construct the other half. Symmetry provides for extremely strong graphic form and stable visual imagery (figure 1.6). Together, similarity and proximity form pattern. A pattern is, in a sense, a homogeneous visual field; it is made up of discrete visual elements that are similar in character and placed near each other in a regular spacing. It should be noted that similarity in visual imagery can extend to meaning. For example, a distinct shape that is similar to another form can take on the meaning or character of that form (figure 1.7).

The principle of continuity states that visual elements requiring the fewest number of interruptions will be grouped to form continuous straight or curved lines. People seek simplicity and economy in the structuring of the visual world. Given a choice, the visual system will usually group stimuli into the simplest possible configuration of lines and shapes. Other alternatives that require more work in terms of bridging interruptions or synthesizing missing pieces of information in a scene will be more difficult to perceive (figure 1.8). Continuity can also influence our perception of single or sequential images in which movement or transition

[figure 1.3]

James Wojcik has crafted an alphabet out of a deck of playing cards. His creatively formed letters clearly demonstrate various Gestalt principles. Here subject and background are brought into proximity in the space of the image distorting our perception of depth and collapsing onto a single plane. The letter U emerges as a dominant form.

Photograph by James Wojcik

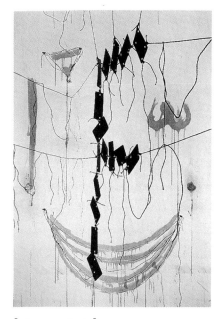

[figure 1.4]

Here, the playing cards, shaped to form the letter F, are brought into spatial proximity with marks on the background. Subject and background interact to create a distorted clown face. We must choose whether to see the letter or the face.

Photograph by James Wojcik

[figure 1.5]

A strong similarity in shape helps us group the two central V forms together. The outlying triangular shapes, even though they are distinctly separated from each other on opposite sides of the frame, are grouped to form a second pair.

Photograph by James Wojcik

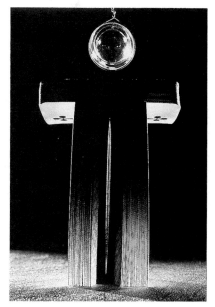

[figure 1.6]

Symmetry creates a powerful, stable form in the shape of the letter T. The central division in part of the figure emphasizes the similarities of each half.

Photograph by James Wojcik

[figure 1.7]

The letter K becomes a running human figure because of our reading of similarity of forms. This recognition animates the image and creates a powerful feeling of movement.

Photograph by James Wojcik

[figure 1.8]

The easily recognized form of the letter L is readily perceived. Continuity of line forms a familiar and meaningful shape. Our visual system works toward simplification and organization.

Photograph by James Wojcik

[figure 1.9]

As we follow the layered rotation of an object through space, we continually rebuild the hidden portions of the overlapped forms. The last is the same as the first, and together, they form the letter X.

Photograph by James Wojcik

[figure 1.10]

The individual cards coalesce into the letter Q. Closure encourages the perception of familiar wholes rather than their component parts.

Photograph by James Wojcik

plays an important role (figure 1.9). One of the most difficult tasks in sequencing a photographic narrative is to insure that there is continuity but not redundancy in the work. Continuity is intimately related to perceived order.

The last of the four principles that facilitate grouping is closure. Closure suggests that nearly complete familiar lines and shapes are more readily seen as complete, or closed, than incomplete (figure 1.10). Closure is one of the ways in which the perceptual system functions proactively. It shows that human beings participate in the act of perception and shape what is perceived. Closure can be easily extended to meaning. The synthesis of incoming visual information into meaningful structures is an example of closure. The ability of the human mind to project into the future and provide a multiplicity of endings for a series of narrative images is closure at work on an intellectual level.

Complex Phenomena

Before ending the discussion of Gestalt, three higher-level perceptual concepts that require the recognition of relationships between stimuli and that are important to photographic imagery should be introduced. Spatial transposition, perspective, and visual illusion are important in the visual process but are not directly related to figure-ground. Gestalt psychology first pointed out the importance of the perception of relations as opposed to absolute, individual features. This means that visual experience is an integrated whole, not a disconnected series of discrete stimuli and reactions. Everything in the perceptual field affects everything else. Interaction, comparison, and contrast are the nature of perception. Without discrimination the perceptual processes cease to function, and it is true that perceptions are as interactive as the processes. These three high-level perceptual concepts illustrate the importance of relationships between stimuli as a component in the final perception.

Spatial transposition of a figure is a complex phenomenon. When viewed in temporal, sequential continuity, most figures, even complex ones, can be transposed, and the perception of those figures will easily accommodate the transposition. However, in a single, two-dimensional image, even partial rotation of a simple figure will often confuse perceptions and delay or prevent recognition (figure 1.11). This is partly due to expectations and to the way in which the perceptual system functions. When something is set in a novel orientation the entire perceptual field must adjust to accommodate that fresh experience. The new orientation of a figure may present the perceptual system with stimuli that are processed in fundamentally different ways, and it may also present information that requires translation to be linked with past experience. The use of novel camera angles to present familiar subjects in an unfamiliar manner is an example of spatial transposition (figure 1.12). The recognition of a

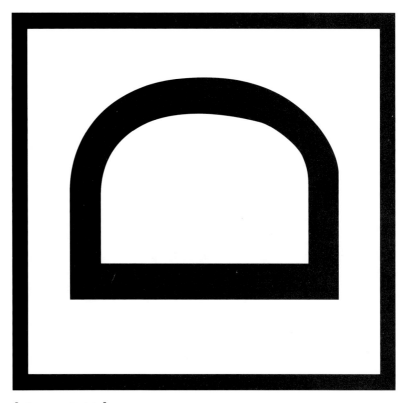

[figure 1.11]

The rotation of even a simple form can cause disorientation for the viewer. Here, the letter D is rotated ninety degrees producing a visual stimulus that does not match a preconceived form. Viewers must reorient their visual fields to accommodate the transposition.

[figure 1.12]

In order to comprehend Joe Ziolkowski's figure study, we must accommodate the novel orientation of the figure and the unusual camera angle. Only when we realize that we are viewing the form from underneath do pose and point-of-view reconcile. This photograph is from Ziolkowski's "Pressure Series," a visual embodiment of the stresses of dealing with the AIDS epidemic.

Photograph by Joe Ziolkowski from "The Pressure Series," "910908–E–3"

a.

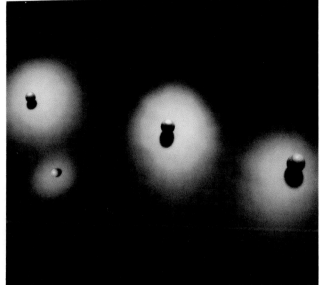

b.

[figure 1.13]

In a related phenomenon, the spheres on the left side of figure a. appear to be all of the same size, yet they seem to recede from the camera creating a visual paradox (similarity and proximity versus perspective rendering). Seen from above in figure b., the true size relationship and placement of the spheres becomes apparent. Perspective rendering and Gestalt principles can be used to create, destroy, or confuse our perception of depth.

spatially transposed figure requires the perceptual system to define a constancy of relationship between various features of the figure, and the system must also detect a change in relationship between figure and ground.

Perspective is an extremely complex and relational visual phenomenon. It requires the comparison and interaction of many stimuli in the visual field. The introduction of perspective rendering in two-dimensional art was revolutionary. The mimicking of visual experience through perspective rendering produces images of startling verisimilitude. Perspective rendering with a lens is characteristic of both the eye and the camera. Some of the primary clues used to establish perspective in visual experience and in photographs are size, interval, and texture gradient.

Identical objects appear to diminish in size as they become more distant from the viewer. When presented with objects that are identical in every way except size, the perceptual system may become confused and perceive change in size as change in distance (figure 1.13). As identically spaced elements recede from the viewer, they are perceived in closer and closer interval. A photograph looking down a set of model railroad tracks provides an excellent illustration of this phenomenon (figure 1.14). The cross ties appear closer and closer together as distance from the camera increases. Also seen in this illustration is convergence, another characteristic of perspective vision and imagery similar to interval, in which parallel lines appear to become

closer as they recede from the viewer. Texture gradient is a complex phenomenon involving both size and interval as well as the perception of detail. As a textured surface recedes from the camera, the regular, detailed pattern of elements making up the texture decreases in size, decreases in interval, and eventually merges into a homogeneous, smooth surface.

Visual illusion is a failure of the visual/perceptual process to accurately construct incoming visual stimuli. It is the stock-in-trade of the magician and a valuable tool for the studio photographer. Visual illusions can be constructed to be photographed. Impossible spaces, objects, and relationships can be represented in photographs that are crafted to fool the eye (figure 1.15). This is not new; it appeared

[figure 1.14]
The effect of decreasing interval, convergence, and texture gradient on our perception of depth is seen as the model tracks recede from the camera. Depth perception in two-dimensional imagery is based largely on these simple visual clues.

in trompe l'oeil works during the fifteenth and sixteenth centuries.

Illusion is the child of perspective rendering. The more accurately an image can be made to appear consistent with a first-hand visual experience the greater the opportunity for illusion. The ability to craft illusions is based on a sound knowledge of how human visual processes function. Illusion relies on the application and integration of many of the principles of Gestalt psychology to confuse rather than clarify communication; it forms an important extension of the photographer's language. A knowledge of visual perception is a critical tool for practicing photographers.

[figure 1.15]
Glen Wexler's photograph of a baby with butterfly's wings flying through space relies on our perception of depth, relative size, and spatial relationships to create the seamless illusion of an interplanetary environment in the studio (original in color).
Photograph by Glen Wexler

Photographic Representation

It has been said that the history of western painting, from 1350 to 1850, can be seen as a progression of more accurate techniques and styles for representing the world. Photography was the technical and aesthetic child of 500 years of representational art; the automatic fulfillment of the quest to depict the world in a manner closely replicating the visual experience. Indeed, visually scanning the two-dimensional surface of the photograph is not radically different from looking at the world. The close relation between photographic and visual processes is neither accidental nor arbitrary.

The visual world can be read as surely as written text. Text is simply a visual code that humans have learned to dissect according to special rules. Physical reality is also coded, and humans learn to understand visual coding on many levels as they function in the world. Logistically, people develop the ability to orient themselves, recognize familiar stimuli, and to predict events in their surroundings. Psychologically, human beings associate visual experience with past, present, and future events and emotions. And finally, people begin to understand the symbolic language of visual experience in their culture.

Reading photographs is not so different. People first orient themselves to the image; then they explore and integrate its content with past experience; finally they interpret the meaning of the image based on their discoveries and the cultural context in which they and the photograph exist. Two important characteristics of the eye/brain visual system are closely related to photographic representation. The lens of the eye structures the world into a perspective rendering similar to that obtained through the lens of a camera, and the eye/brain system sees the world in continuous tone or color—depending on chiaroscuro, variations in light and shade, for much subtle tonal information—just as the photographic process renders the surfaces of the world. The implication in these associations is that reading a photograph, while not an inborn talent, is dependent on many of the same skills people learn in developing their ability to read the visual world.

Perspective rendering advanced the illusionistic quality of two-dimensional representation. Photography, the

child of optics, provided a precise and direct perspective rendering. What was first considered a revolutionary, new visual experience has become the standard for viewing and imaging the world. In fact, nonperspectival images are considered to be abstract representations of reality. The chiaroscuro style depends on the descriptive action of light on surfaces to create three-dimensional illusions of space and surface. Prior to the introduction of photography this description could only be approximated. This is a critical distinction for the reading of photographs. Photography reveals the action of light upon the world and light becomes the active force in delineating the world for the camera, just as it is the activating energy for the visual system.

The discovery that the world could be imaged to match our visual experience brought the image and physical reality closer together and virtually eliminated the need for the decoding of image into meaning. Coding became transparent to the human eye. The scanning eye can rely on the same clues in the photograph that yield information in the world-at-large. Viewers read the image using the skills developed to read primary visual experience, of which the photograph provides a seemingly exacting translation. Thus, the image becomes the world to the eye.

However, the photograph is not the original and differs from the original in many important respects. This may seem like a self-evident statement, but considering how readily the photograph is accepted as a direct experience of the world, how much visual information derives from photographically generated imagery, and how significant the actual differences between the

photograph and lived visual experience really are, the importance of the distinction is realized.

Photography, like all media, has developed conventions for pictorial representation based on the nature of its materials and operation. The deception of the viewer is a result of how closely the "look" of the photograph resembles the "appearance" of the world. This arises largely from the fact that many of the characteristics of the medium are similar to, though not identical with, those of human vision.

The Locus of Meaning

Perhaps equally important to the question, "Where does the photographic image originate"? is the question, "Where does meaning originate"? Experience and interpretation interact to create meaning. Photographers must recognize that the meaning of their imagery is a subject of critical importance that must be addressed from a multiplicity of perspectives.

A photograph is a formal, structured message for communicating meaning. All photographs—family snapshots to highly crafted illusions—partake of this character; all contain information and transmit messages. The understanding of the meaning embodied in an image depends upon the viewer's ability to recognize and decode the message. What is seen in the world is a visual stimulus. What is constructed in the mind is a visual percept. This process is not a passive activity. The brain is constantly ordering, reacting to, and modifying sensory input. People continually strive to make sense of perceptions; to organize them into meaningful concepts,

[figure 1.16]

In his photograph "Quick Shift of the Head Leaves Glowing Stool Afterimage Posited on Pedestal," Robert Cumming encouraged viewers to use their knowledge of visual perception to solve a conundrum based on the phenomenon of afterimage.

Photograph by Robert Cumming

forms, and experiences—wholes. The percepts constructed in the mind represent the individual interpretation of experience and are the foundation of thought.

The investigation that leads to meaning is an important and characteristic activity of the human species. Images that encourage participation in the construction of meaning are often more engaging, effective vehicles for communication than those that exclude viewer participation by providing obvious conclusions (figure 1.16). Photographers must impart meaning and invite participation and discovery in the crafting of images. Both of these goals can be facilitated by attention to the cultural context in which photographing occurs and in which photographs are intended to function.

It is intelligence that makes meaning out of messages, either through discovery or through synthesis. The mind either decodes and recognizes the intrinsic meaning in a message or constructs a meaning from the information provided. If all viewers in all contexts understood the same meaning from an image, then the meaning could be said to be inherent to the image; if varied interpretations abound then the meaning is necessarily subjective. Photographs are always subject to interpretation and at best serve as triggers for, or pointers to, meaning which is a construct placed on the image.

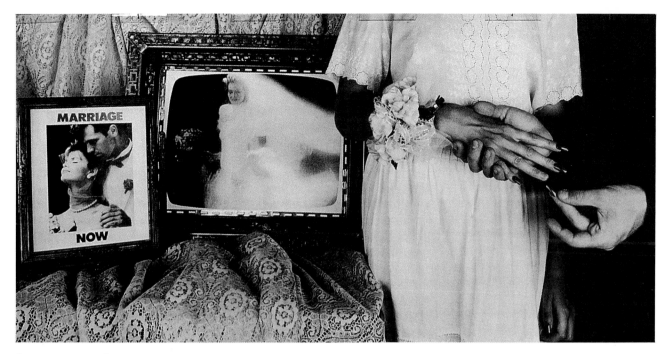

[figure 1.17]

In her image, "Taking the Veil," Laura Bogue turns religious and cultural iconography to her own uses in order to pose questions for her viewers. When dominant beliefs are unmasked and displayed, we must question their authority.

Photograph by Laura Bogue

Meaning is a sociocultural construct that is influenced by complex interconnections. These interconnections imply that the photograph is influenced by, operates in, and influences society. To facilitate communication, photographers must understand the system of signs and symbols available within the specific sociocultural context in which they are working. The knowledge of the viewer, as determined by culture and history, will form the basis for constructing meaning in the image.

Imputing any inherent truth or meaning to the photograph becomes problematic in light of these assertions. The *process* of photography may, in some sense,

be objective, but the *photograph* certainly is not. Yet, photographs can be powerful vehicles for communication. Ideas can be clearly embodied in images and read by an audience. This is not a contradiction. A photograph, like any other form of communication, is a coded message couched in terms of the photographer's intentions, abilities, and culture. The photograph is a manipulation of content and viewer, achieved through an understanding of the codes of culture. Culture provides the framework used for interpreting all messages.

Photographs must be viewed as biased communications representing the interests of their makers. The questions of whose interests are being represented and who can benefit from a believable

representation become vital to understanding the image. This questioning could be called a dialectical process in which the viewer actively becomes involved in deconstructing the codes of the image.

As a critical tool, deconstruction often reveals the implicit assumptions underlying the making and reading of a photograph, and it leads to fresh insights about the role of culture in determining the meaning of any message. Deconstruction can be used as a strategy in crafting, as well as in critiquing, photographic imagery. The dissected beliefs of a dominant culture can be reconstituted to implicate, criticize, and question societal norms, ideals, and values (figure 1.17).

Applications in the Studio

The information about the visual system, the principles of Gestalt psychology, and photographic imagery presented above is applicable to photographing in the studio. First, it should be clear that a great deal of similarity exists between the construction of the human eye and the camera/lens system. The latter is indeed modeled on the former. The implications of this observation are myriad, but most important perhaps is the realization that by understanding the manner in which vision functions, the photographer can predict how a viewer will "read" their photographs.

Direct observation and careful analysis of perceptions are major sources for information about the process of human vision and require no special tools, only attention. The impressionists of the nineteenth century were keenly aware of this. One of the major goals of their paintings was to represent the world as it was experienced by the viewer. This was not considered the same as aspiring to photographic verisimilitude. The impressionists paid a great deal of attention to their own visual experience of the world and developed a unique style of representation based on their direct observations. Creative photographers must learn to use the camera as a means of directing and extending vision. Seeing photographically is a proactive, participatory, conscious experience of the visual. Particularly in the studio environment, where images are literally constructed, application of the basic principles governing visual perception can be productive.

Second, the rules governing visual perception not only suggest the manner in which the world is perceived but also provide a model for how a viewer perceives a two-dimensional image. Much of the terminology of Gestalt such as figure-ground relationship, grouping, spatial transposition, and texture gradient can be applied to the analysis of two-dimensional visual imagery and viewer perceptions. The original visual stimuli form, in the mind of the photographer, an image which is substantiated through available photographic tools and means. This image then becomes the visual stimulus for a viewer, who may act or comment upon the photograph. This cycle of communication involves a common coding of visual experience. The photograph, which simulates the world in much the same manner as does the human perceptual system, is interpreted with the same syntax and grammar as applied to the visual world. This is not to suggest that the photograph and the world provide the same stimulus; however, the same principles and tools are used to interpret both.

Photographs have the power to activate the sensory systems and recall associated real world experiences; they can be rich sources of information, memory, and emotion. The remarkable similarity between photographed and lived visual experience makes the photographic image a powerful tool for visual communication. It is the root of the photograph's truth and the source of the photograph's ambiguity. However, visual perception provides only one layer of the rich experience that forms

life. The photograph is limited to the visual, and therefore limited in its ability to explain and complete lived experience. Photographic truth is limited truth. A clear understanding of how the visual and photographic systems function to create images can aid the search for meaning.

Lastly, an understanding of how the visual, perceptual system functions within a cultural context can be used to map a strategy in photographing. A photographer's images carry the photographer's meaning. Photographers can reinforce preconceptions or challenge them through the visual strategy they employ. They can structure images for the viewer in order to facilitate or confuse certain perceptions. They can also analyze images to determine how the image functions in the communication of their message. This may lead to the adoption of a particular style or visual syntax for certain purposes.

Form is not separate from meaning in a photograph. The formal language of an image can have a great deal of effect upon its interpretation. Not all formal strategies may be appropriate for all content and intentions. The visual form of images is an analog for the visual form of the world. Meaning is transposed from one to the other in complex ways. The world produces image which affects world, etc. An awareness of the strategies employed by the visual system to interpret the world, and of the strategies employed by image makers to represent the world may aid in deconstructing, understanding, and facilitating visual communication.

PRINCIPLES OF LIGHT

The phenomenon of light defines not only the visual processes but also our very being. Light is the source of all life. As such, it has become a powerful physical and psychological signifier for humankind. The physical importance of light to biological life has been well documented and the phenomenon of light lies at the base of the most far-reaching and important physical sense—the sense of sight. As briefly outlined in Chapter 1, the sense of sight allows humans to forge into the world, gather information, and begin the process of synthesizing meaning.

Light forms not only the technical basis of photography but also serves as its primary descriptive element. The metaphor of light as a language element has been explored in visual imagery throughout history. In fact, it would be possible to consider five-hundred years of the aesthetic history of western art, from the beginning of the renaissance to the late eighteen hundreds, as a progression of more accurate styles of representing the play of light on surfaces. Photography was in some ways a culmination of this evolution, and the accurate description of light on surfaces is endemic to the photographic process.

Light functions in photographs as a psychological metaphor and an aesthetic quality. The light of creation, the light of goodness, the light of reason are all metaphorical, visual associations of light with language and meaning. In the photograph, the acute description of light lends it added power as a language element. The subtleties of light enrich the meaning of any photograph. After all, the word photography means "writing with light." Light is never a neutral element in a photograph.

Photographers can learn to control the expressive potential of light in their images. Light functions according to certain basic physical principles that define its character. Photographers can analyze, quantify, and alter light to produce an astounding array of effects. Most importantly, they can use their sense of vision to carefully study light in the studio and become sensitive to its subtleties, beauty, and power. Eyes are the best tools for learning about lighting. In this process, no text can ever supersede the importance of critical observation.

In this chapter, the discussion will focus on the physical aspects of light: its nature, its rules, and its functioning. The discussion will then turn to the descriptive possibilities of various forms of light. Finally, the chapter will more thoroughly discuss the psychological implications of light as related to meaning.

The Basic Nature of Light

Visible light is part of an energy spectrum ranging from short-wavelength, powerful gamma and cosmic radiations to extremely long-wavelength radio waves and beyond. The wavelengths of visible light lie between

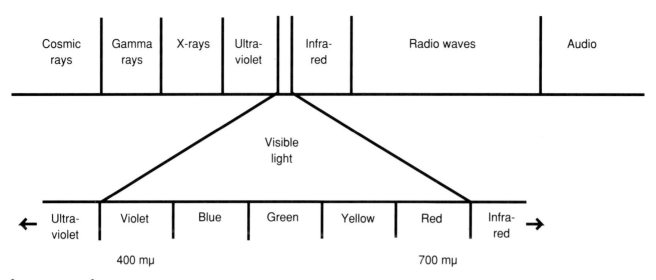

[figure 2.1]

The visible spectrum of radiation is a tiny part of a continuous spectrum of energy ranging from extremely short to very long wavelengths. It is bounded by ultraviolet and infrared radiations.

approximately 400 and 700 nanometers or 4,000 and 7,000 angstrom units (figure 2.1). Human vision perceives the shorter wavelengths in this range as violets and blues, and the longer wavelengths are perceived as yellows and reds. The visible spectrum, as this range is called, is bounded by the ultraviolet and infrared ranges both of which can be recorded on specialized films but neither of which is visible to the human eye.

Photographic systems—cameras, films, papers—have largely been designed to record the visible wavelengths of light. Film technology advanced from the simplest film, blue sensitive only, to orthochromatic, and finally panchromatic emulsions. Color was the next step. All of these refinements were designed to bring the photographic rendering of a scene into the range of normal human vision. As mentioned above, some special films are sensitive to other wavelengths of the spectrum, but standard photographic systems are based largely in the visible spectrum. The camera is an

extension of the sense of sight modeled upon the optics and sensitivity of the eye.

For the practicing photographer, the scientific specification of light is not as critical as the way in which light functions and affects photographic materials. However, a few important scientific principles that define the nature of light and limit its functioning are worth mentioning. For the working photographer, these are points of essential knowledge. Three primary principles of light are particularly important.

Three Principles

First, light travels in straight lines. This is not to say that light rays are always parallel to one another—light rays can travel in many different directions but each individual ray will travel in a straight line (figure 2.2). The direction of illumination in a photograph has a great deal to do with perception of volume, contrast, texture, and space. It defines the direction, size, and

placement of shadows in the photograph and serves to lead the eye of the viewer in emphasizing certain relationships. Because light travels in straight lines photographers can work backward in viewing a photograph to determine where the light source was placed in relation to the subject—a valuable technique in analyzing images.

Second, the angle of incidence is equal to and opposite from the angle of reflection. This means a light ray hitting a surface from a particular angle will reflect off that surface at an equal but opposite angle (figure 2.3). The degree to which light obeys this principle depends upon the nature of the illuminating light and the nature of the reflecting surface. Maximum congruence will occur with a contrasty, focused light source emitting parallel rays of light and a highly-polished or mirrored surface reflecting that light. Minimum congruence will occur with a low-contrast, diffused light source emitting scattered rays of light and a highly textured surface reflecting that light (figure 2.4). Other combinations will

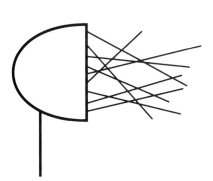

Softlight

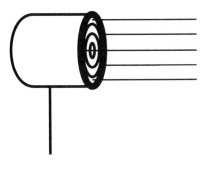

Spotlight

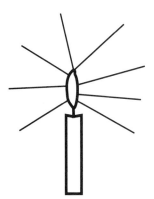

Candle

[figure 2.2]

Light travels in straight lines. Light rays leaving a source can crisscross, travel parallel, or radiate out, but each individual ray travels straight.

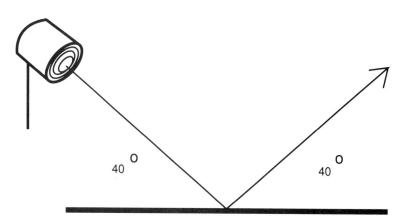

[figure 2.3]

Light reflects off of a flat surface at an angle equal to but opposite from the angle at which it strikes that surface. These angles are called the angle of reflection and the angle of incidence, respectively.

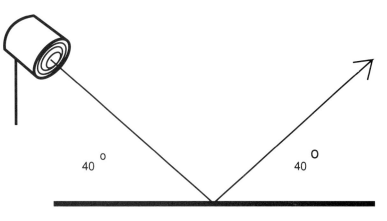

Hard light--smooth surface

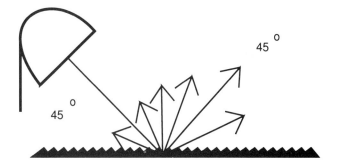

Soft light--textured surface

[figure 2.4]

As a light source becomes less directional and/or a reflecting surface becomes less smooth, the angle of reflection will increasingly diverge from the angle of incidence.

produce a variety of effects. Controlling reflections of various light sources is as critical to the photographer as controlling shadows. Eliminating unwanted reflections that are confusing or disrupting to the flow of an image can be important.

Third, light from a source changes in intensity proportional to the inverse of the square of the relative distance from the source. As an object moves farther away from a light source, the level of the illumination decreases; as it moves closer, it increases. Imagine a light source that casts a square beam; when this light source is placed one foot from a surface it illuminates an area one foot square or one square foot. If the distance of that light source to the surface is doubled, it will illuminate an area two feet square or four square feet. The same amount of light is now illuminating four times the original area (figure 2.5). The illumination will be one-quarter as bright. The level of the illumination is inversely proportional to the square of the relative distance between the light source and the subject. Doubling the distance will cut the level of illumination by a factor of four. Tripling the distance will cut the level by a factor of nine, etc. Conversely, cutting the distance in half will increase the level of illumination by a factor of four.

Brightness adaptation is part of the visual system, and as the eyes scan a scene they adjust for and equalize various lighting levels. Stand outside on a sunny day and scan a shadow dappled landscape for proof of this phenomenon. Photographic materials cannot make these adjustments. Photographers must train their eyes to "see" in the way their materials will record the scene in front of the camera. Photographic materials are extremely sensitive to changes in the level of illumination in a

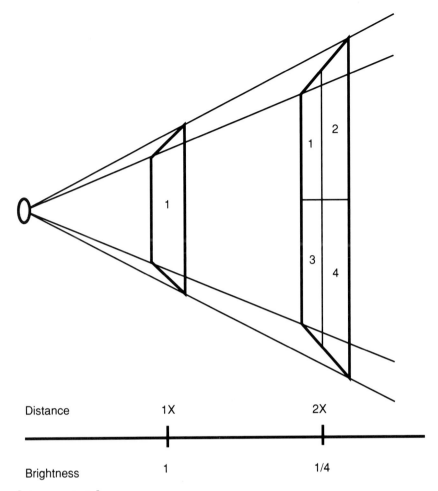

Distance	1X	2X
Brightness	1	1/4

[figure 2.5]

As a subject is moved further from a light source, the level of illumination changes at a rate inversely proportional to the square of the relative distance factor.

scene. Light fall-off sometimes eludes the sense of sight but will always record dramatically on film (figure 2.6).

Direction, angle, and intensity are important aspects of the light in any photograph. The three simple principles stated above form the basis for solving most lighting problems in the studio. Lighting is best learned by developing a solid understanding of the most basic principles of light. If these are firmly grasped, predicting and controlling light can be reduced to logical variables, and solutions to varied problems can be defined in terms of known functions. This is the key to the creative use of lighting tools.

[figure 2.6]

The fall-off of light occurs rapidly over short distances. The first sign is 1 foot from the light source, the second is 2 feet away, and the third is 4 feet distant. Light falls off by a factor of 4 (2 f-stops) each time the distance is doubled.

Four Types of Light

The light used in making photographs can be divided into four basic categories: direct light, reflected light, diffused light, and radiant light. Often combinations of these four basic types of light are found in a single image. Each of these types of light has distinctive qualities that affect the rendering of the subject, the appearance of the photograph, and the meaning of the image. The decision as to which type of light is best employed arises out of a combination of technical, aesthetic, and conceptual concerns.

A photographer's ability to observe and compare various qualities and combinations of lights in the studio is invaluable in developing a sensibility that will allow for informed, yet intuitive decision making. Careful observation cannot be overemphasized, and will lead to an intimate, working knowledge of light that will allow the photographer to previsualize many possibilities.

Direct light is light traveling unimpeded from the light source to the subject. After leaving the source, the light is not filtered, diffused, reflected, or altered in any manner. The light source itself may contain focusing, diffusing, or filtering elements and may emit high or low contrast light. Provided that light proceeds to the subject without additional alteration it is considered direct light. Reflected light can be of two main types; light proceeding from a light source, bouncing off of a remote surface, and reflecting onto the subject or, light reflecting from the subject to the lens of the camera. Diffused light is light having passed through a remote diffusion device or material prior to reaching the subject. The many types of diffusion devices and materials

share certain common characteristics. Light passing through them is scattered, becoming less directional and lower contrast in nature. In addition, they act as filters reducing the intensity of illumination through reflection and absorption. In some cases, they alter the spectral composition of the light.

The fourth type of light, radiant light, is seldom seen in studio photographs. It is light coming directly from a light source into the lens of the camera. Image-degrading effects such as flare, halation, and fogging often result when radiant light enters the lens. Radiant light can be employed for dramatic statements, special effects, and strong silhouettes with back light. A silhouette, although often thought of as clichéd, can be an effective way to define shape information (figure 2.7).

Five Directions

There are five basic directions from which light illuminating a scene can come: front, side, back, top, and bottom. The most common directional lighting that photographers experience is a form of top light, side light, or a combination of these two. Most workrooms, classrooms, and many homes are illuminated with overhead lights. Lights on stage in theaters are usually from above and/or to the side. Sunlight usually comes from above or the side, except at sunrise or sunset when, at certain angles, front or back light may be experienced. Most photographs are also illuminated with a combination of top light and side light. The most uncommon directional light experienced is bottom light. In nature, bottom light occurs rarely and then usually from reflecting overhead light. In studio

[figure 2.7]

Radiant back light creates a silhouette, reducing three-dimensional forms to two-dimensional shapes and creating a graphic image.

[figure 2.8]

Bottom light, though rare, can be used in the studio for effect. As illumination strikes surfaces from unexpected angles, bottom light often creates dimensional forms that offer surprises.

photographs, bottom light is more common, but still rarely used as a main source of illumination (figure 2.8). Because people rarely see an absolute ninety degree side light, an absolute top or bottom light, or an absolute front or back light in life or in photographs, this often makes such light a unique, dramatic statement.

One of the primary characteristics associated with direction of illumination is contrast. Light sources can be constructed to produce high- to low-contrast light. The variable contrast associated with different directions applies equally to all light sources altering the apparent contrast of their particular illumination in the final photograph. Changes in shadow, texture, and shape all help to define this sense of variable contrast.

[figure 2.9]

Front light, like radiant back light, can eliminate dimensional and spatial clues, thus reducing volumes to shapes and flattening space.

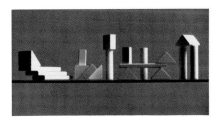

[figure 2.10]

Side light is usually most effective at creating depth and suggesting volume. It helps form distinct spatial relationships and define three-dimensional subjects.

Front light is the least contrasty illumination. It casts few if any shadows, minimizes textures, and flattens forms. It is poor at defining volume and can often create confusing spatial relationships with lack of directional, proportional, and relational clues (figure 2.9). The elimination of shadows with front light deprives the viewer of a primary signifier of three-dimensional form.

Side light is more contrasty than front light. In this category, photographers can include top and bottom light as special cases of side light. Side light creates strong shadows, emphasizes texture, reveals volume and gives good directional and spatial clues (figure 2.10). Side light can be useful in defining spatial relationships. It can be both dramatic and descriptive, making it the most flexible form of directional lighting. The strong shadows created by side light can become important shapes in

[figure 2.11]

Chris Hawker used raking side light to create deep, long shadows that actively characterize this simple still life, adding mood and a sense of morning or evening light.

Photograph by Christopher Hawker

reading a photograph and can actively characterize a subject (figure 2.11).

Back light is the most contrasty directional light. Back light often creates silhouettes of pure black shape and white space. The silhouette, as mentioned

earlier, is often thought of as a cliché. The reason for this is that it is a reduction of reality to a single descriptive component, shape. Shape can be a revealing characteristic, quickly apprehended and easily identified; however, it can also be rejected

[figure 2.12]

Strong radiant back light will bleed around, and in this case through, its subject and become an assertive element in an image. This photograph of paper cups by Todd Haiman uses light as an activating catalyst to transform a banal subject (original in color).

Todd Haiman Studio

[figure 2.13]

Refraction, or the bending of light rays, occurs when light passes from a less dense to a more dense medium, as shown in this photograph where air, glass, and water interact as media of transmission.

quickly for these same reasons. The silhouette is a graphic rather than a photographic form. The nature of the photograph normally embodies tonal description and the silhouette eliminates this complex and intriguing phenomenon. Back light can be used effectively to define shape and can embody the character of radiant light as well. If back light illumination is strong and bleeds or radiates around the shapes it defines, it becomes an active visual element in a photograph (figure 2.12).

Additional Terms

Of the range of technical terms associated with light, the following are particularly relevant to photography. Transmission can be defined as the ability of a material to pass light. No material passes 100 percent of the light travelling through it. Some light is always reflected back from its surfaces and some is usually absorbed by the material. Absorption can be defined as the ability of a material to absorb light energy and convert it, usually to

heat or electricity. Refraction, the bending of rays of light when passing from a less dense to a denser medium or vice versa, can play an important role in photographing transparent media such as water, plastics, or glass (figure 2.13). Dispersion is the distribution of various wavelengths of light, such as the separation of white light into its constituent colors when passing through a prism. Interference is a complex phenomenon that deals with the interaction of various waves of light and makes holograms possible.

Flare and halation are common to photographic systems. Flare appears in the form of well defined spots of light in the negative and print caused by internal reflections in the lens/camera system. Halation, an amorphous diffusion of light around bright highlights in a scene, is caused by stray light penetrating through the film and bouncing back up into the emulsion in the form of diffused fog. Halation often occurs around strongly radiant light sources in a photograph.

A number of terms descriptive of reflection are important. Diffuse reflection is light reflecting from a surface after having undergone changes through absorption by the surface. These changes occur in the intensity, spectral composition, and nature of the reflected light. Specular reflection is light from a source reflecting unchanged from a surface, such as light reflecting in a mirror or off of polished chrome. It is interesting, and occasionally important, to note that all specular reflection from non-metallic surfaces is to some degree naturally polarized. Finally, selective reflection is a special form of specular reflection from metals in which the spectral composition of the light may be changed. In general, diffuse reflection is what allows the visual and camera systems to see tonal information. Specular reflection changes with the nature of the light source, may provide shape information, and may add a sense of life and vibrancy to an image.

A final and wonderful term that should be noted is penumbra. Penumbra is the space between light and shade at the edge of a shadow—the half-light transition at the edge of darkness. Visually, penumbra is related to contrast. Psychologically, it is a magical area of potential transformation. A softlight creates a large penumbra and a spotlight creates a small penumbra (figure 2.14).

Contrast

In defining appearances, the single most important characteristic of the illumination in a photograph is its contrast. As previously noted, the direction of the illumination affects contrast. In addition, every light source has a characteristic contrast associated with its illumination. The various types of light sources and their characteristic illuminations will be

a.

b.

[figure 2.14]

a. A penumbra is the transition area from light to dark at the edge of a shadow. A small penumbra provides a rapid transition from light to dark and will form a defined border.

b. A large penumbra provides a more gradual transition from light to dark yielding a soft blending of tone.

discussed in chapter 6. The contrast of any light source is also directly related to its size and the distance of the light source to the subject. At any fixed distance, the larger the light source, the softer will be its illumination (figure 2.15); and, with any light source of a given size, the closer it is to a subject, the softer will be its illumination (figure 2.16). Although the type of light source—spot, broad, or softlight—will have a greater proportional affect upon the contrast of the light emitted than will size and distance, it is necessary to take these factors into consideration when deciding upon a lighting instrument.

The sense of contrast in a photograph is a function of many elements working simultaneously. The sharpness and direction of the shadows, the nature of the reflections in the scene, and the variation in levels of illumination from one area to another are all important indicators of contrast. Already discussed was direction as related to contrast. In general the sharpness of shadows is defined by the construction of the light source and the distances between

the light, subject, and background. These factors will be discussed thoroughly in chapters 6, 8, and 9. The sharper the shadows, the higher will be the perceived contrast of a scene.

Reflections in a scene can be a prime indicator of contrast. As described above, the qualities of the surface and the angle of the illumination determine the type—diffuse, specular, or selective—and, to some degree, the intensity of the reflection. The light source itself will also have an affect upon the nature of the reflections created. A small, direct light source will create bright, pinpoint specular reflections which will heighten the appearance of contrast in an image. A large, diffused light source will create subdued, broad reflections contributing to an impression of softness in an image (figure 2.17). The variation in levels of illumination is a final, obvious indicator of contrast; an evenly illuminated scene with few extreme darks or lights will appear soft whereas the same scene illuminated to create areas of deep shadow and strong highlight may appear contrasty.

a.

b.

[figure 2.15]

a. At any given distance, a larger light source will provide softer illumination, creating a shadow with a large penumbra.

b. At the same distance, a smaller light source will yield more contrast, creating a shadow with a smaller penumbra.

a.

b.

[figure 2.16]

a. The closer it is used, any given light source will create a softer shadow with a larger penumbra.

b. As the light source is moved farther away, the shadow becomes harder with a smaller penumbra.

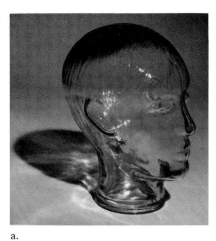

a.

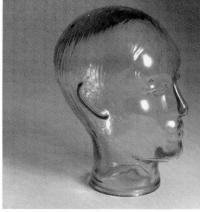

b.

[figure 2.17]

a. A small, direct light source will create focused, brilliant reflections that will heighten the apparent contrast of an image.

b. A large, more diffuse light source will create broad, less brilliant reflections that will contribute to an overall impression of softer volume in an image.

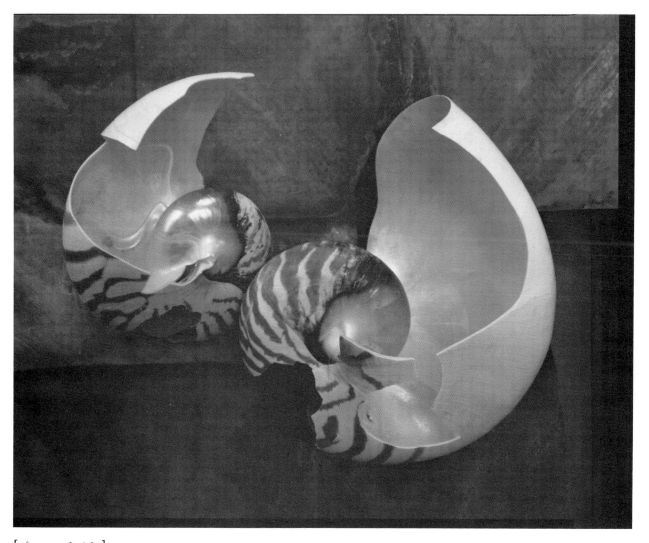

[figure 2.18]

In this image by Olivia Parker, the description of content is critical to the meaning of the photograph. The soft, enveloping light allows the content to reveal itself through the precision of the photographic process.

Photograph by Olivia Parker, "Broken Nautiluses"

The Role of Light

Several visual scales could be developed on which the quality of light could be plotted. These scales might include passive to active or descriptive to transformative. Light can function as passive illumination to allow the visual and camera systems to function and to describe what is being viewed or photographed. Light can also function as an active, transformative force to alter perceptions and play a major

role in shaping photographs. Certain types of light are more effective than others for particular characterizations. Defining the intent of the image aids greatly in deciding whether to employ a descriptive or a transformative light.

Descriptive, passive light is generally soft light. It creates few strong shadows and controlled, broad reflections. It is light that wraps around and embraces the subject, revealing its character and making the relationships in the

photograph visible. It describes the volumes, surfaces, and shapes of the content enabling all the power and precision that photography is capable of delivering (figure 2.18). This light is transparent; the viewer does not sense the active presence of such light in an image. It is present, yet not assertive. Descriptive light plays a supporting role in an image.

If the content of an image is critical to its meaning, then it may be best to employ a passive light

[figure 2.19]

In the image "Training," Parker again utilizes a soft, embracing light. The meaning of this image rests partially upon the identification of content and the linkages between symbolic objects and references in the frame. The light plays a supportive, passive role.

Photograph by Olivia Parker, "Training"

that describes the content and renders it as neutrally as possible. The job of the light in such an image is to illuminate or make visible the subject of the photograph. The meaning of such a photograph rests largely in the content. The photograph becomes a vehicle for effectively describing the content. The assemblage and photographing of the content is a creative act in itself and can engender complex meanings as well as simple descriptions. The encounter between the objects in the frame becomes an important consideration as does the construction of their environment (figure 2.19). Such images often evoke a meaning related but external to the photograph.

Transformative, active light is generally harsher, more contrasty light. It creates strong shadows that become active shapes in the photograph and small, bright reflections that energize the image. This light alters the viewers perception of the content by aggressively defining the reading of the image (figure 2.20). Objects are reduced or enhanced, dimension is sometimes confused, and the meaning of the image often resides within its own borders, utilizing the transformative power of light to create a new visual world within the photograph.

Of course, exceptions to these examples abound. Soft light is not always revealing—sometimes it simply flattens and reduces; and contrasty light is not always transformative—sometimes it brings out textures and shapes that are important to the description of content in the image. In any case, the stronger the role of the light, be it soft or harsh, in defining the viewers perception of the content, the more transformative and active a role that light plays in an image.

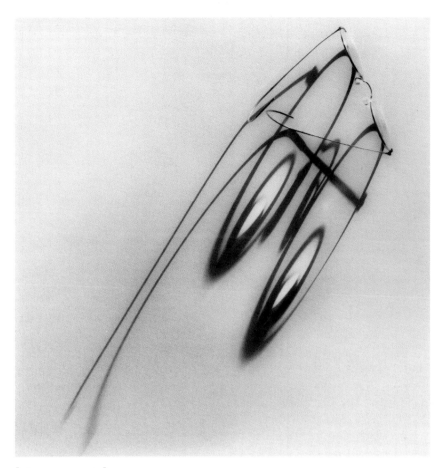

[f i g u r e 2 . 2 0]

R. J. Muna has used a strong, raking light to transform an ordinary object. In this photograph, the light creates defined shadows that aggressively assert themselves in the reading of the final image. The light plays an active, transfiguring role.

Photograph by R. J. Muna

The intent of the image maker toward the role and importance of content may define the choice of light.

Light and Intent

A great many varieties of lighting exist in everyday life. People begin to associate different experiences of light with various situations, environments, moods, and activities. This is a culture of photographic-image consumers, and they have learned to read light in photographs based on their experience of light in the world. In the studio, the photographer can use this as an advantage. The viewer's

expectations in reading an image can be confirmed, tricked, or denied depending on the characteristics of the illumination. Consistency, discontinuity, and surprise are all elements to be considered when constructing a lighting design for an image. Three image-descriptive terms can be considered when deciding upon a lighting design: fact, fiction, and fantasy.

What is the intent of the image? How can this scene be lighted to best communicate this intention? These are two critical questions in lighting design. If the intent of the image is to re-create a factual representation of a real space in the confines of the studio, then certain restrictions

automatically apply to the lighting design. As informed image-consumers, viewers are adept at reading the light in an image, even on a subconscious level. If the prevailing illumination in an image does not agree with the environment being depicted, this discontinuity will register with the viewer. If a sunlit, outdoor environment is created and illuminated with soft, directionless light, the viewer will recognize the discrepancy.

Even if the discrepancy between realistic and actual lighting is not consciously registered, the message and intent of any photograph will be weakened if the light does not characterize the scene properly. An image is limited to one sense; it is dependent upon visual cues for all of its communicative power. These visual cues must communicate clearly, and the quality of light in an image is one of the primary visual cues a photographer can control.

Duplicating "factual" lighting, re-creating the ambient light of a location, can be a difficult task in the studio. It first requires photographers to be aware of the qualities of light that exist at a given location—this requires careful observation and visualization. Next, they must be able to re-create this light in the studio—this requires technical skill and the creative use of tools (figure 2.21). The light in such an image plays an important but not dominant visual role—it is used to reinforce the authenticity of the image.

Perhaps the photographer is not interested in re-creating an actual location in the studio but rather in building a synthetic environment. In this case the lighting requirements may provide more latitude for creativity. The range of probable or possible environments is much greater than the narrow description of any

[figure 2.21]

Ray Perkins re-created this curbside scene in his Chicago studio. His careful attention to the low key light becomes an important element in transporting the viewer to a nighttime, urban street. Light helps specify meaning in this re-creation of an environment (original in color).

Ray Perkins Photography, Chicago.

particular location. The photographer can synthesize a "fictional" environment and lighting design from many diverse elements.

If re-creation of a specific location is not a primary concern, then the concept of the photograph, rather than the notion of a specific ambient light, dictates the lighting design. Usually the viewer can still synthesize a realistic environment in such an image. When a light is not associated with a specific location, a general sense of experienced reality is perceived.

The light in such an image supports the photograph's message. It becomes a tool used to heighten the communicative potential of the photograph (figure 2.22).

In such a photographic fiction, a strict visual analysis of the lighting might reveal inconsistencies. However, in the perception of the viewer, the light and the construction of the photograph function together to form a Gestalt of meaning that supports the intent of the image, and overshadows any inconsistencies and

discontinuities. The viewer perceives a whole rather than its component parts. The light in such an image, as in a factual re-creation, plays a supporting rather than a dominant visual role—it is used as a creative element in the formal design of the photograph.

A third possibility is that the photographer wishes to create an unreal environment in the image—a "fantasy" in which whimsy dominates the construction of the photograph. In such an image no rules apply to the content, space, or lighting design. The light itself may be the

[figure 2.22]

Bruce Charlesworth used light as a formal and directive force in shaping our reading of his metaphorical fiction. The light, like the other elements of the scene, becomes part of a set created for the purpose of conveying meaning (original in color).

Bruce Charlesworth, #39 from Man and Nature, *1989 cibachrome print, 40 in. × 40 in., Copyright © 1989 by Bruce Charlesworth, all rights reserved. Courtesy Jayne H. Baum gallery, New York, New York*

[figure 2.23]

Bob Forrest uses light as an elemental form of energy to help shape his fantasy image of a futuristic plane over an imagined city-scape (original in color).

© 1992, Bob Forrest

source of visual discontinuity, as in a science fiction world with three suns or a fanciful re-creation of Dante's realms of hell. All aspects of the photograph become subject to creative manipulation in service of the concept of the image (figure 2.23). Of course, if the image is to be readable, the viewer must be presented some cues to help build meaning, rules that are consistent with some imaginable reality or internally coherent to the image. The light in a fantastic image may be a dominant, aggressive element in creating a fresh visual experience—it is used to reinforce the fantastic message portrayed in the photograph.

These three terms, fact, fiction, and fantasy, are not exclusive. Other descriptive terminology can be imagined, and occasionally a fact, a fiction, and a fantasy will be portrayed in the same image. However, determining the basic visual form of an image and how that will best be supported by a particular lighting design is simplified when the intent and message of the image are clearly defined and the restrictions of concept identified.

The Meaning of Light

As briefly noted and explored in Chapter 1, much visual language is culturally defined. The time and place in history, the heritage of the culture, and the knowledge of other cultures made possible by the advent of modern communications technologies have a profound affect on the reading of visual imagery. With the entire history and cultural diversity of visual imagery available it is important to note that light has long been a primary signifier. The meaning of light changes depending on historical setting, cultural significance, and context of use. However, the communicative importance of light as sign and symbol is omnipresent in visual art. This observation should come as no surprise, considering that light is the root of life and the visual process.

Light can be both sign and symbol. As a sign, light is the manifestation of a presence, the embodiment of a being, quality, or power. It is specific in the image (figure 2.24). As a symbol, light stands for something else; it represents an entity or concept by reference, not by presence. It is relative to the image. This is a subtle but important semantic distinction.

As symbol, in western culture, light is associated with truth, goodness, knowledge, power, passion, safety, investigation, revelation, holiness, and love

[f i g u r e 2 . 2 4]

*Scott Olsen used the reflected light from an overhead mirror to indicate the existence of
another world beyond the darkness of the present reality. A person gazes into this world,
longing for its warmth and freedom; ironically, this release lies within the reflected self.*

Photograph by Scott Olsen

(figure 2.25). Light takes on much of its meaning relative to its antithesis, darkness. The very concept of light depends upon darkness for its definition—it is devoid of meaning without darkness as a counterpart (figure 2.26). Light in the darkness is the basic distinction from which all else arises. In Genesis, God first creates light from the dark void. Light plays a primary role in many other creation myths ranging from Egyptian, to Native American, to pre-Columbian. These belief structures and their symbolic representations in visual art have helped to shape the modern understanding of light as sign and symbol.

Photography, coming late in the histories of arts, has the enviable advantage of being able to borrow from the past. When a photograph uses light as sign or symbol it references the visual heritage of the culture of both maker and viewer. The photographer and the audience come to the image already educated in the language of light. Through association, the photograph is imbued with much meaning.

Psychologically, light is associated with reason, understanding, and security. People do indeed derive physical security from light. The threat of darkness lies primarily in its depriving humans of a major source of information about their surroundings. Darkness represents the unknown in life and in imagery. Centuries ago René Descartes defined the connection between reason, understanding, and sight. He constantly referred to metaphors of light and vision in defining his concepts of rationalism, a philosophy which is at the base of much contemporary western culture. The light of

[figure 2.25]

Paul Elledge has used light as a symbolic element in his photograph of a man and baby. The glowing illumination surrounding the figures represents the private, emotional bond of love between the two. Light tells us what we cannot see—the inner, emotional state of the spirit.

Photograph by Paul Elledge

[figure 2.26]

Eileen Cowin's lighted characters are connected both formally and conceptually. They are starkly defined in contrast to the enveloping darkness that suggests isolation, fear, and furtive surveillance.

Eileen Cowin, Untitled, 1988

[figure 2.27]

In Martin Brief's photograph, darkness represents the loss of reason; the empty void of loss of self. The scream of the individual is lost in the distancing silence of the darkness.

Photograph by Martin Brief

reason is a human hold on the world. It is our way of constructing a sensible and controllable reality. Darkness is madness and loss of control (figure 2.27).

Light is an emotional catalyst as well as a cultural and psychological force. Emotion and meaning are connected though discrete aspects of an image. The bright light of day, the magical moonlight of night, the warm intimacy of candlelight all affect emotional states. Part of this is culturally defined. However, recent research has demonstrated the importance of light levels to physical and emotional well being. The basic connection between light and life registers in both the physical and emotional beings. Light can be used as an emotional cue in a photograph, nudging the viewer toward a specific response of feeling as well as meaning (figure 2.28).

[figure 2.28]

Ken Perrin has used raking, hard light, characteristic of evening or morning, to evoke a sense of stillness and suspension in this portrait. The ambience of the image connotes feelings of sanctuary and solitude as the figure rests contemplatively in a space defined by light.

Photograph by Kenneth Perrin

LIGHT AND COLOR

It is assumed that the reader has a basic working knowledge of color photographic materials, processes, and theory. In this chapter, the fundamental aspects of color imaging in technical, formal, and psychological terms specifically related to photographing in the studio will be explored. Color is a powerful visual and psychological tool for the studio photographer. It also requires a somewhat different application of lighting than does black-and-white photography. An invaluable reference for photographers working with color materials is the book *Colour Photography In Practice* by D. A. Spencer. It provides an in-depth analysis of color materials and processes in exhaustive, well-written chapters dealing with all aspects of color photography. An excellent introductory work for color photography is Robert Hirsch's *Exploring Color Photography*; see the Bibliography for additional references.

Description of Color

Terms used for specifying color vary greatly. Three main characteristics of color are identified in descriptive terms. These include: hue—the color name, identified with a particular placement on the color wheel or in the spectrum; saturation—the intensity of a given hue, in pigment media often controlled by adding a pigment to a white base, the saturation increasing with the pigment content; and, value—the relative brightness of a color, in pigment often controlled by adding black to a color base.

Three other important terms are primary, secondary, and complementary. The primary colors in pigment media are red, yellow, and blue. All other hues can be made from variously proportioned mixtures of these three colors. The secondary colors in pigment media are green, violet, and orange. They are equal mixtures of the primary colors red,

yellow, and blue. Every color has a complement directly opposite to its placement on the color wheel. In pigment media, mixing complements depresses value and eventually results in neutral gray or black as the colors negate each other's hue. Though photography deals in light, not pigment, these terms can be usefully applied to the visual experience of looking at a photograph in the same manner as they are applied to other media (figure 3.1).

Photographic Color

Color in photography is based on the mixing of light in additive and subtractive combinations. Color films and papers are sensitive to red, green, and blue light. These colors are said to be the additive photographic primaries. Three separate red, green, and blue light beams when overlapped in specific combinations and ratioed in brightness can form all of the

[figure 3.1]

In pigment, the three primary colors are red, yellow, and blue; the secondary colors are green, violet, and orange. All hues can be imagined as circling a color wheel, blending from one to the next in a continuous circle. In this image, Arthur Tress has playfully used the three primaries as a base for his color scheme and composition.

Photograph by Arthur Tress

possible colors. White light is an equal mixture of red, green, and blue wavelengths (figure 3.2).

The dyes that form the final photographic color negatives, transparencies, and prints are cyan, magenta, and yellow. These colors are the subtractive photographic primaries. Various combinations and densities of cyan, magenta, and yellow filters placed in the path of a single white light beam can also produce all possible colors (figure 3.3). The subtractive primaries are said to be the complements of the additive primaries: cyan is the complement of red, magenta is the complement of green, and yellow is the complement of blue (figure 3.4). Filter combinations of complements or all three subtractive primaries placed in one light beam will produce neutral density or black. All color photographic technologies are based on these additive and subtractive principles. In addition to having its own sets of primary colors, photography has developed its own technical and descriptive specification of color. This is embodied in the concept of color temperature.

Color Temperature

Color temperature is a descriptive evaluation of the dominant hue of a light source. Though its scale of measurement, the Kelvin scale, is a real cold/hot temperature scale, the color temperature of a light source has little to do with measurement of heat. Physicists use what they call a "blackbody" to specify color temperature. This black body reflects no light falling on it and emits radiation relative to energy in the form of heat applied to it. As it is heated from 0 degrees Kelvin (°K) it emits shorter and shorter wavelengths of radiation. At about 1,000 °K it begins to emit wavelengths of visible light and is seen to glow dull red. As more energy is applied, the glow changes from red to yellow and moves on up the spectrum through white to cool blues at around 10,000 °K (figure 3.5).

The color temperature of any given light source is defined as the temperature in °K at which a heated blackbody would emit visible light of a similar spectral distribution and hue. Color temperature measurements can only be accurately applied to light sources emitting a continuous spectrum such as tungsten filament bulbs, candles, and the sun. A discontinuous light source that emits light at enough different wavelengths can affect photographic materials in a manner similar to a continuous spectrum light source. These light sources, including electronic flash tubes, arc lights, and a few fluorescents, can be said to have an "equivalent" color temperature. Certain light sources, such as sodium and mercury vapor lamps and many fluorescent tubes, emit discontinuous light of such limited wavelengths that the concept of color temperature becomes meaningless when applied to their illumination. These light sources often cause significant color distortions in photographic materials and are rarely suited for color photography, though to the adaptive human eye they may appear neutral.

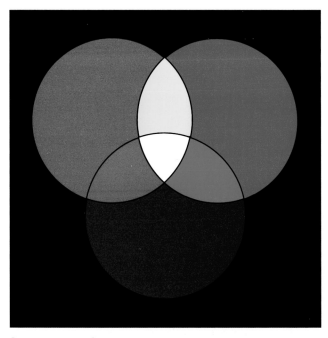

[figure 3.2]

Overlapping red, green, and blue light beams form cyan, magenta, yellow, and, in the center, white light. All hues can be derived from variously segmented combinations of red, green, and blue light. This is the principle behind additive color systems.

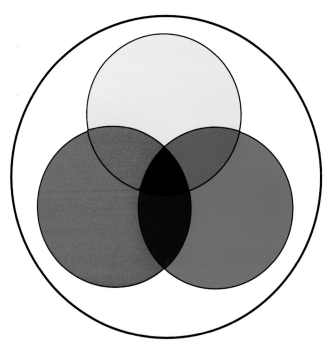

[figure 3.3]

Cyan, magenta, and yellow are the complements of red, green, and blue, respectively. When placed in a single beam of white light, variously blended combinations of cyan, magenta, and yellow filters can produce all hues and black. This is the principle behind subtractive color systems.

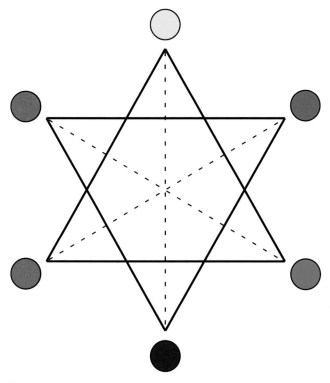

[figure 3.4]

Red and cyan, green and magenta, and blue and yellow are complementary pairs of additive and subtractive primaries. Pairs of complementary additive and subtractive filters form neutral density. A color wheel for photography can be developed with these juxtapositions at its root.

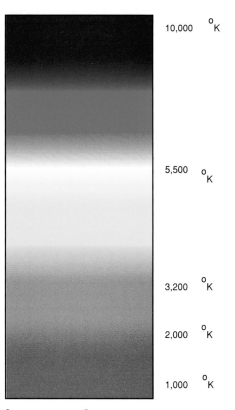

[figure 3.5]

The Kelvin temperature scale with associated colors

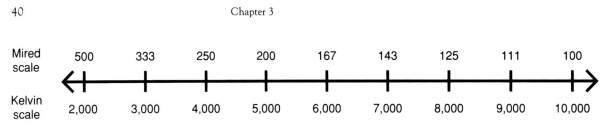

[figure 3.6]

The Kelvin scale as it is compared to the Mired scale. Note that the Kelvin and Mired scales are inverted in terms of their progression from warmer to cooler color.

Most color temperatures encountered in photographing range between 2,000 (candlelight) and 10,000 (clear blue sky) °K. Standard daylight has been specified as 5,500 °K. Another scale has been adapted to describe color temperature and is often used in specifying light-altering color correction filters—this is the Mired scale. Mired units are equal to °K divided into 1,000,000. Therefore 2,000 °K would be 500 Mired units and 10,000 °K would be 100 Mired units (figure 3.6). For added convenience, Decamired units, ten Mired units, are often used converting 2,000 °K into 50 Decamired units. Note that the Mired scale is inverse from the Kelvin scale.

Light and Color Films

Both light sources and color films are specified in terms of color temperature. In studio photography, three commonly encountered color temperatures are associated with specific light sources. Most tungsten and quartz bulbs are nominally rated at 3,200 °K. Some photofloods and quartz bulbs are burned at a higher power and yield increased light output and a higher color temperature of 3,400 °K. Electronic strobe lights are rated equivalent to daylight, between 5,500 and 6,000 °K depending on the manufacturer.

Tungsten lights are similar to regular household light bulbs. They vary in color temperature as they age. This change can range from a new bulb with a color temperature as high as 3,400 °K to a bulb near the end of its life with a color temperature as low as 2,700 °K. This change is gradual, though more rapid at the beginning and end of the bulbs life. Quartz-halogen bulbs are special tungsten bulbs. They have a large filament, are filled with a halogen vapor to inhibit deterioration, and are made with high-temperature quartz glass. They burn intensely, putting out a great deal of light for their size and burning off any filament residue that might cause a change in the color temperature output of the bulb. Quartz lights have an essentially constant, usually 3,200 °K, light output over their entire life span except for perhaps the first and last half-hour of operation. They have a fairly long life span, ranging to 100 hours or more. Photoflood bulbs are tungsten bulbs that operate at a higher power and produce more light than normal tungsten bulbs. They have a fairly constant color temperature of 3,400 °K over their short, 2 to 8 hour, life span. Again, they may vary in their first and last half-hour of operation.

Electronic strobe lights have an essentially constant color temperature output throughout their long life. Some strobe tubes can become discolored near the end of their useful life and this will cause a slight degradation in their color temperature. The color temperature of various electronic strobes differs depending on the manufacturer's specification of daylight. Most fall between 5,500 and 6,000 °K. They produce a highly repeatable and predictable light output and color temperature through the discharge of a measured electronic pulse through a gas-filled tube.

One type of special purpose light available is the HMI light. This stands for Hg medium-arc iodide light, referring to the filament and gas used in the lamp. These lights are extremely expensive. They are useful because they provide a continuous light source of exceptional brilliance balanced to approximate the color temperature of daylight. They are particularly valuable for film and video makers who require a continuous, daylight-balanced, artificial light source. They have a limited but unique application in still photography.

Various color films are available to match the corresponding color temperature output of these light sources. These films are designed to respond with neutral color renditions when exposed to illumination of specific spectral distributions. Tungsten color films are balanced for 3,200 °K, Kodachrome Type A film is balanced for 3,400 °K to be used with photofloods, and daylight color films used with electronic strobes are balanced for 5,500 °K. Matching the correct film to the correct light source is the beginning of achieving acceptable color balance in an image; unfortunately, it is often not enough as other factors may intervene.

Critical Color Balance

In achieving critical color balance, the three major factors of concern for the working photographer are bulb variations, emulsion characteristics of various films, and exposure times. Other factors, such as line voltage fluctuations, discoloration of reflectors and diffusers, and processing variations, can also produce significant color shifts. For critical color balancing, the color temperature of the light source and the color response of the film must be closely matched. Additional tests must be run to account for processing variations and various emulsion characteristics such as color shifts, reciprocity failure rates, and variations between stated and actual ISO.

Similar bulbs of different ages can produce illumination of significantly different color temperatures. As noted above, tungsten, quartz, and strobe lights can all be subject to various degrees of discoloration due to age. For critical color balance, it is recommended to start a shoot with all new bulbs or to keep records of how long each bulb has burned so that its color temperature can be predicted based upon experience. It should also be noted that bulbs and strobe tubes from different manufacturers may vary in terms of light output and color temperature, even though they are nominally rated exactly the same.

When working with tungsten lights, line voltage fluctuations can significantly affect color temperature. These fluctuations are actually quite common and are the reason why color enlargers are normally equipped with voltage stabilizers. Voltage stabilizers are available for lighting equipment but can be quite expensive. Voltage fluctuation is not a problem with strobe equipment because strobe tubes are actually powered by capacitors rather than the incoming line voltage.

Each batch of film produced by a manufacturer has a discrete emulsion number assigned; different emulsion batches of film vary in their color response to light. For critical matching, it is not enough to assume that tungsten film and tungsten lights will yield neutral balance. With some film, certain data is included regarding the precise response of the particular emulsion batch to a standard light source. This is normally true of color sheet film. If this data is not packaged with the film, it can sometimes be obtained from the manufacturer. The data will recommend certain color compensating filters that must be used to match the emulsion response to a light source with a standard color temperature such as 3,200 or 5,500 °K.

With extended or extremely short exposure times, reciprocity failure can become a major factor affecting color balance. Each color film is designed to be used within a specific range of exposure times. Two major film groups exist—type S films, which are designed to be exposed between 1/10,000 second and 1/10 second, and type L films, which are designed to be exposed between 1/50 second and 60 seconds. When used outside of their recommended exposure ranges, films respond slower to exposure than their ISOs would indicate. This is reciprocity failure. With black-and-white films this can be compensated for through increased exposure and decreased development. With color films the problem is more serious and more difficult to correct.

Modern color films are made up of three separate layers of emulsion—red, green, and blue sensitive respectively. These three layers must all react to exposure in a balanced, coordinated manner to render neutral color balance. Each of these layers is subject to a different rate of reciprocity failure. Therefore, when reciprocity failure occurs, the emulsion layers react to exposure individually, not compositely, and produce a color shift in the film. As with black-and-white film there is also an overall loss in ISO.

If neutral, adequately exposed negatives or transparencies are to result, correction must be made for both the color shift in the film and the loss of ISO. Data packaged with most professional films indicates the ISO correction and the color correction that must accompany extended exposure times. The effective ISO and necessary color correction will continue to change with lengthening exposure times. Though reciprocity failure occurs with extremely short exposures as well, correction information is not readily available because these exposures are rarely encountered in normal working situations.

If a choice is possible, it may be preferable to increase exposure by using a larger f-stop rather than risk reciprocity failure with a long exposure time. The ISO and color correction recommendations packaged with film are meant as guides for accurate color rendition. Because every different emulsion batch of film will react individually, for critical work, tests must be run with a number of different ISO/filter combinations.

The processing of color films is much more restrictive than that of black-and-white, but it is possible to vary the development to achieve some contrast and exposure changes. Most professional labs will "pull" or "push" development by up to one stop or more. In addition, each lab will process color film somewhat individually, resulting in varied color casts particularly in transparencies. To assure high quality, tests should be run to find the best quality lab with the most neutral and consistent processing. Color correction is usually made with color compensating or CC filters. These filters are used on the camera when photographing and can also be used as viewing filters when assessing test shots for additional color correction.

Filters for Color Photography

More detailed information on filters is contained in chapter 7. This discussion will summarize certain filters that are particularly applicable to photographing in the studio with color films. The first important principle about filters that the photographer must remember is that filters always subtract, they never add. They may subtract spectral components and/or intensity. Four main types of filters are used in color photography—color compensating filters, light balancing filters, ultraviolet filters, and polarizing filters. The nature and use of polarized light and polarizing filters will be discussed thoroughly in chapters 7, 8, and 9.

Color compensating filters are available in a wide range of colors and densities to cope with almost any color shift required to balance light and film. These filters are designed to absorb specific wavelengths of the spectrum. They are useful in correcting for color shifts due to fluorescent lighting, processing and emulsion variations, and reciprocity failure. Standard filters come in cyan, magenta, yellow, red, green, and blue and vary in density from a pale .025 to a saturated .50. Usually thin, gelatin or polyester, these filters are normally placed in a holder in front of the camera lens. Glass filters are available but expensive.

Another type of filter available for color photography is the light balancing filter. These filters are designed to alter the spectral distribution of a light source. Available sets normally consist of amber and bluish filters of various densities. Decamired light balancing filters are also available. Changes in color temperature as stated in °K are more noticeable at lower color temperatures. For example, at 3,200 °K a shift of 100 degrees produces a noticeable visual change while at 5,500 °K a shift of 300 degrees is needed before any change is visually detectable. When color temperatures are rated in Mired units these shifts even out so that a shift of 1 Decamired unit (100 °K) at 3,200 °K is visually equivalent to a shift of 1 Decamired unit (300 °K) at 5,500 °K. This is due to the nature of the inverse mathematical relationship between the Kelvin and Mired scales, and makes specifying light balancing filters in Mired units a convenient visual reference.

Color conversion filters are also available for radical shifts in color temperature. These light balancing filters are designed to alter the light so that daylight color film can be shot under tungsten or photoflood light or vice versa in any combination. In practice, matching the balance of the color film as closely as possible to the color temperature of the light source is always preferable to using a conversion filter.

Color film is more susceptible to ultraviolet exposure than black-and-white film. High levels of ultraviolet light will register as exposure in the blue sensitive layer of color film. In studio photography this is not a major concern because high levels of ultraviolet light are rarely, if ever, encountered. However, on

location this may be an important filtration consideration. To remove excess ultraviolet light, an ultraviolet-haze filter is often employed. This is essentially an optically clear filter though it may have a slight warm cast. It requires no exposure compensation. A skylight or 1A filter can also be used. A skylight filter has good ultraviolet absorption and a slight pinkish color to "warm up" shadow areas and overcast daylight.

Lighting

Lighting for color photography differs from lighting for black-and-white photography in both technical and aesthetic considerations. The contrast range of color materials, particularly transparency films, is quite limited. Lighting contrast must often be reduced to match the scene contrast to the contrast range of color films. It is interesting to note the trend toward softer, diffused lighting that developed in the 1960s and '70s as color asserted its presence in studio photography. This is not simply an aesthetic trend but also a practical necessity, particularly in working with color transparency materials. Prior to that time, most studio photography was executed in black and white which accommodates a higher contrast range and depends upon tonal separation alone for definition. Today, with the exception of some portraiture, the vast majority of studio photography is executed with color materials, necessitating softer lighting if a realistic, descriptive rendering is to be achieved (figure 3.7). As with black and white, hard, contrasty light can be used to achieve dramatic effects with color, increasing saturation and contrast at the expense of descriptive renderings (figure 3.8).

[f i g u r e 3 . 7]

Raymond Meier used a soft, enveloping illumination to reveal the subtle color and surface qualities of his subject. The contrasting, yet related, shades of cool blue and warm purple provide a visually active palette of soft contrasts.

Photograph by Raymond Meier, "SEXY EXPLOSIVO"

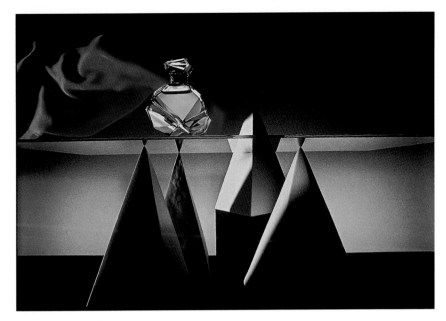

Mixed light sources of varying color temperature can prove a problem when working with color materials. Because films are balanced or can be corrected to respond neutrally to light of only one color temperature, a scene in which there is illumination of two or more color temperatures can be difficult to render in a neutral palette. Certain modern color negative films have a fourth emulsion layer, a negative-red-sensitive layer, that is designed to alter the response of the film in discrete areas of an image affected by sources of illumination having varied color temperatures. These films are designed to render a "visually neutral" image. That is, the scene in the print will look substantially the way the eye would perceive it in terms of color relationships (figure 3.9). This is not 100 percent effective, and one must accept compromises in quality and color rendition.

For simplicity, it is by far best to avoid mixed light sources. However, in practice this is not always possible. Two methods can be used for balancing the color of illumination from mixed light sources to match one film type. The first is to filter the various light sources with conversion filters to balance their color

[figure 3.8]

Jim White used hard light and hot color to create a passionate, dramatic statement in his geometric landscape with perfume bottle.

Jim White Photography, Chicago

a.

b.

c.

d.

[figure 3.9]

Kevin Mooney used Fuji's Reala color negative film, designed with a negative red-sensitive emulsion layer to help balance for mixed light conditions, in his photograph of a Chicago subway (a.). The subject was illuminated with fluorescent, sodium vapor, and tungsten lights. Mooney also shot the scene with Fuji Velvia, a daylight-balanced transparency film; the transparencies were shot with no filter (b.), an FLD filter (c.), and a CC40 magenta filter (d.). All renditions provide a compromise—the photographer must choose the most appropriate solution to a mixed-light problem such as this.

Photograph by Kevin O. Mooney

temperature to the sensitivity of the film. The second is to utilize multiple exposure techniques, exposing for one light source at a time and filtering the camera to correct for the various color temperatures.

Filters for lights are available in many forms. Glass and gelatin are the two most common. In the sizes required for filtering light sources, glass filters are extremely expensive. The use of gels is much more common. Roscoe and other companies make lighting gels in hundreds of colors. Often used to gel theater lights, gels are also available as conversion filters to alter the color balance of tungsten to daylight or vice versa. Polarizing filters are also available in gel form. The most common forms of mixed light encountered are tungsten with strobe and tungsten with daylight. The tungsten lights can be gelled in either case to achieve an overall equality of color balance throughout the image. It is possible to gel strobes and small windows as well to match them to tungsten balance; however, gelling daylight becomes problematic with large windows or outside.

In balancing color with multiple exposure techniques, separate exposures are made for different areas of a scene illuminated by various light sources with different color temperatures. This technique works most effectively when the light sources illuminate discrete areas of the scene and do not significantly overlap. Separate meter readings are taken, exposures calculated and light sources turned on and off independently as the filtration on the camera is changed to balance each incoming light for the chosen film. Multiple exposure techniques will be more thoroughly explored in chapters 12 and 14.

[figure 3.10]

Ray Perkins employed strong complementary colors to create an active image space with advancing figure and receding ground.

Ray Perkins Photography, Chicago

Although techniques for lighting in black and white and color share many similarities, when lighting for black and white, tonal separation is responsible for delineating all shape, detail, and volume. With color materials, color itself takes on a delineating role. Areas of color that might render as similar tones with little contrast or separation in black and white may be dramatically contrasted in color. Color helps to define the shapes of objects and areas in the image. It also adds an additional variable the eye can utilize in defining detail and volume. Shifts in hue and saturation may enrich and soften or exaggerate tonal transitions in the image. Color can be used to effectively structure an image in terms of active and passive colors, advancing and receding space, and visual linkage (figure 3.10). In black and white, tonal transition alone must take on all of these burdens.

Color as Form

As a formal, structural element in a photographic image, color can be extremely powerful. A quick survey of contemporary studio photography will reveal the ubiquitous use of economical, graphically strong, primary color statements. Red, green, blue, and yellow are predominant among simple, tight compositions, with clean lines and saturated color also prevailing. Color is used to communicate, to direct the viewer's eye to certain content, or to set the tone of the image, and it serves these ends effectively (figure 3.11).

Systems of color theory were mapped out as early as the sixteenth century when Goethe developed his nine-color pyramid based on the use of primary, secondary, and tertiary colors (figure 3.12). As opposed to photographic practice, most color theory systems are based on the painting primaries of red, yellow, and blue. As noted earlier, secondary colors in these systems—orange, violet, and green—are fifty-fifty mixtures of the primaries. Tertiary colors are fifty-fifty mixtures of the secondaries.

Many contemporary systems are used for identifying or specifying color. Some, like Goethe's, are based primarily on simple mixing; others are based on the color wheel and incorporate factors such as hue, saturation,

[figure 3.11]

Susan Friedman used the photographic primaries to structure the space of her image into planes, volumes, and splashes of interactive color.

Photograph by Susan Friedman

[figure 3.12]

Goethe's nine-color pyramid is based upon the primaries red, yellow, and blue and their secondary and tertiary combinations. It is one of the earliest visual formalizations of color theory.

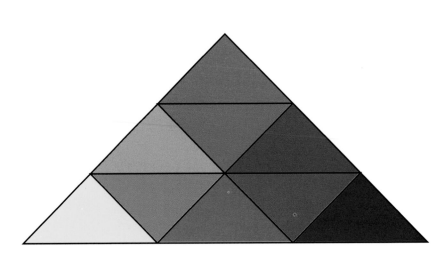

and value in their descriptive vocabulary; still others depend on the scientific specification of wavelength and brightness. The purpose of these systems is usually to help set standards, analyze data, or establish aesthetic principles. While the first two functions may concern photographers as technicians, it is the last that concerns photographers as image makers.

Many theoreticians have proposed systems that define "proper" or "acceptable" color relationships—which color complements or contradicts another. The limitations implied by these restrictive systems seem to negate the free exploration of color and reduce it to predictable, static possibilities. One can approach color theory in a more fluid and dynamic fashion. This is clearly demonstrated in the work of Josef Albers. Albers, a painter and color theorist, published a book and series of color studies under the title *The Interaction of Color*. Albers encourages the free exploration of color relationships and demonstrates their inherent flexibility in a series of often surprising exercises and illustrations. The basis of his theory is that color is almost always seen in an interactive context. This leads to an exploration of the interactive principles that arise between myriad colors rather than a system of rules limiting those potential encounters.

Albers' theories encourage experimentation and visual sampling of color relationships. The portfolio that accompanies his book is, in itself, a wonderful visual experience. It leads the viewer through illusion, science, and fantasy. He concludes his color studies portfolio with a series of silk-screen reproductions of free-form studies made from leaves and colored paper scraps.

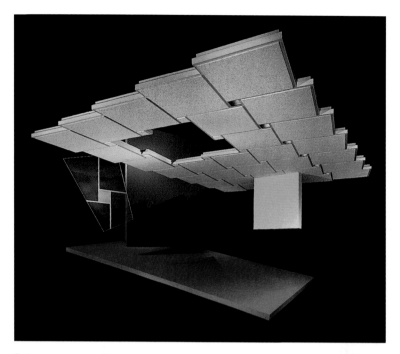

[figure 3.13]

In Barbara Karant's image for U.S. Gypsum, the primary colors red, yellow, and blue play a dynamic, formal role, adding stability and power to the composition.

Photograph by Barbara Karant

Albers' work is refreshing and invigorating. While not invalidating the systematization of color theory for specific purposes, Albers does manage to complement the rigorous definition of color with whimsical observations and joy.

Some simple principles underlying color theory can be directly useful in constructing photographs. These observations are based on the traditional red, yellow, blue primary structure of pigment media rather than the red, green, blue additive primaries of photography. Visually, red, yellow, and blue are the only three pure colors; all other colors are mixtures of these with the addition of white and black to control saturation and value. These three primary colors, red, yellow, and blue, are extremely immutable and powerful compositional elements. They maintain their character in interaction and form a commanding triad. Their use adds formal stability to an image (figure 3.13).

The secondary colors, green, orange, and violet are active mixtures of the primaries. They each lie midway between two primaries and are pulled equally toward their poles. This lends secondaries a stability in their own right but makes them susceptible to influence by other strong colors. The secondaries in combination with the primaries or with each other are vibrant and unstable. Witness the use of secondary colors in combination with primaries in much op art of the 1960s or in "black-light" posters and velvet paintings. The secondaries are unique in that each one contains a component of and the complement of the other two, making their juxtaposition visually active and disquieting (figure 3.14).

[f i g u r e   3.14]
Joe Vitone exploited the inherent instability of the relationship between the secondary colors green, orange, and violet to enhance the uneasy suspicion implied in his image "Shady Dealings #4."   © 1985 by Joseph Vitone, "Shady Dealings #4—Finding the Letter."

Colors lying between the primaries and secondaries tend to be easily influenced in combination. As a rule they do not possess the strength of the primaries or the energy of the secondaries due to their tendency to give their character to a stronger color. Oddly, as Albers demonstrates in his color studies, certain combinations of these colors can be quite vibrant even at low levels of saturation and value.

Using Color Theory

In the studio, color theory can be directly applied to the construction of sets and images. The choice of background color, the coloring of various surfaces, and the selection and preparation of props are just a few of the elements that can be manipulated Color rendering can be controlled by the selection of film, the choice of light source, and the filtration of lights or camera. Complex interactions can occur through varying the color combinations of light sources with illuminated surfaces and multiple exposure techniques (figure 3.15). The possibilities are endless. Experimentation will reveal that all of these variables can be controlled and previsualized to "color map" a formal structure. The studio photographer has the opportunity to exercise strict control over this color-mapping, which is a powerful, communicative tool.

The viewer will make connections between areas of the same or similar color in an image. Indeed, color can be used to lead the eye through an image, to pull various parts of an image together, or to imply formal relationships between different objects or planes of space (figure 3.16). Because color is normally perceived in interaction, the introduction of a monochromatic color scheme can in itself be a powerful statement (figure 3.17). Sets constructed to take full advantage of color are sometimes highly imaginative, manipulated, and fantastic (figure 3.18). In other images, color serves strictly as a compositional element, creating formal dialogue.

In photography, the hand-coloring of black-and-white photographic prints provides the opportunity to add color in a controlled manner after the fact of exposure (figure 3.19). The use of spot color in black-and-white images has recently been popularized through the application of sophisticated computer imaging and video techniques. If color is to be added to an image, the original lighting scheme should be designed to accommodate this manipulation. To function effectively, hand-coloring often requires soft tonal transitions and high-key renditions. The aesthetic effect of adding color without attention to the original image can be seen in many colorized versions of classic films. It is often visually disruptive, not suited to the

David Haxton structured the space of a large set with various planes of colored light and paper. The resulting images are formal exercises defined by the color and spatial relationships within the frame.

Photograph by David Haxton, "Torn Orange Front and Rear," 1979

Kip Swehla's still life of guitars uses color to unify receding planes of space. The warmer and lighter colors in the middle ground advance while the cool blue and green in the foreground and background pull together. All of this compresses the image depth and focuses our attention on shapes.

Photograph by Kipling Swehla

original lighting, and considered an aesthetic violation of the filmmaker's intent and craft. Applied color can be used creatively, but it must be considered carefully.

Color as Meaning

Often in common language color is associated with concept: red hot with anger or passion; green with envy or jealousy; yellow with fear; blue with cold or depression. All of these affect the visual perception of color. Not innate psychological responses, these associations are rather learned cultural meanings that influence the response to color. In addition to these conceptual relationships, some psycho-physiological reactions associated with color have been proved.

It has long been believed that warm colors motivate toward passion, anger, or action while cool colors evoke mental states of calm and relaxation. Actors have their green room where they wait and compose themselves before a performance on stage. Many police stations house blue rooms where violent prisoners are held for "cooling off." Red is often associated with power, sexuality, or speed. Recent research has indeed shown marked changes in brain activity related to color perception. However, not all of these reactions are predictable. For example, when a person is exposed to a hot-pink stimulus that person experiences a substantial drop in respiration, brain activity, and metabolism. Here, a "hot" color produces a "cool" response. Generally speaking though, the use and perception of color is more influenced by the cultural understanding of its meaning and importance than by the specific psycho-physiological response to given stimuli.

[figure 3.17]

Ray Perkins used a monochromatic color scheme to enhance impact in his still life of a banana. Since color is normally seen in complex interaction, the reduction of a scene to one color can create visual imbalance that will draw attention to itself through absence.

Ray Perkins Photography, Chicago

[figure 3.18]

In her 1983 composition "Maybe Babies," Sandy Skoglund uses the complementary colors green, orange, and violet to structure a formally active space. Our eye is drawn to the warm orange window glow in the background, while the cool greens, blues, and purples provide a tension of contrast in the foreground.

Photograph © Sandy Skoglund, "Maybe Babies," 1983

[figure 3.19]

Paul Elledge's use of subtle, hand-applied color in this portrait adds depth and intimacy to the subject. The soft, selective color melds well with the subdued light in the image creating an overall feeling of quiet contemplation.

Photograph by Paul Elledge

Modern, western society has a fairly sophisticated descriptive language to specify color. Approximately thirty names are frequently used to describe color. However, the ability to identify color remains rather vague. Most of us can form a mental image of red, green, or blue; but what about mauve, chartreuse, puce, or teal? Linguistic discrimination breaks down quickly even though the visual sense is acute. As mentioned, designers have developed a number of systems for specifying color relative to their requirements in order to facilitate communication. Culture specifies color in terms of its own needs as well, and these have as much to do with meaning as with hue.

Color can be used as a signifier in images if its significance is understood in a societal context. Defined meanings vary from culture to culture and evolve as each culture changes. It is important to understand the transcultural, historical, and contemporary significance of color. For example, in western culture the color white is associated with the purity and celebration of life, while in the east it is the color of mourning; historically, the indigenous peoples of the great plains of North America associated the colors white, black, green, and yellow with cardinal points on the spiritual wheel of the universe and in the character of human beings; and, the color green has become closely associated with environmentalist groups and political movements whose agenda involves environmental preservation. Color can be associated with cultural meaning in many other instances.

If color is to be used intelligently in photography, practitioners must also be aware of the viewers' knowledge of and associations with particular colors. Photographers will not elicit a

[figure 3.20]

Patrick Nagatani and Andree Tracey used color as a metaphor and a warning in their 1985 composition "Unsafe Light." The association of red with danger and the linkage of photographic chemistry with industrial waste implied through the formal structure of the image function together to create a meaningful whole.

Patrick Nagatani and Andree Tracey, "Unsafe Light," 1985. Courtesy Jayne H. Baum Gallery, New York, N.Y.

response from a viewer who has no knowledge of the photographers' codes. When using color as a formal element to structure an image, photographers can proceed more intelligently if they consider the culturally defined responses that certain colors are likely to elicit from viewers. If photographers use color as a meaningful aspect of content, they must give the viewer access to the meaning either through using familiar codes or through defining their terms in the work itself (figure 3.20). Josef Albers' theories operate both in the internal context of the image and in the relation between image, viewer, and meaning.

CAMERAS IN THE STUDIO

It is assumed that the reader has a basic knowledge of camera formats and operation. Two excellent books that can supply general information are Arnold Gassan's *Exploring Black and White Photography* and Phil Davis' *Photography*. Of the many fine books detailing view camera use, a particularly good one for studio photographers is *View Camera Technique* by Harvey Shaman; refer to the Bibliography for further references. This chapter will examine some general concerns that, while not exclusive to any one environment, may take on special importance in the studio.

Historically, the camera most closely associated with the studio is the large format view camera. In contemporary studio practice all types and formats of cameras from 35mm to 20″ × 24″ view cameras are in use. The view camera remains dominant in most situations. Its unique abilities in controlling shape and depth of field make it a valuable tool for

many applications. However, the view camera is expensive, static, and slow. It must be tripod-mounted and is limited in quick response situations where movement and changing point of view might be important. The nature of the task and the requirements of the image generally define the choice of format.

Camera Format

Available formats can largely be divided into three major groups: small format 35mm cameras, medium format 120/220 roll film cameras, and large format view cameras using cut sheet film. Each group has several types of cameras to offer. These vary in their capabilities, construction, and usefulness. The choice of camera format begins with the analysis of the shooting situation and the requirements of the final image. Several factors must be taken into consideration.

First is camera mobility. One of the unique features of photography is its ability to forage into a scene and visually explore its geography. Early filmmakers discovered this technique realizing that the camera could abandon its static "observer's" point of view in favor of a "participator's" interaction with a scene. The still camera is no different. The photographer, the camera, and the viewer can be spectators to or participants in the image. Point of view makes its visual presence felt in every photograph, just as the tense of writing defines the nature of a novel.

If the camera is to become an active participant in the scene, it must normally be hand-held. This immediately suggests a small or medium format camera. If the camera is to be hand-held and the image is to be sharp, either the level of ambient light must be sufficient to permit the use of short shutter speeds, or strobes must be employed. With most cameras, hand-holding at shutter

a.   b.   c.   d.

[figure 4.1]

Cedric Chatterley used the blur of motion created with a long exposure to enhance
feelings of charismatic catharsis in his series of photographs dealing with religious ecstasy.

Photographs by Cedric Chatterley from the series Ambivalent Ecstasies/Converging Energies

a.   b.   c.

[figure 4.2]

Steve Nozicka used a 35mm camera and motor drive to capture rapid changes in pose
and expression as his model acted out various roles and emotions in front of the camera.

Photographs by Steve Nozicka

speeds over 1/125th second may result in blur due to camera vibration. Some 35mm cameras, especially rangefinder cameras, can be hand-held up to 1/30th second with satisfactory results.

Light levels in the studio are generally less than outdoors. In a large set, it can be difficult to attain the level of tungsten illumination necessary to permit the use of short shutter speeds and apertures small enough for adequate depth of field. Electronic strobes overcome much of this difficulty with brief flash durations and high light output. Conversely, image sharpness may not be a requirement. Many images can effectively utilize the longer exposure of the blur (figure 4.1).

Second, and related to camera mobility, is the level of spontaneity required in photographing. Will it be important to respond quickly to momentary poses, expressions, or dynamics of the situation? If so, speed of camera operation becomes an issue. A large format view camera is neither responsive to changes in the scene nor capable of quick-paced, successive exposures. Again, a small or medium format camera offers much more flexibility in these situations. These cameras can be quickly positioned and focused, can be easily exchanged or reloaded, and can be equipped with motor drives for rapid or sequential exposures (figure 4.2). Another difference lies in the interpersonal dynamics between a subject and photographer working with a small, hand-held camera versus a subject and photographer working with a view camera on a tripod. Thirty-five millimeter cameras offer the greatest mobility, the fastest camera operation, and the most spontaneous responsiveness.

A third factor to consider is the level of description involved in the image. The photographic process is capable of great detail and subtlety of tonal rendition. These aspects of the medium reach their zenith in the large format image. The view camera is also capable of rendering shapes with little apparent distortion. Therefore, in an image where the description of content is of primary importance, a large format view camera is often the best tool for achieving the desired end (figure 4.3). The same considerations often apply to an image in which the photographic print as an object in itself is the goal. The rich beauty of a large format image gives the print a sense of presence and seductive power. The large format camera expresses formal photographic vision to its fullest.

A fourth factor to consider when working on location is portability. A view camera is a large, heavy piece of equipment requiring a large case and many accessories. The set up time is extended, and the process is rather invasive. View cameras are not discrete, nor are they unintimidating to nonphotographers. Small and medium format cameras, along with their many accessories, can be carried almost anywhere, can be set up quickly, and can be unobtrusive.

Often, a medium format camera is an excellent compromise, satisfying all of the above requirements to some degree. The camera is small enough to be portable and spontaneous in demanding situations, yet it provides a large enough negative to yield rich prints with great detail and tonal

beauty. Some medium format 120/220 cameras have built-in bellows for close-up work and even allow moderate view camera swings and tilts of the lens. Combined with their range of accessories, including motor drives and interchangeable camera backs, the unique capabilities of the medium format camera may provide solutions to a wide range of problems.

Camera Supports

Two types of camera supports are regularly utilized in the studio— tripods and studio stands. Tripods used in the studio are often sturdier and heavier than those taken on location. This extra stability accommodates the larger format cameras and extended exposure times encountered in studio work. Tripod heads are often equipped with geared movements to facilitate precise angle adjustments. Often, when working with a stationary camera, photographers will opt for a studio stand rather than a tripod.

Studio stands are composed of a central column, ranging up to eleven feet in height, and a cross arm that slides smoothly up and down along the column and that can also be shifted horizontally (figure 4.4). Tripod heads may be mounted at the end, or ends, of the cross arm. The stands themselves are usually equipped with a heavy-duty caster base that can be locked in position. Other accessories such as cross arm extensions, equipment trays, and low angle adapters are available for many studio stands. These stands are much more stable than a tripod and increase productivity by simplifying precise and flexible camera positioning.

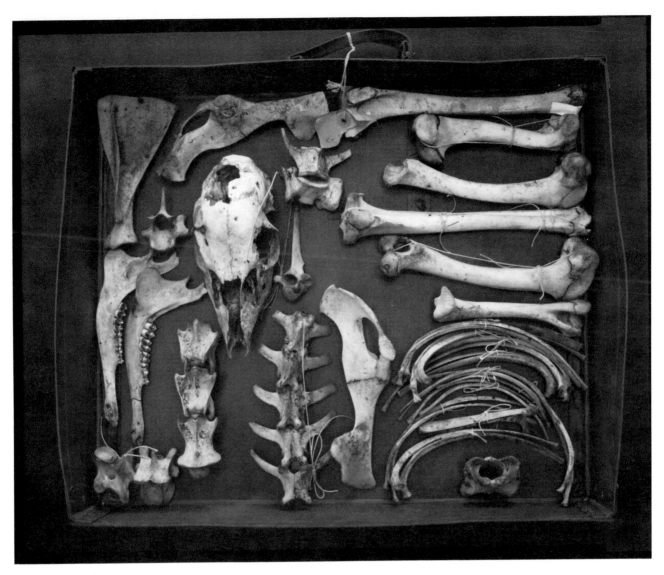

[figure 4.3]
In Olivia Parker's photograph of the skeleton of a deer, the description of content is of the utmost importance. The strange beauty and fascination that we find in the skeleton is the source of the photograph's power. The large format camera allowed Parker to evoke nuance of her subject in exquisite detail.

Photograph by Olivia Parker, ''Deer''

Lenses, Perspective, and Related Concerns

The notion that the selection of a lens defines the perspective of a photograph is not true. Perspective is defined by the position of the camera relative to the subject. It describes the relationship in size and position of various objects within the frame to one another. It is always relative to distance and point of view. The lens controls the size of objects in the frame. This is true of any format. The proper image-perspective is the primary decision the photographer makes. This will determine camera position. The correct lens is then selected to fill the frame with the desired image.

With any given image, if foreground objects are to be exaggerated in size compared to background objects, the camera must be positioned near the foreground, often requiring a shorter lens to expand the field of view and to accommodate the reduced camera-to-subject distance. If all objects are to be rendered accurately in relative

[figure 4.4]

A 4″ × 5″ view camera mounted on a studio stand. Note the accessory tray, adjustable cross arm, and tall central column.

Photograph by Guy Hurka

[figure 4.5]

In Leasha Overturf's photograph, the depth of scene and the close positioning of the camera to the near subject distort the true size relationship of cat to man. If Overturf had moved the camera back significantly and used a longer lens to achieve the same framing, the cat and man would have been rendered in their true size relationship, yielding a much less dramatic image.

Photograph by Leasha Overturf

size, then the camera must be positioned farther from the foreground, generally requiring a longer lens to reduce the field of view and to fill the frame with the image (figure 4.5).

Related to perspective is shape distortion. If one part of an object is proportionately closer to the camera than other parts, its shape will be rendered in a distorted manner. The foreground areas will be much enlarged relative to the whole object. If shapes are to be rendered accurately, the camera must be moved away from the subject and a longer lens used to fill the frame adequately. This is

particularly important in still life and portraiture, where compositions are often tight and, with shorter lenses, camera-to-subject distances will be greatly reduced thus introducing shape distortions (figure 4.6).

The reduced distances and light levels involved in studio photography necessitate attention to depth-of-field calculations. It is useful to know that depth of field is not evenly distributed around the plane of focus. It exists one-third in front and two-thirds behind the plane of focus. This phenomenon leads to the rule of focusing one-third of the way into

the subject to attain maximum depth of field at any given aperture.

A useful, important accessory for the studio photographer is a good lens shade. The purpose of the lens shade is to keep stray light from reaching and reflecting off the surface of the lens or filter and thereby degrading the image contrast, color saturation, and detail. In the studio, the lens shade can serve as a gobo, or light blocker, to shield the camera lens from lighting instruments. Small format cameras normally have individual lens shades designed specifically for each lens. A special

[figure 4.6]

Keith Cotton's portrait of Maynard Bluelight relies on both facial expression and camera distance to distort the subject's features. In this case, the camera distortion complements, rather than contradicts, the intentions of the photographer, which shows how rules can often be violated to the benefit of a successful photograph.

Photograph by Keith Cotton

[figure 4.7]

A compendium lens shade mounted on a view camera. Note the shade's adjustable bellows and filter holders.

shade called a compendium lens shade is available for view cameras and some medium format cameras (figure 4.7).

Compendium lens shades have an adjustable bellows to shield a maximum amount of light from lenses of various focal lengths and angles of view. The longer the lens and the narrower its angle of view, the more the bellows are extended; overextension of the shade will cause vignetting in the corners of the image. Some compendium lens shades are equipped to hold filters and can be moved out of the way for lens adjustments. Proper use of a good lens shade can add the equivalent of one grade of black-and-white paper contrast to a negative and will significantly increase color saturation in a transparency; an increase in sharpness and detail may also be evident.

Shutters and Flash Synchronization

Electronic strobe is the dominant studio light source, making an understanding of flash synchronization imperative. All cameras contain a shutter mechanism, and when it is used with a flash, either bulbs or electronic strobe, it must be synchronized with the peak of light output of the flash. This requires a slight delay between the tripping of the shutter release and the opening of the shutter. During this delay the flash is triggered and attains maximum brightness. The time varies with bulbs and electronic strobes. Flash bulbs actually contain a burning filament foil or thread and take a certain time to reach maximum light output. Electronic strobes are gaseous discharge tubes and reach maximum light output almost instantaneously. On the shutter, bulb synchronization is labeled M and electronic strobe synchronization is labeled X.

Two major types of shutters are available. Focal plane shutters are built into the camera body and are normally found in 35mm and some medium format cameras. These shutters consist of two curtains that regulate the exposure time as they pass the film plane. Leaf shutters are built into the lens and are normally found on view cameras and some medium format cameras. They consist of several overlapping blades that open and close behind the lens aperture.

Focal plane shutters normally have a maximum flash synchronization speed. This ranges from 1/60th second to 1/250th second depending upon the camera design. Leaf shutters can be synchronized at any shutter speed, usually ranging up to 1/500th second. At shorter than recommended shutter speeds, a focal plane shutter will only expose a portion of the negative at any one time. A leaf shutter exposes the entire negative as soon as it opens, regardless of shutter speed, allowing for faster synchronized flash speeds. This may be helpful in balancing exposures in which both flash and ambient light are involved.

Photograph by Christopher Hawker

LIGHTING IN PRACTICE

[chapter]

MEASURING LIGHT

Quality is more important than quantity. Though this simple principle of lighting design will be emphasized throughout the text, the implicit knowledge of how to achieve desired exposure levels is a critical, practical matter. What constitutes proper exposure is, of course, a subjective judgment and may have as much to do with aesthetic decisions as with objective standards. The ability to previsualize results and achieve well-exposed images is an important part of the craft of photography. Fortunately, photographers have a variety of tools to help them. In studio photography, two tools are often used to aid subjective judgment in arriving at proper exposure: the light meter and Polaroid materials. The use of Polaroid materials as an aid in determining exposure levels will be thoroughly discussed in chapter 13. The drawback to using Polaroid materials is their expendability and expense; the advantage lies in the purely visual nature of the testing procedure. A

light meter represents a major, one-time investment that, with reasonable care, will have a long useful life.

The use of in-camera light meters is not fundamentally different from the use of hand-held light meters. For the purposes of this text, a working knowledge of in-camera metering systems is assumed. The principles discussed below refer specifically to hand-held meters; photographers using in-camera metering systems will need to exercise some interpretation for their specific circumstances.

Types of Meters

The two basic types of light meters are reflected light meters and incident light meters (figure 5.1). All in-camera metering systems employ reflected light meters. Reflected light meters actually measure the specific amount of light reflected from a particular surface or surfaces in

the scene. Incident light meters measure the amount of light emanating from a light source that reaches or is present at various planes within the scene. The two types of meters have various forms and are used in significantly different ways. They also yield different information, all of which needs to be interpreted by the photographer. Combination meters that function in both reflected and incident modes are available, though usually not as effective as dedicated, single-mode meters.

Both reflected and incident light meters can be designed to measure either continuous light as from tungsten light sources, or discontinuous light as from electronic strobes or flash bulbs. Many of the high-quality light meters available for studio use measure both continuous and discontinuous light; some are capable of averaging these two readings together to arrive at a cumulative exposure recommendation. Meters

63

[figure 5.1]

Clockwise from upper right: a reflected light, spot meter capable of 1° readings; an incident light/reflected light, ambient/flash meter fitted with an incident light diffusion dome; an incident light/reflected light, ambient/flash meter fitted with a reflected light aperture; spot and incident metering attachments for the meter at lower left.

Incident light meters are designed to measure the amount of light present at a given point in the scene in front of the camera. These meters normally have a white, half-spherical diffuser over the light-sensitive meter cell. They are intended to gather all of the light at a particular point in the scene from a 180° sweep of vertical and horizontal angles, to blend the light into an average brightness, and to give a measurement of the total quantity of light present at that point. Attachments that replace the diffusion sphere with a flat diffusion disc are available for certain models of these meters. This is valuable for metering flat, two-dimensional surfaces.

Some light meters are particularly useful for a specific task. Certain meters are designed with built-in scales referencing brightness ranges and tonal rendering. Reflected meters are suited to judging overall scene brightness relationships, while incident light meters are preferred for establishing lighting ratios. Individual working habits will define personal preference in the choice of a light meter. It is best to start with a meter that has maximum flexibility.

measuring continuous light are normally referred to as "ambient light meters," and those measuring discontinuous light are referred to as "strobe or flash meters." Ambient light is simply light which exists in a scene in an encompassing, constant manner—continuous illumination. The type of light meter purchased, ambient or strobe, depends largely on the working circumstances of the photographer. Obviously a meter capable of measuring both types of light is ideal.

Two types of reflected light meters are available, averaging and spot meters. Averaging meters measure the light over a relatively broad area of a scene with a fairly wide angle of view, sometimes 30°

or more. Spot meters measure the light from selected small areas of a scene with very narrow angles of view, often as little as 1° (figure 5.2). Certain meters are convertible between averaging and spot configurations. A spot meter allows one to remain at the camera position and, without moving into the scene itself, measure the light reflected from many varied surfaces within the picture space. A special type of spot meter for use in view cameras is a film-plane meter. A through-the-lens metering system for view cameras, this meter has a probe that, like a film holder, is inserted into the camera back. The probe can be moved to any position in the frame and take restricted and accurate spot readings.

Meters, Light, and Film

A common misconception among beginning photographers is that a light meter tells the proper exposure for a scene. This is not the case. A light meter gives specific, repeatable, and predictable information that can be used in determining exposure, adjusting lighting ratios, or creative visualization. No light meter will ever tell a photographer the definitive "proper exposure" for a scene. The light meter must be regarded as a tool to be intelligently used. The more a photographer comes to rely on a

[figure 5.2]

A simple still life with spot meter readings indicated by white circles. Spot readings allow for accurate comparison of brightness levels in restricted areas of a scene.

light meter to dictate exposure, the more creative control is sacrificed to electronic predictability and averaging. This practice leads to banal, naive conclusions when judging lighting and exposure. Meters have, after all, a limited vision. Their entire world is 18% gray.

Middle gray, or 18% gray, has been adopted as a standard point of reference by the photographic industry. This is a neutral gray tone, reflecting 18 percent of the light that illuminates it. Photographic paper speeds and contrast grades are based around the rendering of a middle-gray tone. Some systems of film exposure and development are also based around similar principles. Light meters see 18% gray; that is all they see. They see no texture, no color, no shading,

no nuance; only 18% gray. A reflected light meter pointed from the camera position at any surface in a scene will tell the photographer what exposure to use for rendering that surface as a middle-gray density in the negative. An incident light meter placed in a scene and pointed toward the camera will tell the photographer what exposure to use for rendering a middle-gray tone at that plane in the scene as a middle-gray density in the negative. That is the essential function of a light meter. Predictability is based on standards, and the standard is 18% gray.

This information is valuable, but it will yield creative results only if interpreted intelligently. In establishing exposure, consideration must be given to

the contrast and exposure range of the film being used, the overall contrast of the scene in front of the camera, the final form of presentation for the photograph, and the desired placement of tones in the scene. These factors must be interrelated and creative decisions made to arrive at the desired exposure for any particular scene. It must always be remembered that exposure is one of the primary creative controls available to the photographer; most photographs are not subjected to an objective standard. Some exceptions might be found in highly technical or precisely descriptive images in which some external factors could dictate a particular level of exposure as the only acceptable solution.

A meter will only work effectively if it is calibrated properly. This includes both the calibration and zeroing of the meter itself, and the selection of the proper ISO film speed. The ISO rating of any film is based on an average of many tests. In order to accurately predict exposure, each photographer should establish their own "system ISO" based on their meter, camera, darkroom technique, and other individual variables. Other texts, particularly those dealing with sensitometry and the zone system, provide much detailed information on establishing a system ISO. See the Bibliography for references.

Contrast and Brightness Ranges

Descriptive language tends to vary from author to author; therefore, for the purposes of this text, certain terms should be defined. It will be helpful if the reader understands the terms "lighting contrast," "subject contrast," "scene contrast," and "brightness range." These terms are not interchangeable and should be understood to describe specific conditions.

Lighting contrast is related to the various levels of illumination present in different areas of the scene. If the entire scene is evenly illuminated, with the same amount of light reaching every plane and every surface, then the lighting contrast is nil. Conversely, if certain areas of the scene receive a great deal of illumination and other areas receive little light, then the resulting lighting contrast will be high. Lighting contrast can be expressed in more technical terms of "lighting ratios." A lighting ratio of 1 to 1 would indicate totally even illumination. A lighting ratio of 2 to 1 would indicate that one area of the scene is receiving twice the illumination of another area. It must be remembered that when calculating lighting ratios f-stops represent a geometric and not an arithmetic progression. For example, a 1-stop difference in meter readings indicates a 2-to-1 lighting ratio. A 2-stop difference in meter readings indicates a 4-to-1 lighting ratio, and a 3-stop difference in meter readings indicates an 8-to-1 lighting ratio. Each change of one f-stop either doubles the amount of light or cuts it in half. Incident light meters are ideal tools for measuring lighting contrast. When used properly, they will yield information regarding the levels of illumination in various areas of the scene. This comparative information can be used to establish overall exposure as well as lighting ratios.

Subject contrast is defined by the reflectivity of the various surfaces within the scene itself. Some surfaces are smooth and light in tone or color, while others are deeply textured and dark in tone or color. Various combinations of these factors provide an almost limitless array of possible surfaces—each with a unique reflectivity. Subject contrast is the difference in reflectivity between the most reflective and the least reflective surfaces assuming that all surfaces receive equal levels of illumination.

A reflected light meter is necessary to determine subject contrast. It will measure the actual amount of light reflected by a surface in the scene toward the camera. Comparative information obtained from metering various surfaces in the scene will allow the photographer to determine subject contrast.

Despite the above observations, it must be remembered that the definition of subject contrast is also relative to black-and-white or color materials and not simply a matter of reflectivity. For example, two widely varying hues such as red and green can provide great contrast in a color image, yet they can also record as relatively similar densities and tones with black-and-white materials. The photographer must take this into consideration when structuring and lighting the image. The world is in color, and photographers must translate to brightness levels and tones when using black-and-white materials. Filtering with black-and-white materials for subject contrast changes can be extremely useful and will be discussed in chapter 7.

Scene contrast is an overall description of the total range of illumination and reflectivity in a scene. It takes both lighting contrast and subject contrast into consideration. Low lighting contrast and high subject contrast or high lighting contrast and low subject contrast may produce similar results. A light surface in a shadowed area of a scene can record as a tone similar to a darker surface in a bright area of the scene, thus reducing perceived scene contrast. Conversely, the highest possible scene contrast would result from a light surface in a bright area of a scene contrasted with a dark surface in a shadowed area of the scene (figure 5.3).

Because scene contrast is inevitably tied to lighting contrast as well as subject contrast, a reflected light meter must be used to establish the overall scene contrast range. The reflectivity of various surfaces will play an important role in this determination. In color, scene contrast is intimately related to lighting contrast and color interactions. Even under relatively low-contrast lighting conditions, active color combinations can, on their own, produce extreme scene contrast . In any case, it is vital that important information in the image fall within the range of the photographic materials being used. High-scene contrast often translates into loss of detail in the shadows or compression and loss of information in the highlights.

Lighting contrast, subject contrast, and scene contrast are all essentially descriptive terms. A light meter actually measures the brightness of various surfaces in the scene or various levels of illumination. A more technical terminology for describing contrast is to refer to brightness range. Brightness range is directly related to meter readings and can be expressed in f-stops of difference between one reading and another. Other specifications for brightness in terms of footcandles, foot-lamberts, exposure values, etc., abound. In the context of this book, brightness range is a technical specification of the descriptive term "contrast" expressed in the language of some established, standardized system of light measurement.

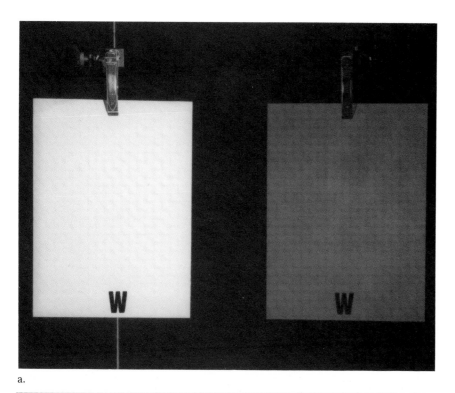

a.

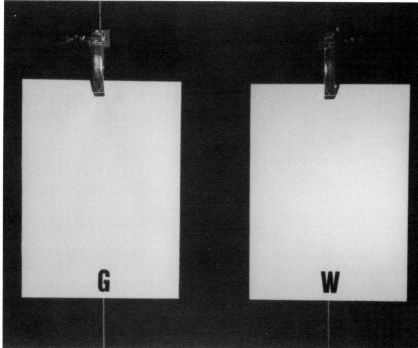

b.

[figure 5.3]

a. In black-and-white photographs, tonality is related to surface brightness. Surface brightness is determined by the reflectivity of a surface and the amount of light falling on that surface. Here, two identical white cards are placed side by side but in different levels of illumination. The resulting photograph appears to be of a white card next to a dark-gray card. The subject contrast is nil, but the lighting contrast is high.

b. Here, an 18 percent grey card and a white card are placed side by side in different levels of illumination. The resulting photograph appears to be of two light-gray cards. In this case, both subject contrast and lighting contrast are high, yet they contradict each other with the darker subject in brighter illumination, thus creating matching tonalities on the two cards. Combinations other than these two (a. and b.) can be imagined.

"Brightness" as a term can be applied to a light source, a level of illumination, or a reflective surface. Each of these uses involves specific terminologies and systems of measurement. The measurement of light or photometry, is based upon standard units and principles. Emission of light from a source is normally measured in candlepower units, which are defined in accordance with international standards. If a 1 foot-square card is placed 1 foot away from a light source emitting 1 candlepower of light, the card will receive a total of 1 lumen of light and will have a brightness of 1 footcandle. The lumen is the measurement of the amount of light falling on a surface and is related to the size of the surface as well as the candlepower of the light source. The footcandle is a measurement of the brightness of the surface illuminated and is related to the candlepower of the light source and the distance from the light source to the surface. If the light reflected from a surface is to be discussed, the foot-lambert needs to be introduced. The foot-lambert is a measure of the light reflected from a surface and is related to the candlepower of the light source, the distance from the light source to surface, and the reflectivity of the surface.

The mathematical formulas are as follows:

$$footcandles = candle\ power/distance^2$$

$$lumens = foot\ candles \times area\ (sq.\ ft.)$$

$$foot\text{-}lamberts = footcandles \times reflectivity$$

The technical specification of these lighting units is not directly applicable to practical working situations; however, such knowledge can serve to explain certain observed phenomena and add to the photographer's understanding of light (figure 5.4).

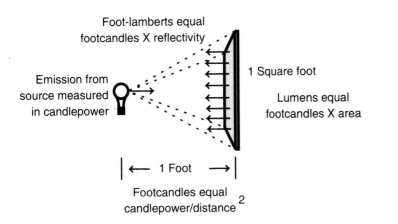

Foot-lamberts equal
footcandles X reflectivity

Emission from
source measured
in candlepower

1 Square foot

Lumens equal
footcandles X area

|← 1 Foot →|

Footcandles equal
candlepower/distance^2

[f i g u r e 5.4]

A visual representation of the formulas presented in the text, showing footcandles, lumens, and foot-lamberts.

Using a Reflected Light Meter

A reflected light meter, as indicated above, measures the amount of light reflecting from a surface in the scene. Assuming that the ISO has been determined and set properly, a well-calibrated, reflected light meter will tell the photographer how to expose the film to render a metered surface as a middle-gray density or value in a negative, or as a middle-brightness value in a color transparency. The function of a reflected light meter is to inform the photographer how to expose film to match a metered surface with a standard tone or brightness value.

Meter readings must be interpreted to yield creative results. They can be used to determine contrast ranges and placement of various tones or values within the image. A reflected meter reading will always try to match the metered surface to a middle-gray tone. If the photographer wishes that surface to fall below middle gray, then it must receive less exposure than indicated by the meter. If the photographer wishes that surface rendered above middle gray on the tonal scale, then it must receive more exposure than indicated by the meter.

A reflected light meter must be used at a suitable distance from and angle to a surface to obtain accurate readings. The distance is dependent upon the angle of view of the meter and the size of the surface being metered. The narrower the angle of view and/or the larger the surface area being metered, the farther away from the surface the meter can be used. For maximum accuracy, the meter reading should derive from specific areas of discrete tone. Therefore, meter readings of restricted areas in the scene that correspond to restricted tonal areas in the final image will be more accurate and useful than meter readings that encompass many different areas of varying brightness. The latter readings will yield averaged information and may be misleading in judging exposure and contrast range (figure 5.5). For example, an averaged reading of an overall bright scene may lead to underexposure due to the meter's tendency to compensate and expose for middle gray. Similarly, an averaged reading of an overall dark scene may lead to overexposure as the meter attempts to compensate for and shift the dark tones in the scene.

Exposure for negative materials is based upon minimum light readings in shadow areas, while exposure for transparency materials is based on critical highlight readings. These areas might be quite small in the scene but require accurate metering. The spot meter is an ideal tool for metering small areas. Spot metering from the camera position also aids in maintaining the correct meter-to-surface angle necessary for accurate readings. Light from many surfaces will be reflected with different brightnesses depending upon the angle of the viewer, camera, or meter to the surface. A measurement with a reflected light meter at 30° to a surface may yield a different brightness reading than a measurement of the same surface taken at 60°. Whatever reflected light meter is used, it should be positioned, as closely as possible, on the axis from the surface being measured to the center of the camera lens (figure 5.6).

A spot meter used at the camera position will always remain close to the correct angle/axis for accurate readings. A film plane meter will automatically see the scene from the same angle as the lens. In addition, spot and film plane meters allow the photographer to stay behind the camera and out of the scene while taking meter readings. This may be necessary with small still life photographs; it will also facilitate working and avoid unnecessary intrusions into any set. If it is necessary to approach a surface to make a meter reading, care must be taken to avoid blocking any of the light illuminating that surface, thereby causing an inaccurate measurement.

Reflected light meters are necessary when metering for subject contrast and scene contrast. They have not been

[figure 5.5]

The still life from figure 5.2 with an average reflected meter reading from approximately 4 feet, which is indicated by the large white circle. Average readings such as this, which encompass many brightness levels, provide information regarding overall exposure but are not very effective for calculating brightness and contrast ranges.

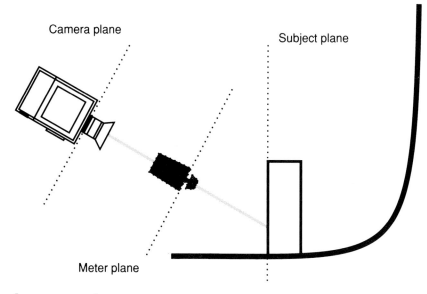

[figure 5.6]

A reflected light meter should be positioned on axis between the lens and the surface being metered and be pointed at the subject. The lens plane and the front plane of the meter should both be parallel.

traditionally associated with studio work. Using an incident meter to adjust the lighting contrast, or ratio, has long been a popular method of working in the studio. Despite this tradition, a photographer should not ignore the usefulness of reflected light meters in specific situations or for certain purposes. They yield a great deal more specific information than incident meters and can actually be utilized in place of an incident meter; the reverse is not true. A proper reflected light reading off of a gray card placed in the scene at a right angle to the axis from the lens should be the same as an incident meter reading taken at that spot.

Using an Incident Light Meter

An incident light meter is designed to measure the intensity of illumination at a given point within a scene. Again, it must be assumed that the proper system ISO has been established and that the meter is well calibrated. Incident meters are designed to gather light hitting the surface of their diffuser from all directions, to average that light, and to yield an exposure recommendation based on that average. The standard that the meter is calibrated to is the 18% gray card. If a gray card is placed in a scene at the meter position and at a right angle to the meter-to-lens axis, an incident meter reading is taken, and an exposure made based on the meter's recommendation; the gray card in the final image should have the same value as the original.

An incident light meter is placed in the scene with the base of its diffusion dome perpendicular to an axis drawn from the meter to the center of the lens. In other words, the meter is pointed toward the camera (figure 5.7). The only exception is when metering a scene illuminated entirely with back light and intended to record as a silhouette. In this case, the meter is placed behind the subject and pointed at the light.

A proper measurement with an incident light meter will tell how to expose the film for rendering an "average contrast" subject at the meter position as an "average" range of densities and/ or brightness values in a negative or transparency. An incident light meter primarily tells the photographer how to expose film for a standard rendering given a specific level of brightness. The meter makes assumptions about the contrast ranges of the subject and illumination.

First, the meter is assuming the subject is of an average contrast range. This may be true depending upon the reflectivity of various surfaces within the scene. With an exposure based on an incident reading, values outside of these average limits may be lost in black or white at different ends of the tonal scale. Also, a single incident reading essentially assumes the entire scene is illuminated with light of the same intensity. It is more common to have a scene in which the intensity of the light varies in bright and shadowed areas. This points to the necessity of comparative readings when using an incident light meter.

By taking an incident reading in the darkest area of the scene and another in the brightest area the photographer can establish the lighting ratio of the scene. Determining the darkest and brightest areas of the scene is a subjective endeavor. Areas that are to render as pure black or pure white in the image are not areas of important tonal information. Lighting ratios, though valuable,

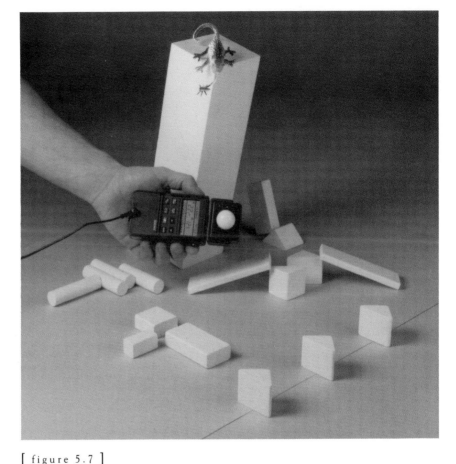

[figure 5.7]

The diffusion dome of an incident light meter should be pointed toward the camera lens from the point in the scene where the meter reading is taken.

do not take subject contrast into account, and are not useful indicators of overall scene contrast.

Exposure Placement

Exposure placement is largely a matter of aesthetic sense. In certain images, technical or illustrative requirements may necessitate a certain tonal placement. However, exposure placement is also a primary creative tool. Exposure will determine the overall sense of light and dark in an image, and no such standard as "proper exposure" can be universally applied. The requirements of each photograph and the photographer's sensibilities will

define the best exposure for each image from a broad range of possible interpretations (figure 5.8).

Generally, with negative materials exposure should be sufficient to record detail in all of the important areas of the scene. The negative must be given at least a threshold level of exposure in the shadows. Below the threshold level, no detail will be recorded in the negative. In order for negative detail to be printable, it must achieve a certain level of density and separation above the threshold level of negative exposure/density. Visual inspection of a negative may reveal detail in the lower densities that is not printable. The human eye is more acute than photographic materials that

[figure 5.8]

Martin Brief purposely underexposed this scene to allow only the hand and small photograph to record on the film. Suppressing the other detail in the scene focuses our attention on gesture and the relationship between the hand and its image, which are both floating in a dark void.

Photograph by Martin Brief

require definite levels of separation between discrete areas of tone to form detail. Visible separation may not be printable separation. Information that falls below 2 stops under middle gray will likely be compressed and dark—not clearly defined as detail or substance. Adequate negative exposure is assured by proper placement of important shadow detail.

Transparency exposure should be such that important highlights in the scene are rendered with detailed substance and colors are rendered with rich authority. Overexposure will cause a loss of detail and color in the highlights of a transparency or overall weak

color saturation. Underexposure will produce dull highlights and colors of low value that will appear dark. The minimum density in the highlights of a transparency calls for accurate exposure placement. Generally, transparency material must be exposed to within 1/3 stop for rendering bright highlights in the desired manner. Though this is also a subjective judgment, latitude with transparency materials is limited. Exposure bracketing is a common practice with color transparencies.

Exposure bracketing involves making more than one exposure of a scene. Normally a minimum of 3 exposures are made,

sometimes as many as 5. The desired exposure is calculated and one image exposed at the indicated camera settings. Additional images of the same scene are then exposed usually in 1/3- or 1/2-stop increments—for example a three-shot bracket would include the calculated exposure, 1/3-stop underexposure, and 1/3-stop overexposure, etc. This produces a range of transparencies from which to choose the final image and avoids reshooting. Exposure bracketing is sometimes employed with negative materials as well; however, more leeway is possible with negatives, which are an intermediate step to a print, than with transparencies which are considered a final product.

When using a reflected light meter, exposure may be calculated keeping certain factors in mind. With negative materials, first make a decision as to what represents the darkest surface in the scene where detail is to be rendered in the print. Take a meter reading of this area; this represents the darkest detailed shadow in the scene. Remember, the meter will indicate how to expose this area for a middle gray. It should be rendered as a darker tone, so exposure must be adjusted. Set the camera 2 stops less than the meter reading indicated. This will place the metered surface two stops below middle gray, the proper placement for a detailed shadow area. For example, if a meter reading of the darkest detailed shadow was f-8 at 1/30, then the camera should be set to f-8 at 1/125.

With a reflected meter and transparency materials, first make a determination as to the lightest detailed surface in the image. If no light colors or tones exist, a piece of textured, white material placed in the scene may be substituted. The meter will indicate the exposure to render this surface as a middle gray; again this information must be interpreted. The textured, white surface should be placed 2 stops above the indicated exposure reading to render as a white with detail and substance. If the meter reading was f-8 at 1/125, then the camera should be set to f-8 at 1/30.

An alternative method with a reflected light meter and negative materials would involve taking a meter reading off of a gray card placed in the darkest area of the scene where detail must be recorded and using that reading for the exposure settings. A similar alternative with a reflected meter and color transparency materials would involve taking a meter reading off of a gray card placed in the brightest area of the scene and using that reading to set the camera f-stop and shutter speed. These methods assume that the lighting and subject contrast are average.

When using an incident light meter with negative materials, exposure may be calculated by taking a meter reading in the darkest area of the scene where detail is to be recorded. With transparency materials an incident meter reading would be taken in the brightest area of the scene. These readings would yield the camera settings for the respective exposures. Again, this method assumes an average lighting and subject contrast. Compensation for various lighting contrasts can be achieved by taking incident meter readings in the darkest and brightest areas of the scene, deciding where the most important information lies, and making an exposure based on weighted averages of the readings. For example, if most of the important information was in the brighter areas of the scene, then

the averaged exposure should be weighted toward the high reading and vice versa.

The above methods for determining exposure with an incident meter do not take overall scene contrast into account. With a reflected light meter, measurement of the darkest and lightest important surfaces in the scene will yield a measure of overall scene contrast. This will be expressed in terms of f-stops. Ideal scene contrast with black-and-white and color negative films is 5 f-stops of difference and with color transparency films, 4 f-stops of difference. With black-and-white materials scene contrast can be compressed or extended in development using standard compaction and expansion processes. The books listed in the Bibliography that deal with sensitometry and the zone system contain information on these techniques. With color materials, especially color transparency materials, contrast must largely be adjusted by manipulating the lighting of the scene prior to exposure. Excessive scene contrast is likely to result in a loss of shadow or highlight detail and is a common problem for novice studio photographers.

Again, the final arbiter of proper exposure is the photographer. Despite all the tools, rules, and systems, unless image requirements dictate otherwise, aesthetic principles should remain the guiding force in exposure determinations. Creative decisions are always subjective decisions.

Color Temperature Meters

Color temperature meters are specialized tools designed to yield a description of the color of illumination in a scene. Color temperature meters normally

contain three sensitive cells and/or take three separate readings of the light. These red, green, and blue readings are averaged together to yield a single, interpretive reading expressed in °K. A color temperature meter measures the relative component amounts of red, green, and blue—the photographic primaries—contained in the illumination and derives its color temperature measurement from averaging these three colors. Though not a precise technical process, actual °K are never measured at any source; it is a descriptive process that tells what the illumination "looks" like in terms of a standard reference. This information can be useful to the photographer.

Some studio photographers regularly use color temperature meters. When exact color description is an image necessity, color temperature readings can be of use in narrowing and speeding testing procedures and in maintaining consistent results. Due to unpredictable variations in emulsion color and speed characteristics, lab processing, lenses, exposure, and lighting equipment color temperature meters cannot altogether eliminate the need for testing.

As a shoot progresses, accurate monitoring of the color temperature of the illumination can aid in avoiding reshooting due to shifting in the color of the light. This may be a problem, particularly in relatively long shoots with tungsten lights—quartz bulbs are relatively stable after an initial burn-in period and the color temperature of a strobe tube should remain constant over the life of the tube. The color temperature of tungsten lights may change quite radically and rapidly. Color temperature readings of the illumination will aid the photographer in establishing and tracking filtration requirements.

[chapter]

6

LIGHTING INSTRUMENTS

In this chapter, the types of lights available for use by the studio photographer will be discussed. They will be examined in terms of their construction, functioning, and particular useful potentials. The characteristics of the illumination produced by each light will be explained and safety considerations will be emphasized. Chapter 2 laid out the basic rules and definitions of light; now their operation when embodied in specific lighting instruments will be investigated.

Most studio lighting equipment will be either tungsten, quartz, or electronic strobe light. Certain fluorescents can be used in specific applications, but that is rare. Arc lamps, vapor lamps, and alternative light sources are rarer still but may occasionally be encountered. Electronic strobe is by far the most common light source employed by studio photographers in developed nations. It has the advantages of high light output with comparatively little bulk, low power consumption, and little

generation of heat. It has the disadvantages of being expensive and technically complex; electronic strobes are not normally user-repairable.

Tungsten light is a good learning tool. It can be continuously observed as it is manipulated to create various effects. The effects of strobes can often not be seen until a Polaroid, transparency, or print is processed. Tungsten light is physically hot; in fact, studio photographers often refer to tungsten lights as "hot lights." Tungsten lights also consume a great deal of power and are heavy. The choice of which type of light source to use is sometimes defined by the requirements of the photograph. More often the choice is an expression of the photographer's preferences. Usually, in the final image, the viewer will never be aware of the type of light used to expose the photograph.

One good reason to learn how to control tungsten lighting is that a continuous light source is necessary for film and video work.

Many contemporary studio photographers are making a transition into film and video or are incorporating it into multimedia contexts with their still photography. Though the principles of light are the same, tungsten equipment is functionally quite different from strobes. The photographer should be familiar with both systems.

Safety

Studio lighting equipment often involves high-voltage or high-amperage electrical current. Shocks from such current can be dangerous or fatal. Many studios have continually observed unsafe and foolish practices involving lighting equipment that put photographers, assistants, and models at risk of electrocution. It is critical that common sense and safety precautions be strictly enforced to avoid injury. As water amplifies the effect of electric current and increases the possibility of accidental shorting,

73

situations involving electricity and water are especially dangerous. A photographer must also anticipate the power demands that lighting equipment can make on wiring circuits and be certain that the building is properly equipped to handle such loads. Power overloads are a prime source of fire in older buildings.

A studio photographer should know enough about electricity to understand basic wiring, warning signs of malfunctions, basic safety procedures, and first aid for electrical shock. In addition, the electrical system in a studio should be wired with the general illumination on a circuit separate from the studio lighting equipment. The lighting equipment requires special power circuits equipped with ground-fault interrupt circuit breakers that will kill the power instantly in case of a short circuit or accident. Everyone working in the studio should know how to cut the power to the lighting circuits at the main electrical box. This will kill the shooting lights but leave general illumination in the studio, so the room will not be plunged into darkness in case of an emergency. The mains should always be kept clear of obstructions that might hamper access. The studio should always be kept clean and well organized. All electrical equipment should be regularly checked for safety. These precautions are basic; even one shock can kill. Safety should always be a prime consideration.

Tungsten Lights

The four main types of tungsten lights are: spotlights, broadlights, softlights, and bulbs in reflectors often called "scoops." Each of these lights has its own unique design and characteristic illumination. As defined in

chapter 2, these would all be considered direct light sources. A combination of different types of light is emitted from each of these sources. The only true, direct tungsten light source is a bare light bulb. However, since we treat the light source as a whole, we call the light coming from any lighting instrument direct light.

To review, tungsten lights have a nominal color temperature of 3,200 or 3,400 °K, though their true color temperature may vary considerably from these standards. Quartz lights are a type of tungsten light that incorporate special glass and gasses in the bulb. HMI lights are special filament lights that burn at approximately 5,500 °K to balance with daylight illumination. All of these lights are available in various wattages. As mentioned in chapter 3, variations in incoming line voltages can alter the color temperature of tungsten lights.

Circuits used for powering tungsten lighting equipment must be capable of handling the total wattage of the lights on line. In the studio, this is usually accommodated by special circuits designed to handle a great deal of wattage; however, on location this can present a problem. A circuit will safely handle a total wattage equal to volts $\times$ amps. Most household and commercial circuits are 110 volt and either 15 or 20 amp circuits. Overloading a circuit will create a dangerous situation that could lead to short circuits and fires from overheated wiring. Always be certain that the electrical requirements of lighting equipment do not exceed the rated capacity of circuits utilized. Heat generated by tungsten lights can also pose a hazard. It will quickly melt and/or scorch vulnerable surfaces at close distances, and it can inflict severe burns.

Special precautions must be taken with quartz lights. Quartz bulbs must never be touched with bare hands as this will deposit light skin oils on the bulb surface. The bulbs heat up quickly and any dirt or oil on the surface of the glass can create uneven heating and cause the bulb to explode. These lights also get extremely hot and are actually capable of melting their own expensive lighting fixtures.

Tungsten lights should not be moved or jolted while burning. The hot filament is quite fragile and does not withstand shocks. The life of a tungsten bulb can be shortened by as much as 95 percent if the light is constantly moved, raised, or lowered while still being used. The bulb should be turned off and allowed to cool until its color fades; then the light can be safely moved. This simple practice will avoid costly bulb failures.

Spotlights

Spotlights are designed to focus their light on a small area. They usually incorporate a bulb, reflector, and condenser-like lens in a deep housing (figure 6.1). These elements work together to produce the characteristically bright, contrasty light of the spotlight. The bulb puts out light in all directions, including front and back. The reflector is designed to reroute the light rays traveling backward from the bulb straight out of the front of the light. The lens is designed to align all of the light rays and focus them at a spot in front of the light source. A spotlight, like a camera lens, can actually be focused at a specific distance. Deeper housings are required for long-throw spots, such as follow spots in theaters and arenas, that can focus small beams of light at great distances.

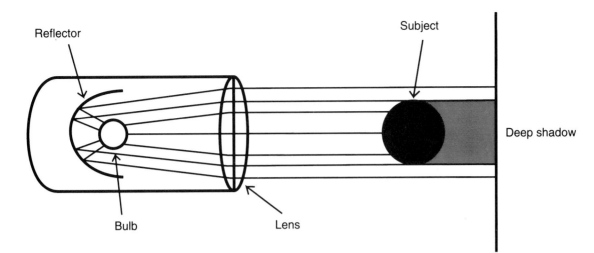

Reflector

Subject

Deep shadow

Bulb

Lens

[figure 6.1]

A stylized, schematic drawing of a typical spotlight that shows how individual rays of light are directed and redirected into parallel lines that form a focused spot. The light from a spot does not wrap around a subject.

The light coming from a spotlight is actually a combination of direct light from the bulb and reflected light from the reflector; all of which is focused by the lens. A spotlight is considered the most contrasty light source available. This is mainly due to three factors mentioned in chapter 2: the sharp, directional shadows cast by the focused light; the nature of the specular reflections in the scene; and the concentrated brightness of the illumination.

The individual rays of light in the focused beam leaving the spotlight lens are traveling parallel to one another. Coupled with its small size, this allows the spotlight to cast sharp, directional shadows as the light has little tendency to wrap around objects in its path. The shadows cast by a spotlight also tend to remain constant in size independent of the distance between subject and background. The parallel nature of the rays of light emanating from the source ensures shadow uniformity. Sharp shadows have little penumbra, the transition area between light and dark, and are therefore evenly dark from edge to edge (figure 6.2).

[figure 6.2]

A spotlight casts a contrasty, deep, and even shadow with little or no penumbra. Its illumination is focused into a small area thereby creating extreme contrast between highlights and shadows in the scene.

The specular reflections of a spotlight will be sharp, small, and extremely bright. They function in localized areas of the scene to add a sense of brilliance and energy to an image. The reflections can be placed through the positioning of the light source; however, they are not easily controllable in terms of brightness, always tending toward extreme.

The spotlight focuses all of its light output into a small area. This leads to extreme differences

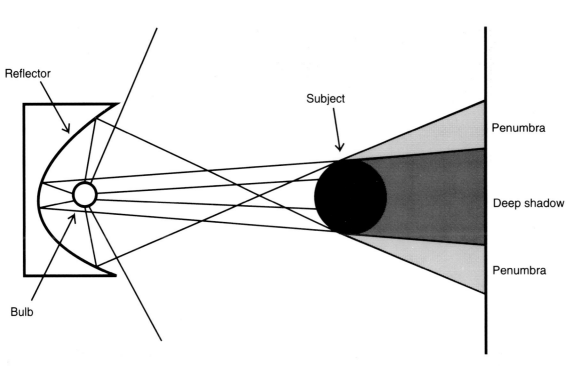

Reflector

Bulb

Subject

Penumbra

Deep shadow

Penumbra

[figure 6.3]

A stylized, schematic drawing of a typical broadlight shows how individual rays of light are caused to diverge after leaving the lighting instrument. The light from a broad tends to wrap around a subject and create a small but noticeable penumbra.

in levels of illumination between bright surfaces that the light strikes and dark surfaces outside of the beam of light or inside shadows cast by the light. Contrast must be understood in terms of all of the above factors, which each affect perception in a different manner and combine to create overall scene contrast.

Broadlights

Broadlights are designed to spread light over a large area. They usually incorporate a bulb and reflector in a shallow light housing (figure 6.3). Most broadlights are rectangular in shape and radiate light in all directions. The textured, silver reflector takes light from the bulb and throws it out in a broad, forward arc. A broadlight will cover a great angle with even illumination. Similar to a spotlight, a broadlight actually

emits a combination of direct and reflected light. The rays of light flowing out of the broad are not focused by a lens and are not parallel, as those from a spotlight, but rather crossing and divergent in an expanding arc. The broad has some tendency to wrap around objects due to its less-directional nature (figure 6.4).

Because of the expanding arc of the illumination, shadows tend to increase dramatically in size as the subject moves away from the background. The specular reflections of broadlights will be brilliant and relatively small. Because the broad spreads its illumination over a large area, it is never as bright as the spot at any given point. This reduces the difference in levels of illumination between light and shadow. As perceived contrast is a function of all of these factors, a broad is considered a moderately contrasty light source.

Variable Spot/Floodlights

Many photographers have found that variable spot/floodlights are versatile instruments. These lights, similar in appearance to standard spotlights, mimic the illumination of spots or broads. Their angle of illumination is variable, focusing light into a small area or spreading it over a larger expanse. These lights will never focus a spot of light as intense as a true focusing spotlight, nor will they spread light over as large an area as will a dedicated broadlight. The variable spot/flood is a compromise light giving added flexibility at the expense of extremes.

The glass lens element of a spot/floodlight is usually a Fresnel lens. This is a stepped, curved surface lens of limited quality but adequate for lighting instruments. Either the mirror, the bulb, or both move in relation to the Fresnel lens and/or each other.

[figure 6.4]

A broadlight casts a fairly sharp, even shadow with a small penumbra. The diverging rays of light cover a large area, reducing the intensity of illumination at any one point, and therefore reducing the contrast between highlights and shadows as compared to a focused spotlight.

This produces a variable angle of illumination dependent upon the positioning of the various components (figure 6.5). Not all spot/flood combinations have lenses; some simply move the bulb in relation to the reflector to vary the angle of coverage.

The light emanating from a spot/floodlight will be directional in nature. The rays will vary from nearly parallel to divergent depending upon the adjustment of the light. The illumination will be moderately contrasty in terms of sharpness of shadow, with little tendency to wrap around and soften shapes. The specular reflections will be similar to those from a spotlight—brilliant and tiny. At the same time, the level of light in any one area of a scene illuminated by a variable spot/floodlight will change dependent upon the coverage of the light, thereby varying the brightness range.

Softlights

Softlights incorporate a diffuser and/or a reflector in the construction of the lighting instrument (figure 6.6). Larger in size than spotlights or broadlights, softlights are designed to spread light over a large angle of coverage. As mentioned in chapter 2, the contrast of a light source is directly related to its size and its distance from the subject. A large light source will produce less contrasty illumination. Because the effective size of a light source is related to its distance from the subject, the farther away it is placed the smaller its relative size. A softlight that is small in relation to the subject illuminated, or that is used at a great distance will lose its unique character.

Though it is considered a direct light source, the light emanating from a softlight is

actually either diffused and/or reflected by the design of the lighting instrument itself. The light rays emanating from a soft light source will be scattered in different directions by the diffuser and/or reflector. Coupled with the larger size of the light source, this creates a minimally directional illumination that tends to wrap around objects.

The shadows cast by a softlight will have a large penumbra (figure 6.7). They will be uneven in brightness from edge to edge, darker at the center. The specular reflections from a softlight are unique. They are large, like the light itself, and tend to spread over reflective surfaces, delineating shape and volume quite beautifully. These reflections are also easily controllable in placement; small changes in the positioning of the large light make little visible difference in the reflections.

Because a softlight, like a broad, spreads its light over a large area, the illumination at any one point in its field will be diminished. Additionally, much of the intensity of a softlight's illumination is lost in the diffusion and/or reflection of the light in the instrument. A third factor that diminishes the amount of illumination from a softlight is the nature of the reflector employed in the light source. It is usually a matte surfaced reflector, either silver or white, that reflects less of the light falling on it than does a polished reflector in a spotlight.

Bulbs in Reflectors

The specification of available bulbs could be an endless task. Many different types and wattages are available for various applications. Tungsten and quartz bulbs are the most common.

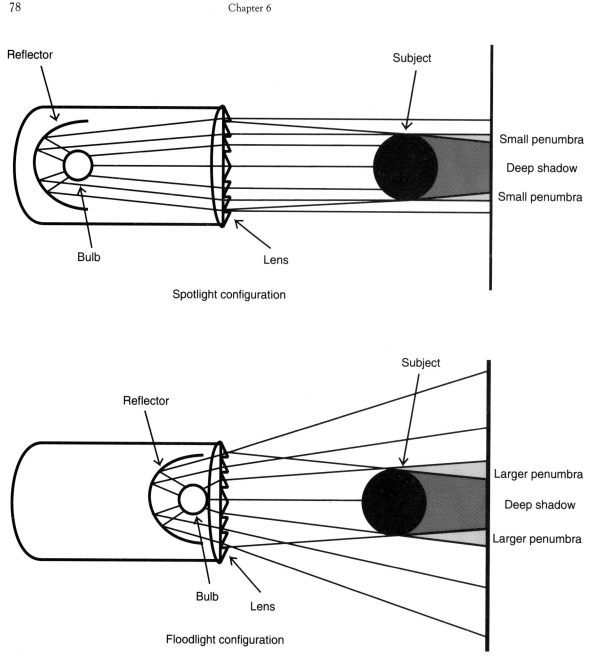

Reflector

Subject

Small penumbra

Deep shadow

Small penumbra

Bulb

Lens

Spotlight configuration

Subject

Reflector

Larger penumbra

Deep shadow

Larger penumbra

Bulb

Lens

Floodlight configuration

[figure 6.5]

A schematic drawing that shows a typical spot/floodlight with a Fresnel lens. As the components of the lighting instrument change position relative to the lens, and sometimes each other, the coverage of the light is expanded or contracted.

Three major types of reflectors, or scoops, are available. These vary in terms of shape, and each is designed for a specific purpose. They are spherical, parabolic, and elliptical.

Spherical reflectors are designed to spread out rays of light. Similar to broads in their function, these reflectors are good for illuminating large areas.

Parabolic reflectors are designed to reflect light out in straight, parallel lines from the light source. Similar to spots in general function, concentrating light in a small area, these are the type of reflectors used in the optical system of most spotlights. Elliptical reflectors are designed to angle the reflected light to converge at a specific distance in

front of the reflector. These reflectors are similar to focusing spotlights in their function, not only concentrating the light into a small area but having a specific focal length.

In a bulb/reflector combination, the whole unit acts together as the light source. A larger reflector will cast a softer light than a smaller reflector. The

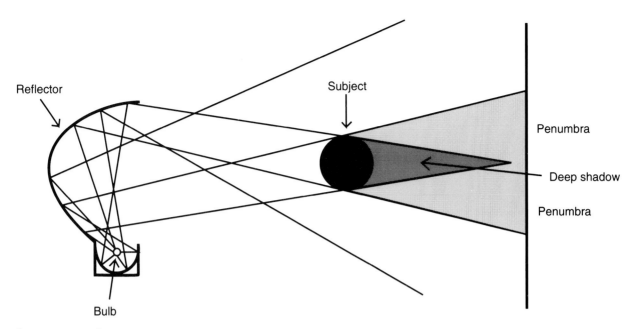

[figure 6.6]

A schematic drawing of a typical softlight that shows how individual rays of light crisscross at random angles forming a "multidirectional" or "directionless" light source that tends to wrap around a subject.

[figure 6.7]

A softlight casts an ill-defined, uneven shadow with a large penumbra. The rays of light are spread over a large area and travel in many different directions from various points of this often large light source.

surface of the reflector will also have an effect on the contrast of the illumination. Highly polished chrome surfaces will produce more contrasty light than will matte metallic or reflective white surfaces. Likewise, a reflector with a smooth curvature will produce more contrasty light than a reflector with embossed ridges.

Electronic Strobe

The electronic strobe is an incredibly versatile light source. Small in size and light in weight, it can be configured in the same types of lighting instruments as tungsten bulbs, from focusing spots and broads to softlights, and bare bulbs in reflectors. The rules governing the nature and action of light, the use of the various lighting instruments, and the essential character of light will remain identical whether utilizing strobe or tungsten illumination.

The electronic strobe produces a great intensity of light for its size and is power efficient due to its design. Power is stored in capacitors and then released through the strobe tube causing intense bursts of light. The speeds of electronic strobes can range from as long as 1/250 second to as short as 1/50,000 second or less. These characteristics offer great advantages in utilizing smaller f-stops for increased depth of field and in stopping motion.

The light or power output of electronic strobes is measured in many different scales. The most common references are to "guide numbers" and "watt-seconds." Guide numbers were commonly utilized before the advent of automatic thyristor strobes and flash meters. Guide numbers are a reference to light output as it affects film exposure. They were used to calculate appropriate f-stops at various strobe-to-subject distances or appropriate strobe-to-subject distances at various f-stops. The larger the guide number of a strobe unit for a given ISO of film, the more powerful is the strobe. Guide numbers vary proportionately with ISO; the higher the ISO of the film, the larger the guide number of a given strobe. In manufacturer's literature, guide numbers are often stated for ISO 25 and 100 films.

The guide number of a strobe is dependent upon the strobe design and any reflectors or diffusers utilized. The same strobe tube in two different reflectors will have a different guide number. The advantage of using guide numbers as a measurement of light output is that they refer directly to the exposure of the film and therefore give a true assessment of the actual level of illumination generated by a particular strobe configuration. BCPS (Beam Candlepower Seconds) and ECPS (Effective Candlepower Seconds) are two scientific specifications that, like guide numbers, measure actual light output as it affects film exposure. Despite their accuracy, guide numbers are rarely used to calculate strobe exposures in the modern studio.

Watt-seconds are a rather abstract reference to strobe power output. In Europe, the term "joule" is used to substitute for watt-second. One watt-second is equal to one joule. Watt-second ratings actually refer to the ability of the capacitors of a strobe unit to store available energy. They do not address the efficiency of energy usage and light output. Watt-seconds are not always an accurate benchmark for comparing various strobes; however, in general, the higher the watt-second rating of a particular strobe unit the greater the nominal light output. Studio strobes can range in their ratings from as low as 200 watt-seconds to as high as 9,600 watt-seconds. The advantage of using watt-seconds as a measurement of power output is that they remain constant across different strobe units and different unit configurations. Watt-seconds are not dependent on reflectors, diffusers, etc., because they measure power at the electrical source, not light at the destination.

Because strobes require a large amount of stored energy to be discharged in a short burst, they must restore that energy between bursts. The time required for the strobe capacitors to recharge is called the "recycle" time of the strobe. Short recycle times are often desirable in situations requiring multiple exposures, sequential images, or quick reactions to fluid scene dynamics. Many studio strobes have fast and slow recycling times and draw more current in the fast mode. All strobes should be allowed to fully recycle before being fired again. Premature firing can damage the strobe circuits and cause overheating. Most studio strobes up to 2,400 watt-seconds can run on a standard 15 amp, household circuit. This can be an advantage when working on location. Some of the large 4,800-watt-second-and-above strobe systems require a 220-volt circuit.

Studio strobes have both a xenon-filled strobe tube and a tungsten modeling lamp in the same light housing. The strobe tube provides the illumination for picture making, while the modeling lamp provides illumination for light and camera setup. The modeling lamp is usually a 250-watt quartz bulb surrounded by the strobe tube. Although strobes are usually adjustable in light output, modeling lamps may not be. This creates a deceiving situation when lighting a scene. The visual appearance of the lighting balance from the modeling lights may have little relationship to the actual light levels from the strobes. Some modeling lights can be ratioed along with the strobe tube output to give a more accurate picture of lighting balance.

Modeling lamps, like all quartz lights, produce a great deal of heat. Most high-quality strobes have fans built into the light housings allowing heat to dissipate. Otherwise, damage to the wiring, strobe tube, or housing may occur. Repeated, rapid firing of a strobe tube can also produce a great deal of heat and may burn out the light. If modeling lamps are turned off, check to make sure that the fans are still operating or give the strobe tubes some time to cool off between repeated firings.

Synchronization

Strobes can be triggered in numerous ways. The most common method is to utilize a synch-cord between the camera and the strobe's power unit. As explained in chapter 4, the camera shutter is synchronized to the flash unit with certain delays built into the sequence to insure that the strobe flashes when the shutter is open. The synch-cord is a physical connection between the camera and the strobe. It can be extended with long extension cords to provide for flexibility of movement and camera placement. Strobes can also be radio controlled from remote locations, or they can be triggered by light-sensitive slave units.

Radio control devices consist of two components, a transmitter and a receiver. The transmitter is placed with the camera or at a remote location, and the receiver

is placed with the strobe. The transmitter can either be triggered by the camera or independently operated. If triggered by the camera, it sends a pulse at the proper time to flash the strobe in synch with the shutter. If operated independently, it can be tripped to trigger the strobe at the discretion of the photographer or by a second remote device such as an infrared beam-trigger or a motion sensor. In this latter mode, the shutter on the camera might be locked open, and the strobe might provide the only illumination for the scene.

Most strobes will also accept light-sensitive slave triggering devices. Like flash meters, these devices are sensitive to short blasts of strobe light, not to ambient illumination. When they sense the light from another strobe, they automatically trigger the strobe to which they are connected. In such a situation, one "primary" strobe is usually connected to a camera in normal fashion and is responsible for firing the entire strobe "system." The light from the primary strobe triggers the remote strobes so quickly as to cause a negligible delay in firing; for all practical purposes, all the strobes flash at once.

Normally slave triggers plug into the synch-cord or the synch-cord receptacle on a strobe unit or power pack. Some strobes have slave triggers built-in. Slaves can also be mounted on the end of long synch-cords, which are then connected to the strobe unit, allowing the slave to be carefully positioned to catch the light from a primary strobe. Slave triggers vary in sensitivity and some are adjustable to a "hair trigger" margin. Infrared slave triggers will respond only to a specific, coded pulse of infrared light, thus eliminating misfires due to strobes flashing from other photographers'

cameras; such a device is particularly handy at press conferences and public events. Obviously, combinations of all of these triggering devices can further extend the flexibility and control of a strobe system.

Monoblocks and Power Packs

Two main types of studio strobes are available: those with integrated power/light modules and those with separate power packs and strobe heads. The former are often referred to as monoblocks, having only one component. Each type of system has its advantages. Monoblocks are lightweight, sometimes quite powerful, and often the lower-priced alternative. Separate power pack/strobe head systems are usually more powerful, all controlled from the same central power unit, and more widely available.

Monoblocks are excellent strobes for location photography. They are small, easily transported, and can be set up on individual light stands placed at diverse locations in the scene (figure 6.8). These strobes are sometimes battery powered. The largest monoblock systems are rated at 1,800 watt-seconds; their power limitation is due to their small size. This small size may be their greatest weakness in terms of general in-studio photography, which often requires more power and light output. To compensate for this and to add flexibility, many component monoblock systems can be linked together, either physically or with slave triggering devices, to function as integrated systems. Some can be regulated and individually power-ratioed from a central control module. One disadvantage of monoblocks is that their power

[f i g u r e 6 . 8]

A monoblock system set up with accessory reflectors and a soft box. This system is a
White Lightning, Ultra 1800 from Paul C. Buff, Inc. of Nashville, Tennessee. Each light
contains its own 1800 watt-second power pack, strobe tube, and modeling lamp. They
have a built-in slave trigger and can function independently or can be linked together and
controlled from a central command unit.

cannot be rerouted from one strobe head to another to provide maximum flexibility and power when ratioing strobe heads.

Separate power pack/strobe head systems are available in a wide range of watt-second ratings and system configurations (figure 6.9). The power packs can be quite large and weighty, often making these systems difficult to transport. Two main types of power packs are available: symmetrical and asymmetrical. Each power pack is capable of accommodating a number of strobe heads at one time, usually from three to six. Symmetrical power packs distribute power evenly between all of the strobe heads plugged into the pack. The

pack is sometimes adjustable in total power output. With a 2,400 watt-second symmetrical pack operating at full power, one head would receive 2,400 watt-seconds, two heads would receive 1,200 watt-seconds each, three heads would receive 800-watt seconds each, etc.

Asymmetrical power packs can be ratioed and combined between separate circuits to vary light output to each strobe head (figure 6.10). The circuits themselves are often separately controlled in terms of individual power output, full, half, quarter, etc. A 2,400 watt-second asymmetrical power pack operating at full power can put 2,400 watt-seconds or less into

one head depending on the circuit used. With two heads, one might receive 1,200 watt-seconds and another 400 watt-seconds. With three heads, one might receive 800 watt-seconds and the other two 400 watt-seconds each. The combinations are almost endless and provide for a great deal of flexibility when establishing lighting designs. Again, modeling lamps may vary with the power ratioing of the strobe head.

Normally, when strobes are set at less than full power, their flash duration is decreased proportionately. The same is true when more than one flash tube is being powered by a single source. Four strobe heads or tubes hooked to four separate power outlets on one symmetrical power supply, and thus all operating at 1/4 power, would provide the same amount of light as, and a shorter duration than, one of the strobe tubes hooked to the same power supply and operating at full power. Accessories such as bitube and quadtube light heads are designed for such applications. Certain power supplies and strobe heads are also designed to operate at higher than normal voltages, yielding increased intensity of light with reduced duration. When photographing moving subjects, a short flash duration may be necessary to stop action (figure 6.11).

Strobe Tubes and Safety

Strobe tubes are available in many different shapes and configurations. Some tubes have multiple elements integrated into a single unit, which provide even light patterns. Tubes are available in circular shapes, for ring lights, or long and thin, up to four feet in length, for strip lights. Custom shapes can also be designed for special-purpose lighting instruments.

a.

b.

[figure 6.9]

a. A single, separate power pack powers all of the light heads in this Speedotron 4,800 watt-second system. The light heads each contain a strobe tube, modeling lamp, and cooling fan. They are linked to the power pack by heavy-duty cables. This is an asymmetrical system, and the light heads can be ratioed in numerous configurations.
b. This Balcar strobe system is a hybrid, combining features of both monoblock and power pack systems. Each individual light head produces 1,600 watt-seconds of power, while the central unit is necessary for controlling and ratioing the light heads.

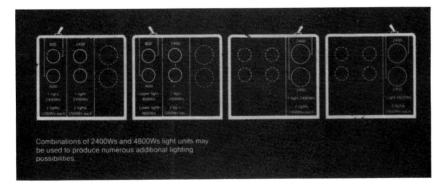

[figure 6.10]

A diagram of the Speedotron asymmetrical power switching system that, for easy reference, appears on the side of the power pack.

Electronic strobe power units and light heads must be treated with great respect. These instruments are prone to electrical arcing thus discharging their power through the best-available ground—possibly the photographer's body. Hand-held units can short and discharge under certain conditions, but studio strobes are riskier. These units carry a great deal of power and can be dangerous, even fatal, if handled inappropriately. Read all safety precautions and follow these simple rules: never plug in or unplug a strobe head cable while a power pack is turned on or charged; always discharge a power pack with a test button after turning the pack off and before unplugging any light heads; never use strobe equipment around

Strobe tubes are rated in terms of watt-seconds to accommodate a specific power burst. Pushing 4,800 watt-seconds through a strobe tube designed to handle 2,400 watt-seconds will destroy, or perhaps explode, the tube. Similar to quartz lamps, strobe tubes should never be touched with the bare hand. These lights heat up quickly and dirt or oil on the surface of the bulb could cause uneven heating and explosion.

[figure 6.11]

Normal studio strobes may have a flash duration as long as 1/250th of a second. This is not always fast enough to freeze action. As can be seen in Joe Ziolkowski's photograph of a running figure, rapidly moving subjects can blur at normal studio strobe speeds. For freezing fast action, a strobe system that operates at a higher than normal voltage, thereby reducing the flash duration and boosting the intensity of the illumination to achieve proper exposure, must be employed.

Photograph by Joe Ziolkowski from the "Diuturnal Series," "Option A"

water without stringent safety precautions; and, never touch a strobe tube or modeling lamp. This is not a comprehensive list of safety precautions, just a few warnings.

Alternative Light Sources

Fluorescent light sources are occasionally found in the studio. Fluorescents can be used to provide a soft, even source of

direct light. The most common use of fluorescents is in light boxes where the diffused surface of the box, illuminated from behind by fluorescent tubes, burns out to a solid white in the exposed

a.   b.

[figure 6.12]

a. The overhead skylight in Paul Elledge's Chicago studio could be used as a large softlight on sets in the studio below.
b. When totally artificial light is employed, the light well can be covered with a tarp to block the overhead illumination.

Photographs courtesy Paul Elledge Studio

image. If color materials are being exposed, using fluorescents as light sources becomes problematic because of their discontinuous spectrum and the consequent color shifts in negatives or transparencies; black-and-white materials will not be subject to this failing.

Other possible sources of light in the studio are numerous: flash bulbs, candles, flares, video monitors, etc., can all function as alternative light sources. As with fluorescents, color temperature can be a major concern when employing any of these alternative light sources as main illumination. One final source of light in the studio that must not be overlooked is daylight. Many photographers take advantage of large skylights or windows as

functional light sources in their studios (figure 6.12). The traditional north-window light that artists have sought for centuries for its soft, embracing quality is a valuable tool. Windows and skylights should be considered in studio design as potentially important sources of illumination.

Accessories

There are numerous accessories for studio lighting. The lighting support is an accessory critical to the flexibility and usefulness of any lighting system. Two main systems of lighting support are used in the studio: light stands and ceiling mounted rail systems.

Ceiling mounted rail lighting systems are flexible and keep the studio floor clear of cords, power packs, and stands (figure 6.13). They can be configured to serve almost any imaginable studio need. Their largest drawback is that they are permanently installed in one area of the studio and cannot be moved or taken on location. Many photographers work on numerous shots simultaneously, each on a different set, in various bays of one large studio space. Light stands can be moved back and forth or allocated as needed among bays. Rail systems cannot be redistributed in this manner.

Light stands are available in many sizes and configurations. Some stands designed for location

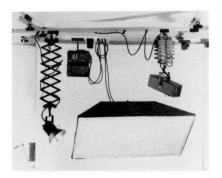

[figure 6.14]
A boom light stand allows the photographer to position a light directly over a set; some more expensive booms provide for controlling the angle and direction of the light using geared controls at the opposite end of the boom.

work are compact and lightweight yet sturdy. Other stands designed primarily for studio use are heavier and not easily transported. Obviously, heavy tungsten lights are going to require large, heavyweight stands for support; another reason why strobe equipment is desirable for location work.

Most light stands are one of two types: straight, vertical stands or offset booms. A boom stand is designed to suspend a light at a distance along a horizontal arm extending away from the vertical column of the light stand (figure 6.14). The horizontal arms are usually adjustable and/or counterweighted to support various lighting instruments. Some boom stands have control arms that allow the photographer to rotate and direct the light from the opposite end of the boom. Booms are useful when the light is positioned directly over the set or in an inaccessible location. They also allow for small adjustments of the angle of the light without resetting clamps or mounting screws. Certain large softlights are designed with integrated stands that allow for extremely flexible positioning of the light source.

These lights are not portable and are meant for studio use only mimicking overhead rail systems in their flexibility.

The choice of support system, rail, or stands, is often a matter of preference. Rail systems can be expensive, but they are extremely flexible once in place. Stands are relatively cheap, but they do clutter the studio floor and are easily tipped. Stands are the obvious choice for a system that will be used both in the studio and on location. A rail system may be particularly useful for a studio table-top product or portrait photographer. Both alternatives should be investigated in designing a studio and choosing a lighting system.

Many other lighting accessories include numerous clamps, pole support systems, extension cords, etc. They are available in any good studio supply house or catalog. Sometimes, the hardware store provides the most effective answer to a lighting accessory problem at a nominal cost. Flexibility and functional ease of use are important considerations in lighting equipment. The easier the lights are to use and the more flexible the lighting system, the more chance the photographer has to play creatively with the lighting design. The right light, the right stand, and sometimes even the right clamp can make studio life more enjoyable and productive.

LIGHT MODULATORS

Regulate, moderate, modify, restrain, and temper are some of the synonyms for modulate. Light modulators may take the form of filters, scrims, grids, diffusers, reflectors, or any devices that modulate light—altering its spectral distribution, contrast, direction, or pattern. In combination with the various lighting instruments described in chapter 6, light modulators define the character of light in a scene. Light modulators can play a subtle or pronounced role in lighting design. Though they don't supply the light, modulators often redirect and are responsible for the skillful fine-tuning of the illumination in a photograph. At the other extreme, modulators can be used to radically alter the light, creating entirely new interpretations of form and content.

Components integral to lighting instruments such as the lenses, reflectors, and diffusers of spotlights and softlights are actually light modulators in their own right. However, for the

purposes of this text, these elements are considered part of the lighting instrument or light source. This chapter will investigate modulators that are not integral to lighting instruments. Some of these modulators, such as filters, screens, and diffusers, are accessories that attach directly to lights or cameras; others, such as reflection and diffusion panels, are discrete devices. In addition to their more obvious effects, modulators can absorb light, play an important role in controlling reflections, and greatly simplify lighting design. Modulators are diverse tools with one common purpose—to extend the photographer's control over individual lighting instruments.

Filters

A myriad of filters are available for use in photographing. Some are designed to mount on the camera, some mount directly on lights, and some, like large

lighting gels, fit in separate frames and are placed in the light path. These filters are usually made from glass or gelatin. All filters are light modulators. They operate on subtractive principles; all subtract intensity and some absorb specific spectral components of light. In chapter 3, a brief discussion covered filters for color photography; now filters will be examined in more depth with specific attention to studio applications. Many photographers divide filters into two groups, those for black-and-white photography and those for color photography. Filters can be more accurately divided into three classes: those that alter the spectral composition of light, those that evenly reduce light intensity across the spectrum, and polarizing filters.

Filters can absorb wavelengths of light in the visible and the invisible portions of the spectrum. Both the color compensating filters and light balancing filters mentioned in chapter 3 alter the spectral composition of visible light. The ultraviolet filters discussed absorb wavelengths of light outside of the visible spectrum. In any case, the effect is to change the distribution and proportion of various wavelengths of light through subtractive absorption. Colored filters employ various dyes to absorb light of their complementary hue; these dyes can be in coatings on the filter or integral to the glass or gel material of the filter. Some filters absorb light through the use of interference coatings rather than dyes. These thin coatings are used in the dichroic filters of color enlargers. For practical purposes, each of these different types of filters act upon light in the same manner.

A colored filter, in eliminating certain wavelengths from light, reduces its intensity and necessitates longer exposures. With camera-mounted filters, this exposure increase is expressed in terms of a filter factor which is usually supplied by the manufacturer. A filter factor indicates the amount of exposure increase needed to adjust for the loss of light through absorption. Factors are expressed mathematically. A factor of $2\times$ indicates a doubling of exposure or a 1 f-stop increase; a factor of $3\times$ indicates a 1 1/2 f-stop increase; a factor of $4\times$ indicates a 2 f-stop increase; etc. Factors are generally applicable to panchromatic black-and-white and color films but can vary depending upon the type of illumination and sensitivity of the emulsion in use. Filter factors for lighting gels are not stipulated and must be arrived at through testing. It should be noted that in-camera light meters designed to read a full spectrum of white light may not give accurate readings of colored illumination. It is preferable to take a white light reading without

a filter, then apply the filter factor to arrive at the correct exposure. When this is not possible, testing may be necessary to determine correct exposure levels.

As discussed in chapter 3, the spectral composition of light can have a great effect upon the rendering of colors, with various color films responding differently to given illumination. Each color film is designed to respond correctly to a particular spectral balance of wavelengths. Although not often discussed, it should be understood that panchromatic black-and-white films are also designed to respond to light of a particular color balance. The spectral composition of the exposing light will affect both the contrast and speed of a black-and-white film depending upon the sensitivity of the emulsion. Most black-and-white films are essentially balanced for daylight and generally gain contrast while losing approximately 1/2 f-stop or 25 percent of their ISO when exposed to unfiltered tungsten illumination. The "correct" response of panchromatic black-and-white film can be measured in terms of the reproduction of tones and colors as negative densities.

While the effect of colored filters on color films, as discussed in chapter 3, is apparent and obvious, their effect upon black-and-white films is less commonly understood but surprisingly pronounced. With black-and-white materials, colored filters can be used for two basic purposes: to balance the response of the film and light so as to render all colors and tones in a scene in their proper, monochromatic brightness-relationship; or, to alter tonal relationships in the negative so as to separate specific areas of color as different negative densities. In the first case, certain colors, such as greens and reds,

may render as near or identical tones of gray on the negative. While this may be densitometrically correct in terms of the brightnesses of these colors, it may prove confusing to a viewer attempting to read information or separate shapes in the photograph (figure 7.1). If the intent of the photographer is to convey certain information clearly, then filters can be effectively used to separate and define areas or objects of a particular color. In this second instance, numerous choices are available to the photographer.

When used with black-and-white materials, a colored filter will proportionately lighten surfaces similar in hue to the filter and darken surfaces of complementary hues. This observation assumes that the filter factor has been calculated and applied to the exposure. It is possible to radically change the rendering of surfaces in a black-and-white photograph through the use of filters. Many renderings are possible, particularly with strongly colored subjects (figure 7.2).

Color filtration can be accomplished at the source of light as well as at the camera. Given a single source of illumination, a red filter placed between a lighting instrument and a subject will have the same visual effect as a red filter placed in front of the camera lens. The filtration is accomplished at a different point in the process, and the mechanics of the relationships are altered, but the light reaching the film is the same. Objects in the scene of similar hue to the filter will reflect proportionately more light and be rendered lighter, while surfaces of complementary hue will absorb illumination and be rendered darker. If multiple light sources are involved, each source can be filtered independently with varying colors to create effects not possible with one on-camera filter. Multiple exposure techniques using various colored filters are also possible with both black-and-white and color films.

Neutral density filters absorb light evenly across the visible spectrum; many also absorb ultraviolet wavelengths. They reduce the amount of light reaching the subject or the lens. Neutral density filters are available in numerous densities and can be combined to produce a full range of light-reducing effects. The most common filters have factors of $2\times$, $4\times$, and $8\times$, though filters are available up to $1,000,000\times$. These filters are useful when the normal adjustments of lens and shutter speed are not sufficient, or when they must remain fixed. In this context, neutral density filters are especially useful in film, where frame-per-second requirements often limit available exposure ranges. In still photography, images utilizing multiple exposure techniques sometimes require consistent apertures and shutter speeds necessitating exposure control through other means such as neutral density filters.

Various films of different ISO can be exposed using identical lighting and neutral density filters to adjust for the higher ISOs. Many photographers employ this method when testing for exposure with Polaroid materials. Neutral density filters can also be employed when extended exposure times are needed to record movement. The filters reduce the

[figure 7.1]

An unfiltered black-and-white photograph and a schematic drawing of a child's puzzle made up of geometric shapes of various saturated colors. Hues are indicated on the schematic. Note the separation of the various colors in the unfiltered photograph.

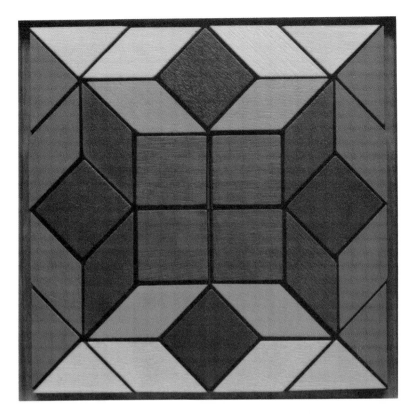

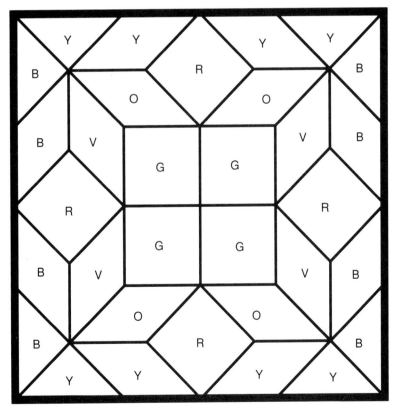

R = Red   G = Green
B = Blue   O = Orange
Y = Yellow   V = Violet

a.

b.

c.

d.

[figure 7.2]

Four additional exposures were made of the puzzle from figure 7.1: a. was made with a red filter; b. was made with a yellow filter; c. was made with a blue filter; and d. was made with a green filter. Note the variation in the rendition of color as tone achieved through the application of the different filters. Colors similar to the filter are rendered as lighter tones while complementary colors are rendered as darker tones. When using black-and-white materials, filters provide a valuable means of controlling tonal placement of various colors.

[figure 7.3]

A neutral density filter applied to the camera lens allowed for a long shutter speed and the balancing of tungsten and strobe illumination in this photograph incorporating movement as an important image element.

amount of incoming light allowing long exposures with given f-stops (figure 7.3). Finally, neutral density filters can be used to reduce depth of field when the shutter speed cannot be changed—denser filters allowing larger f-stops. Like colored filters, neutral density filters are available in glass for cameras and lights as well as in large gels.

Polarizers

Polarizers are special-purpose filters that, like neutral density filters, can be essential tools. Though most often thought of as a tool for eliminating reflections on glass and water or darkening skies in color photographs, a polarizer is particularly valuable in the studio under controlled lighting conditions. To understand the functional value of a polarizer, photographers must

first understand the nature of polarized light—where and when it exists, and how it can be controlled with a polarizer.

As light travels, it vibrates in all planes perpendicular to its axis of propagation. The vibration of polarized light is restricted to one plane perpendicular to this axis. Light can be polarized either naturally or by a polarizing filter. On a microlevel, a polarizing filter can be thought of as a fine series of parallel lines which act like a grille to restrict the plane of vibration of a beam of light (figure 7.4). Light passing through a polarizer will lose intensity as it is restricted; this loss can range from one to two f-stops, a factor of $2\times$ to $4\times$.

When polarized light encounters a polarizing filter, if the plane of vibration of the light and the orientation of the polarizing "grille" are identical, it will pass through the filter or, if

these planes are crossed, be held back. At varying angles in between, more or less of the light will pass through the filter. Two polarizing filters placed in-line and crossed at 90° will eliminate all light (figure 7.5). Polarizing filters used on lighting instruments allow photographers to illuminate scenes with polarized light. The main use for a polarizing filter on a camera is not to polarize light but to control the amount of polarized light that reaches the film.

Before proceeding, the nature of reflected light must be discussed. As stated in chapter 2, there are three types of reflection: diffuse reflection, specular reflection, and selective reflection. Diffuse reflection is light that has undergone changes due to absorption and reflection by a surface. Diffuse reflection allows the visual and photographic systems to function; it is responsible for delineating form, texture, tone, and color. Specular reflection is light reflected from a surface that is unchanged. It can lend a sense of brilliance and vitality to an image in the form of reflected highlights. Specular reflection is similar to radiant light in that it plays no role in defining tonal information; it can degrade and interfere with diffuse reflection causing loss of contrast, saturation, and detail. Selective reflection is a special form of specular reflection from metallic surfaces. It is reflected light that is unchanged except, in some cases, for its spectral composition.

All surfaces produce a combination of diffuse and specular reflection in varying proportions, and all specular reflection from nonmetallic surfaces is polarized to some degree. The degree of polarization changes with the angle of incidence of the illumination, being greatest at 34°. Polarizing

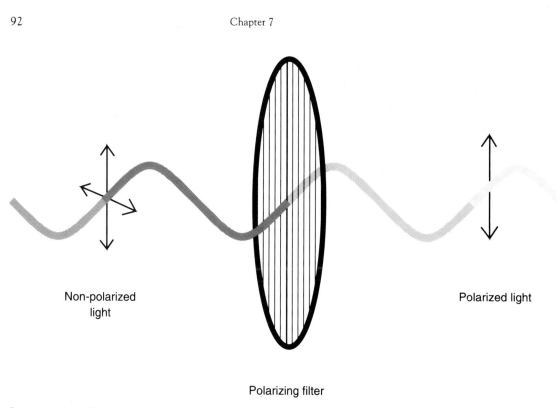

Non-polarized light

Polarized light

Polarizing filter

[figure 7.4]

A polarizing filter restricts the vibration of light to one plane perpendicular to the axis of propagation.

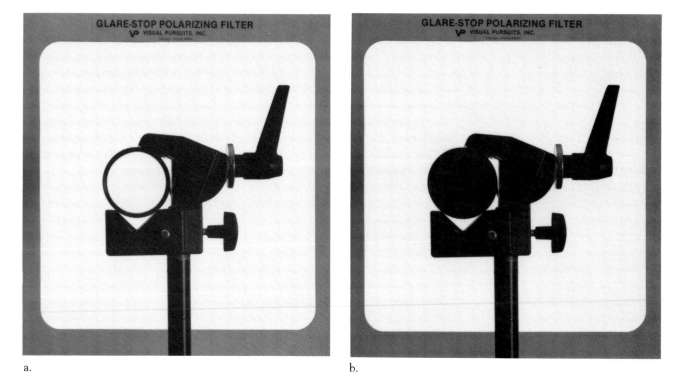

a.   b.

[figure 7.5]

a. Two polarizing filters, a camera lens filter in front of a large gel, with their axes aligned, are placed in front of a light source. Almost all of the light passing through the gel passes through the second filter.
b. When the polarizer's axes are crossed, the back light is entirely blocked by the second filter. A polarizing filter controls the passage of already-polarized light.

a.

b.

c.

[figure 7.6]

Light in the form of specular reflection from nonmetallic surfaces is, to some degree, naturally polarized. A polarizer can be used to control or eliminate this glare from reflections, resulting in increased surface detail, contrast, and saturation of color. These images are shot with no polarization (a.), slight polarization (b.), and maximum polarization (c.).

filters can be used to control the polarized light in specular reflections thus increasing contrast, saturation, and detail (figure 7.6). Unless the illuminating light is polarized, specular reflection from metallic surfaces remains unpolarized; thus the value of polarizing filters and gels for lights. With polarizers on both lights and camera, all specular reflection in a scene will be polarized and can be controlled or eliminated completely. To accomplish this, the polarizers on the lights must all be oriented in the same plane, and the polarizer on the camera must be at a 90° angle to that plane. To facilitate orientation, gels or filters for lights should be mounted in frames that allow for flexible placement; polarizing filters for cameras are normally mounted in rotating rings.

The effect of a camera-mounted polarizing filter can be observed by looking through the viewfinder or ground glass while turning the polarizer. As the maximum degree of polarization is reached, the image will darken and reflections will be minimized or eliminated. Exposure

determination when using polarizing filters is challenging. In-camera or film plane exposure meters will give accurate readings, but readings from hand-held meters must be interpreted. This is difficult due to the variation in filter factors as the camera-mounted polarizer is rotated; as more specular reflection is eliminated, less light remains to expose the film. As mentioned earlier, with one polarizer mounted on the camera an exposure factor of $2\times$ to $4\times$ can be expected. With filters on both the camera and the lights, a factor of $4\times$ to $16\times$ is common. As always, exposure increases can cause reciprocity problems and color shifts which must be anticipated. Experience will resolve some of these difficulties, but bracketing exposures will provide added security.

Eliminating all specular reflections from a scene may not be desirable. These reflections, particularly pinpoint highlights, often add life to an image; they are present in nearly all visual experience, and their absence can make an image appear unnatural. For example, a portrait with no

catch light reflecting from the eyes can appear lifeless, and shiny surfaces with no reflections lose their character.

Filters are often thought of as corrective devices that will allow a photographer to solve a specific problem. They can more productively be thought of as tools that expand creative horizons. Filters, though seemingly diminutive, can be one of the most important tools in defining the appearance of the final photograph. This is true of the common problem-solving filters discussed above as well as the more exotic special effects filters that will be discussed in chapter 14.

Scrims, Grids, and Diffusers

Scrims, grids, and diffusers are accessories that mount on or in front of a lighting instrument. While filters are designed to change the spectral composition, intensity, or polarization of light coming from a source or entering the camera, scrims, grids, and diffusers are designed to change the intensity, character, or

[figure 7.7]

A metallic scrim in position on a small quartz floodlight

[figure 7.8]

Honeycomb grids of various densities. The density of the grid, along with its depth, controls the spread of illumination.

coverage of light from a source. These accessories can also, as a corollary, change the spectral composition of the light; however, this is not their main function.

Scrims are made with fine wire-mesh screen. Various scrims are available as attachments for many lights. They either fit on the light itself or they mount in a frame directly in front of the light (figure 7.7). The purpose of scrims is to decrease the intensity of light. Unlike neutral density filters, which will have no effect on the character of the illumination produced by a light, a scrim will not only reduce intensity but also slightly diffuse and soften illumination. Because scrims are positioned near the light source, light wraps around them, and they cast no visible pattern in the illumination. As light passes through the scrim, a portion of it is reflected back at the light source. It is also reflected forward at various angles from the curved surfaces of the individual wires composing the screen. This results in a somewhat less-directional illumination with slightly softer shadows at the subject plane. A scrim can cut

light intensity by as much as fifty percent, but it is not a terribly effective diffuser and will only soften the light slightly.

The degree to which the light is softened is affected by the material used to make the scrim. Shiny silver or gold material will tend to reflect and scatter more light than matte-white or -black material thus providing slightly more diffusion. The color of the scrim material will also affect the color temperature of the light passing through. When using color films, it is advisable to check manufacturers' specifications or make test exposures to assure that the scrim is not warming or cooling the light it passes.

Grids or honeycombs, also called grid-spots, are designed to restrict the coverage of a light source without substantially changing the character of the light. These accessories are usually constructed of matte-black

material forming a boxlike or honeycomb pattern. They can be any shape and are designed to attach directly to a light (figure 7.8). They can be found for most lighting instruments. The angle of coverage and the rate of lateral light fall-off at the edges of the illuminated area can be controlled by varying the density and depth of the grid pattern. By restricting the light to a smaller area, grids can mimic the coverage of a spotlight (figure 7.9). Grids do not focus light, increase the intensity of the illumination, or alter its color temperature. Because grids do restrict the spread of illumination by blocking light rays not traveling more or less forward and parallel, they may tend to slightly increase the characteristic contrast of a light source. Depending upon the density of the grid, the intensity of the illumination may be decreased significantly by blocking.

[figure 7.9]

Scott Raffe employed a grid spot to focus the hard light from a medium reflector into a narrow stream in which his subject resides. A small fill light provided the rest of the illumination for this photograph made in the studio's basement.

Photograph by Scott Raffe

Diffusers are designed to scatter light, producing less-directional illumination. They can be mounted directly on lighting instruments or be separate panels or disks placed in the path of the light. Numerous materials are used for diffusion purposes. Some of the most common are spun fiberglass, translucent plastic sheeting, translucent coated fabric, and translucent Plexiglas. Each of these materials produces its own unique effect with a distinct appearance; some photographers prefer one to another. Their basic function is to alter or augment a light source to

[f i g u r e 7 . 1 0]
A strobe with a small reflector would normally produce a harsh, contrasty light. By directing the strobe through a diffusion panel, the contrast of the light is reduced. Note the defined, but not razor sharp, shadow.

[f i g u r e 7 . 1 1]
The same setup as in figure 7.10 with the strobe moved away from the diffusion panel. Note how a larger area of the diffuser is now being utilized. The shadow is much less defined and contrast is dramatically lowered.

provide illumination with broad highlights of controlled brightness, gradual tonal transitions revealing volume, and soft shadows with large penumbras. A spotlight can be turned into a softlight with a diffusion panel (figure 7.10).

Included in the following discussion are portable, light-weight fabric soft boxes which revolutionized location lighting in the 1980s and are also employed in many studios, replacing larger, less mobile, and less flexible studio softlights. These boxes are a blend between a lighting instrument and a diffusion panel; however, as they have no integral source of illumination they should be considered diffusion attachments. They share similar properties and perform the same function as other diffusion devices.

When a diffuser is placed in front of a light, it becomes the light source in relation to the subject. The lighting instrument

no longer defines the character of the illumination, the diffuser takes on this role. As mentioned earlier in the text, the contrast of a light source is related to its size; the larger the light source, the less contrasty will be its illumination. The same is true of a diffuser; the larger the diffuser in relation to the subject, the softer will be the illumination. In fact, the increase in size of the relative light source may be as important as the actual scattering of light rays by the diffusion material in providing a soft, wrap-around illumination. Even a soft light source will be perceived as quite contrasty if its size is small in relation to the subject.

The size of a diffuser can be controlled in two ways, either by changing the actual surface area of the diffusion device or by utilizing more or less of the existing surface area. This second method involves moving the source of light closer to or farther from the diffuser. As the light

source is moved away from the diffuser, it illuminates a larger area of the diffusion surface thus increasing the relative size of the diffuser as a light source in relation to the subject (figure 7.11).

A diffuser will reduce the amount of illumination that reaches the subject. Some of the light will be absorbed and some will be reflected back toward the light source. The illumination passed through the diffuser will not only be less directional and less intense, but it also can be of a different spectral composition than light from the source. The diffuser is, in actuality, a filter; if it absorbs light evenly across the visible spectrum, it will be similar to a neutral density filter; if its absorption is skewed toward certain wavelengths, it will add a color cast to the illumination. Diffusion materials that appear neutral white to the human eye can shift the color of light significantly in one direction or another. In certain contexts, color casts from diffusion material can be used to the advantage of the photographer to purposely warm or cool illumination. Though certain materials are guaranteed to be neutral, tests should be performed before critical color films are exposed using any diffusion device.

Portable diffusion panels utilizing PVC piping for frames and lightweight coated fabrics have replaced heavy diffusion flats in many studios. These panels are available in a wide range of designs and sizes and can be clamped to light stands for flexible positioning (figure 7.12). The fabrics for these frames are available in translucent neutral-white for diffusion, in opaque neutral-white and opaque silver or gold for reflection, and black for absorption. The same fabrics are used in conjunction with lightweight frames to form many of the portable soft boxes available. These soft boxes collapse for easy transport, are extremely light and flexible, and are available in a wide array of sizes and configurations.

Though each manufacturer offers unique designs in soft boxes, some of the critical components are shared. The fabric composing the box is normally opaque, black on the outside, and white or silver on the inside. Silver-lining fabrics tend to reflect more and harsher light than white fabrics. The front panel of the box is made from a translucent, white fabric. Most of these fabrics are guaranteed neutral; however, variations do exist between manufacturers and, as noted above, testing is recommended. An opening is provided in the rear of the box through which a light source is inserted; usually the light is mounted on a special ring or adapter to which the box itself attaches. Most of these boxes are designed for use with electronic

[figure 7.12]

A lightweight diffusion panel mounted between two light stands. The mounting clamps allow the panel to be tilted around its central axis. The fabric is a translucent synthetic purchased ready-made. The frame for the panel is made of inexpensive PVC plumbing pipe that is fitted, but not glued, together. These panels can be disassembled quickly for easy transport or storage.

strobe equipment. Although most fabric light boxes will accommodate the fan-cooled, tungsten modeling lamps built into strobe heads, only a few are actually designed for use with "hot" lights. Before using any fabric soft box with tungsten or quartz lights, be sure that the manufacturer recommends such a combination.

The various configurations and designs of fabric soft boxes include: internal baffles to insure even light distribution; removable fabric scrims allowing for additional diffusion or light reduction; and, recessed front panels allowing for increased control over the spread of the illumination. Available accessories include extra diffusion panels, honeycomb grids, louvres, barn doors, and assorted mounting rings.

Fabric soft boxes are available in many shapes and sizes. Small boxes are available for hand-held,

camera mounted strobes and huge 15 × 40-foot boxes are available for studio or location work utilizing multiple strobe heads and power packs. Many photographers feel that the light coming from a fabric soft box is harsh in comparison to illumination from large studio softlights utilizing opalescent Plexiglas as a diffusing medium. Though certainly not a panacea, these portable, collapsible, fabric soft boxes have had an impact on photographic lighting, both studio and location. Their versatility and effective operation make them indispensable tools (figure 7.13).

Reflectors

Reflectors are designed to redirect light into or within a scene. They can also be used to soften, color, and concentrate light. Like diffusers, reflectors are available in many sizes and are constructed of many materials. Also as with diffusers, when a reflector is employed to direct light into a scene, the surface of the reflector becomes the light source in relation to the subject. Again, the lighting instrument itself no longer totally defines the character of the illumination. In addition, reflected light is usually less directional and less intense than direct light, except for light reflected by mirrored surfaces. In certain instances, reflectors and diffusers can be used to achieve the same apparent result in the final image, though the means of implementation are considerably different. Generally, however, the purpose of reflectors is not to soften light but rather to function as a source of additional illumination for a scene. Fill cards or reflector panels are placed around, and occasionally inside of, a scene to illuminate shadows or bounce light back toward the camera. The use of these cards

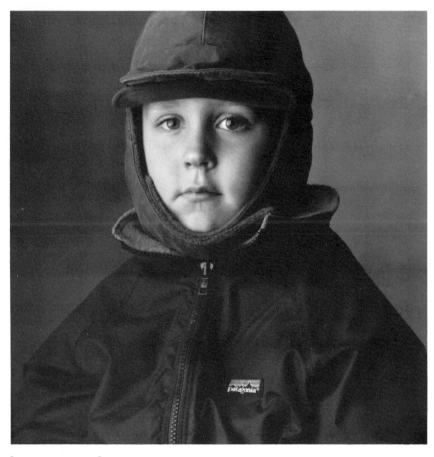

[figure 7.13]

Guy Hurka used a large fabric soft box to light this portrait of his son, Colin. Note the reflections of the large light source in the subject's eyes and the soft, enveloping quality of the illumination.

Photograph by Guy Hurka

and panels greatly expands the potential of a single light source, allowing it to function in a manner suggesting multiple lighting instruments (figure 7.14).

The major factors affecting the performance of a reflector fall into three categories: the size and shape of the reflector, the nature and color of its surface, and its placement in the set. The larger the reflector, or the larger the area of a reflector that is utilized, the softer will be the reflected illumination. Again, this is a product of the rule that larger light sources provide softer illumination. As with diffusers, the size of the area of a reflector being utilized can be controlled by placement of the light source nearer to or farther from the reflector. The shape of a reflector

will affect the distribution of light bouncing off its surface. The basic shapes are concave, flat, and convex. The spherical, parabolic, and elliptical reflectors mentioned in chapter 6 are all concave reflectors. Most studio reflectors tend to spread light to a greater or lesser degree—concave shapes less than flat and convex shapes.

The surface of a reflector will affect not only the directional nature of a light reflected but also its intensity and spectral composition. Highly polished or shiny surfaces will tend to reflect more directional light of greater intensity than will matte-surfaced reflectors. Although rays of reflected light will travel in straight lines, they will not obey the inverse square law nor, as pointed out in chapter 2, be

reflected at only the angle of incidence. The scattering of light by the surface of the reflector is responsible for these anomalies.

The surface of a reflector will also absorb some of the light striking it and can change the spectral composition of the illumination. As with diffusers, neutrality is difficult to judge without comparison and testing. Is a white reflector really white? A visit to a paint store and a glance at the available "white" paint samples will point out the variance that might be encountered. This is, of course, not always negative. Colored reflectors can be used to infuse parts of a scene with color casts to accentuate or offset the dominant illumination. Again, as with diffusion material, testing should be performed before critical color films are exposed using reflected light.

The placement of a reflector in the set is as important as the placement of a light. Placement can affect the reflector's performance in much the same way it affects that of a light source. The farther a reflector is placed from a subject, the smaller is its relative size and more contrasty its illumination. The angle of a reflector to the subject is also important as it will influence the amount and distribution of light in the scene. Reflectors can be used to create shapes and broad reflected highlights on glass or other reflective surfaces; however, the placement of these shapes must be carefully controlled as they influence the appearance of the final image and can be elegant or awkward.

One special type of reflector designed to attach to a light source is an umbrella. Lighting umbrellas are one of the most common accessories in the studio; they vary in size and construction. Lighting umbrellas are, like their

[figure 7.14]

A small still life set with reflector cards in place, redirecting light from the one source back into the scene from secondary angles.

namesake, constructed from lightweight, collapsible, metal skeletons covered with various fabrics. Most umbrellas are specifically designed to work with electronic studio strobes; the strobe head with a reflector in place points up into the umbrella. Some strobe systems have specially designed reflectors that accommodate the umbrella shaft allowing for near on-axis light placement (figure 7.15). Umbrellas increase the effective diameter of a light source and reflect light that is less directional than source light. Depending on their size, shape, and surface they soften and spread the light to varied degrees. Larger umbrellas with matte surfaces soften the light most markedly, and deeper umbrellas spread the light out to a lesser degree.

The most common fabrics used in umbrellas are coated synthetics, which are white or silver on the inside. Umbrellas are also available with translucent fabrics; lights are directed at the subject through these umbrellas which act as diffusers. Some reflective umbrellas have diffusion panels that attach to their open side, essentially forming a light box; these are versatile, multipurpose tools. Umbrellas tend to be more efficient than other light reflectors and can produce a wide range of effects depending upon their individual characteristics and distance to the subject. As with other diffusers and reflectors, umbrellas can change the spectral composition of the light they reflect.

As noted in the previous section, many frame and panel reflector systems are available that consist of collapsible, lightweight frame components and coated-fabric reflectors. Again most of the fabrics are either white or silver with an occasional gold used for warming reflected light. These versatile systems are modular in construction, include many accessories, are readily mounted on light stands or easily joined together to form large "reflector walls," are transportable, and can be flexibly configured. Though valuable in the studio, reflector/diffuser panel systems are, again, tools that have particularly revolutionized and simplified location photography.

Occasionally a reflector will be placed within a scene to reflect light back toward the camera. The most common use for such reflectors is in illuminating glass vessels from behind. Because glass is transparent, it cannot be illuminated directly. It can, however, be accentuated with illumination from behind, which allows the glass to refract and reflect light coming toward the lens. Small, individually shaped reflectors can be placed behind glass containers to reflect light back toward the camera. In this instance, the reflector acts as a source of radiant light. Highly polished reflector surfaces work most effectively in this application.

Mirrors are special kinds of reflectors that have unique uses in studio photography. A mirror will reflect light essentially unchanged from the source. The directional character, spectral composition, and intensity of the source light will remain largely constant. Of course, even a softlight reflected in a mirror will be harsh if the mirror is small in relation to the subject. Mirrors can be used to illuminate small areas of a scene with bright, reflected light. In

[figure 7.15]

*An umbrella mounted on a strobe head. A hole in the reflector to accomodate the
umbrella shaft and mounting clamps built into the monoblock head allow the strobe to
be nearly centered in the umbrella, facilitating even illumination.*

addition, mirrors will reflect light in patterns determined by the shape of the mirror: a circular mirror will reflect a circle of light, a triangular mirror will reflect a triangle of light, etc. (figure 7.16). These characteristics make mirrors particularly affective for creating small highlights and key reflections. Many studio photographers keep small mirrors of various sizes and shapes for such purposes.

Barn Doors, Snoots, Gobos, and More Tools

Though new lighting accessories are constantly being developed and many of the tools that are available today are innovative, most of the devices described above have been in use in various forms for many years. Barn doors, snoots, and gobos have a long history as lighting tools and remain relatively unchanged,

useful accessories. Barn doors and snoots are devices used to restrict the spread of light from a source. They are normally constructed of matte-black metal and attach to the light itself. Barn doors consist of two or four moveable fins that mount to a frame attached to the front of the light (figure 7.17). These fins can be independently opened or closed over the front of the light to cut off illumination in various areas of the scene or to keep stray light from hitting the camera lens. Because the edges of the fins are close to the light source, the lateral fall off of illumination is gradual, creating a large penumbra at the boundaries (figure 7.18). In this sense, barn doors function in a manner similar to grids; however, they are both more and less flexible. Unlike grids, barn doors can be adjusted to restrict the spread of light to a greater or lesser degree, but they are not as efficient as grids as they block more light and the degree of lateral fall-off is not variable. When closing barn doors it is important to be conscious of heat buildup.

Louvres are a variation on barn doors. Louvres are normally designed to attach to softlights. They fit on the front of a light fixture and work in a manner similar to a venetian blind. Louvres can restrict the spread of light but are more useful in reducing light intensity. In a sense, louvres are variable scrims. Set close to the light source, they cast no visible pattern of shadows in the illumination.

Snoots are cylindrical or funnel-shaped devices designed to attach to the front of a spotlight, a variable spot/floodlight, or a reflector. Depending upon their size, they restrict the spread of light to a larger or smaller circle (figure 7.19). Snoots perform a similar function to grids and barn

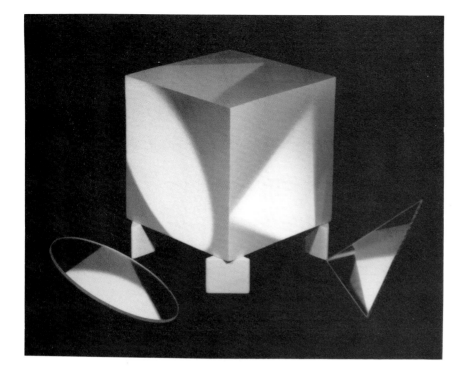

[figure 7.16]
Cut mirrors will reflect light in a pattern matching their shape. This can be useful for illuminating small areas of a scene with bright light. The mirror does not substantially change the character of the light, but it does act as an auxiliary light source and, like any small light source, can be quite contrasty.

[figure 7.17]
Barn doors in place on a spotlight. Each of the four panels can be folded in or out to adjust the coverage of the light.

*In use, barn doors restrict the spread of
the illumination from a light source.
Because they are close to the source and
the light wraps around them, they tend to
feather off the illumination rather than
create a hard edge.*

*A snoot in place on a spotlight. The snoot
restricts the spread of illumination to a
small circle. As with barn doors, the snoot
is close to the light source, thus the edges
of the circle will be softened.*

doors as they reduce lateral light-spread; however, they are not adjustable like barn doors and not as efficient as grids because they block a great deal of light.

Gobos, or flags, are shields that "GO BEtween" a light source and the camera or a light source and a subject. These accessories are made from matte-black material in a wide range of sizes. Many photographers construct their own gobos. The purpose of a gobo is to block light. Stray light reaching the surface of a lens causes flare with a resultant decrease in contrast, saturation, and sharpness. Back light of any sort is most likely to result in such problems. Gobos mounted on dowels attached to light stands can be positioned to effectively block stray light from the lens (figure 7.20). Gobos can also be employed to block light from specific areas of a scene to control highlights and reflections.

As a light modulator, a gobo placed in the path of a light will obviously cast a shadow. It is the nature and control of this shadow that is important. The shadow will be larger as the size of the gobo relative to the light source increases. Not as obvious is that the greater the distance from the light source to the gobo and/or the smaller the distance to the subject from the gobo the sharper its shadow will be. By varying the distance from the light source to the subject, the size of the gobo, and the distance of the gobo from the light and/or to the subject, the shadow cast by the gobo can be tightly controlled to blend in with the subject and the background. Shadows from gobos can be used to reduce the brightness of highlights without substantially affecting other parts of a scene (figure 7.21). A variation of this technique is to use a scrim as a gobo, thereby reducing but not eliminating light from an area.

[figure 7.20]

A gobo can be used to block stray light from the camera lens. This is especially important when using any kind of side or back light directed toward the lens.

Gobos can also be used to eliminate or create reflections in glossy surfaces. A gobo can be positioned to block the light causing a reflection much in the same way that it reduces a highlight. The gobo is actually creating a shadow that is specific to the area of the reflective surface. Another way to think of this is to imagine the gobo itself being reflected in the surface: A reflection of a black gobo appears the same as the absence of reflecting light. Gobos of various shapes can also be used to create "black reflections" in glossy surfaces to help define shape and volume. If a diffuser is being used, these reflections can be softened by placing the gobos between the light source and the diffuser as opposed to between the diffuser and the subject (figure 7.22). Sometimes photographers use black paper to mask off areas or shapes on diffusers or reflectors to create similar effects. This is a variation on the use of the gobo to eliminate or create reflections.

Black reflections can also be created with small cards or large panels placed around or in the set; different from gobos, they do not intercede in the light path at any point—they simply add reflected shapes. These cards and panels can also be placed near a subject to function as light absorbers, eliminating stray illumination that might bounce back on the subject from various surfaces. These absorbers can be used to tone down highlights, darken shadows,

[figure 7.21]
a. A light source placed close and directly above a subject can create extreme contrast as it falls off quickly. This makes balancing exposure for the top and bottom of the scene difficult; detail can be washed out on the top and lost in heavy shadow on the bottom.
b. A gobo placed directly above the subject, blocking some of the light (forming a soft shadow), evens out the illumination considerably, helps reveal detail in all parts of the subject, and separates the subject from the background.

a.   b.

and/or contain light in a scene; they might simply keep light off a background, not affecting the main subject at all. As noted above, black fabrics are available for many of the panel and frame diffuser/reflector devices on the market, increasing the versatility of these component systems.

In essence, any device that blocks or modifies light in any way is a light modulator. In addition to the modulators discussed above, photographers utilize many unique, self-designed tools to control light. These range from simple stencils that create patterns when placed in the light path to pattern masks for optical spotlights to elaborate systems designed to create special effects. Some special light modulators used in the studio will be discussed in chapter 14. At times, the simplest device can provide the most elegant solution, enhancing the form and extending the meaning of an image.

[figure 7.22]
A gobo placed between a light source and diffuser will create a soft, black shape that can function as a soft shadow to control local brightness in an area of a scene, or be reflected in a shiny surface to help define shape and form.

CONTROLLING LIGHT

The most familiar light source in the world is the sun. While this may seem a simple observation, it holds many clues for the studio photographer. As a primary light source, the sun can be a sort of starting point for an investigation of studio lighting. Many of the kinds of light experienced in studio photographs have already been experienced in nature. As humans live and grow, they observe. People develop innate feelings for the conditions under which various types of light occur, the events that can be implicitly associated with them, and the implications they have for humanity. The light of morning or evening; the moon shimmering on the water; the light of a cold, gray winter sky; the light just before a severe storm; the diffuse, enveloping light in fog—all of these become familiar. People know that on a cloudy day they won't cast a shadow, they know to expect bright reflections from the sun, and they know that dusk is a time of illusion and magic.

Photographers and viewers of photographs alike learn to read this natural language of light on a subconscious level.

For photographers, particularly studio photographers, this experiential knowledge base must be used as a foundation upon which to build a conscious understanding of light. The best way for a photographer to learn about light is through direct and careful observation. This can begin outdoors, consciously observing the qualities and effects of different types of light. Sunlight is the most powerful spotlight; with shifting angles and with clouds acting as reflectors and diffusers, even gobos, many studio lighting designs can be imagined in nature. The sun brightens and dims with clouds and time of day; it changes angle in the sky; it casts shadows; and, it reflects off of human-made and natural surfaces. It is a source of illumination, it defines shapes and surfaces, and it affects interpretations of the world. These are the basic

characteristics and functions of any illumination, natural or artificial.

Moving into the studio, the most effective lights to learn with are tungsten lights because of their constant nature; photographers cannot see in the few thousandths of a second in which strobes fire, but their tungsten modeling lamps can serve the purpose. Photographers need to be able to observe and adjust the effects of lights as they work. Knowledge gained with tungsten lights will easily translate to electronic strobes, and observations are much cheaper than test film. Tungsten, or "hot," lights have largely fallen from favor with studio photographers who now mostly employ strobe lights. However, most studios have some tungsten lighting equipment on hand; some photographers prefer tungsten light for certain subjects; some subjects demand constant illumination; and, as pointed out earlier, film and video employ continuous light by necessity.

Underlying Principles

As suggested above in reference to the sun, studio lighting has three main functions in a photograph. First, it provides illumination; making both vision and photography possible. Light facilitates processes. Second, it differentiates the space, shapes, and surfaces in a scene; defining depth and volume, delineating edges, and revealing texture. Light creates form. Third, it manipulates the reading of a subject; acting as a psycho/physical cue in the interpretation of an image. Light influences meaning. Two of these three functions of light have been discussed in some detail—chapter 5 dealt with understanding and measuring general levels of illumination, and chapter 2 investigated the relationship between light and meaning. In this chapter, the concentration will be on light as it defines form in a photograph.

In this context, five important considerations exist: the intensity of a light, the relative size of a light source, the direction from which light emanates, the shadows created by a light, and the reflections created by a light. These are interrelated concerns with many corollaries and interactions. No system of lighting is ever capable of solving all problems; for creativity, it is critical to know when to step outside of systems. However, the five considerations outlined here form the underlying principles of sound, flexible lighting design.

The intensity of illumination in a scene is controlled by the power of the light source and the source's distance to the subject. A powerful light source will raise the overall levels of illumination in a scene and can facilitate various choices in exposure that will radically alter the rendering of the subject. A weak light source can

limit choices for exposure placement and restrict creativity. An obvious corollary to this is the constraining effect of low levels of illumination on shutter speed and aperture combinations, limiting movement and depth of field. For high-contrast effects, a powerful light source is required to accentuate tonal differences between highlight and shadow areas.

The distance of a light source to a scene will affect the relative levels of illumination in various parts of the scene. This is due to the fall-off of the light. Because light intensity decreases with the square of the distance, the distance of a light source to a subject can have a great affect on the levels of illumination in various areas of a scene. For example, if the depth of a scene is 1 foot and a light source is placed 1 foot from the front of the scene, the rear of the scene will be 2 feet from the light source and receive only 1/4 the amount of illumination. This represents a fall-off of 2 f-stops in the space of 1 foot. With the same subject and the light source placed 5 feet from the front of the scene, the fall-off will be less than 1 f-stop from front to rear; with the light source placed 10 feet from the scene, the fall-off would be negligible (figure 8.1). By moving the light source closer to or farther from the subject, the light can be made to fall-off more or less gradually; also, as the light is moved, the overall illumination changes and exposure must be adjusted appropriately.

As previously stated, when a light is moved its characteristic contrast will change because of changes in its relative size. This is a critical point and deserves some further discussion. Contrast is related to a number of characteristics of an image. Along with the range of values, the

a.

b.

c.

[figure 8.1]

Because of the inverse square law, a light placed close to the front of a scene will fall off rapidly over a short distance. The identical white cards in photographs a., b., and c. are numbered relative to their distance in feet from the light source. Note that as the light source is moved back from close (a.), to medium (b.), to far (c.), the difference in tonality between the front and rear cards diminishes to near nothing. The contrast of a scene can, in part, be related to the distance from the light source to the subject.

nature of the shadows and reflections are the most important delineators of contrast. While the range of tonal values in a scene is largely dependent upon the intensity of the light, the nature of

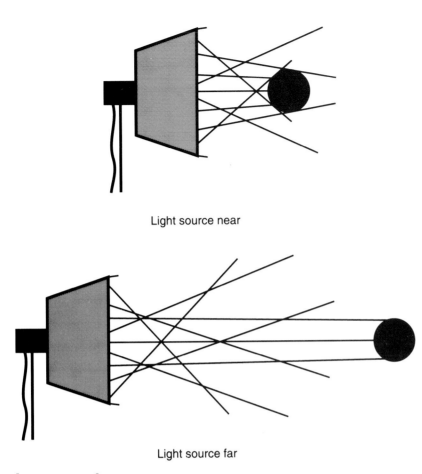

Light source near

Light source far

[figure 8.3]

Here, the subject hides its own shadow which is cast straight back by the frontal light. The relationship between camera, light source, and subject will determine the visibility of the shadows in a scene.

[figure 8.2]

The functional size of a light source is relative to the distance of that source from the subject. As a light source is moved farther away, a smaller percentage of its available light reaches the subject resulting in more directional illumination and more contrast.

the reflections and shadows is largely dependent upon the size of the light source. Other things being equal, a larger light source will produce softer shadows and broader reflections than a smaller light source. However, distance affects relative size. The farther a light is positioned from a subject, the smaller will be its relative size. The more distant the light source, the less of its available illumination is actually being used to light the subject. The light being utilized is more directional, and therefore more contrasty (figure 8.2). If lighting contrast is too high or too low, moving the light source closer to or farther from the subject may solve the problem.

Perhaps the most important consideration in positioning a light source is angle. This includes both horizontal and vertical location and, along with positioning the camera, will determine the size and/or placement of shadows and reflections in the photograph. It will also alter contrast. Recalling chapter 2, the contrast of illumination is related to its direction with regard to the subject and camera position with front light being flattest, side light being more contrasty, and back light being highest contrast. As a light is moved around, the shadows cast by three-dimensional objects and textured surfaces in the scene become more or less pronounced and visible to the camera. The direction and length

of the shadows themselves will be defined by the relationship between the light source and the subject, while the visibility of the shadows will vary according to the relationship between the camera, the light source, and the subject (figure 8.3). The location, size, shape, and visibility of reflections in the scene are dependent upon the same factors.

Deciding how to position a light is sometimes a technical problem-solving exercise, sometimes an aesthetic decision, and sometimes both. Observation is the key to learning about positioning. Referring to the discussion of Gestalt perceptual theory in chapter 1, it should be apparent that shadows and reflections may be read as meaningful shapes in two-dimensional images. Because, with a given camera angle, both of these are dependent upon the placement of the light source, positioning becomes critical to formal construction and psychological interpretation.

[f i g u r e 8 . 4]

In this Raymond Meier photograph, shadow plays a simple, yet strong, graphic role. It creates its own shape and thereby asserts its presence in contrast to the subject (original in color).

Photograph by Raymond Meier, "Black Shoe"

[f i g u r e   8 . 5]

John Divola used a hard, side light to model form in this simple, yet intriguing, still life. The transition from light to dark on the curving surfaces creates the cyclone's volume and helps separate it from the flat background.

Photograph © John Divola, "Cyclone 1986"

Shadows and Shading

In this text, shadow and shading are taken to be different properties. A shadow is a defined shape that indicates direction, depth, and sometimes texture. It can be more or less sharp-edged, vary in depth of tone, and be attached to or distinct from its source of origin; it is a source of graphic, not tonal, information (figure 8.4). Shading is the gradual transition of tone from light to dark on a surface; it is integral to the surface. It indicates angle, volume, and depth. It varies with the angle of the surface to the light source and the camera (figure 8.5). Shading is always perceived as three-dimensional, while shadow may be perceived as two-dimensional. Most, though not all, photographs make use of both of these properties; some images utilize one or the other exclusively. The only exceptions to this rule are photographs of flat, two-dimensional surfaces.

Various lights and the nature of the shadows they cast were discussed in chapter 6. Here are a few more observations about shadows. A shadow implies three major components: a source of light, an object in the light path, and an illuminated ground upon which the shadow is cast. Remove any one of these and no shadow exists. The relationship between these three components determines the contrast, direction, size, and shape of the shadow. Shadows can range from sharp-edged and even in tone to soft-edged and varied in tone; that is from no penumbra to a large penumbra. The contrast of the shadow will be defined by three basic variables: the nature of the light source, the distance from the light source to the object, and the distance from the object to the ground. Each of these variables can be manipulated independently to achieve flexible control over the contrast of shadows in a scene. The first two variables have already been discussed.

Most shadows change relative to the distance between the object casting the shadow and the ground on which the shadow is cast. They become harder-edged when close to the ground (figure 8.6). This is the nature of the penumbra. A penumbra results from light traveling in various, nonparallel directions. Such light projects numerous overlapping shadows from any object it strikes (figure 8.7). The degree to which the light rays and these shadows overlap defines the size of the penumbra. With any given light

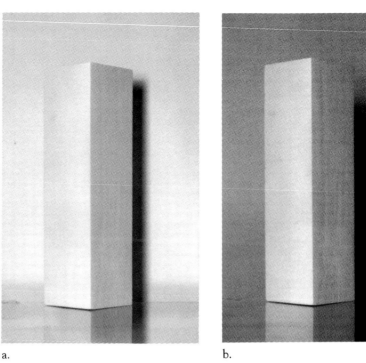

a.   b.

[figure 8.6]

a. The closer the ground, the more defined a shadow will appear. The background in this image stands immediately behind the subject.

b. In this image, the background has been moved back substantially from the subject; note the softening of the shadow.

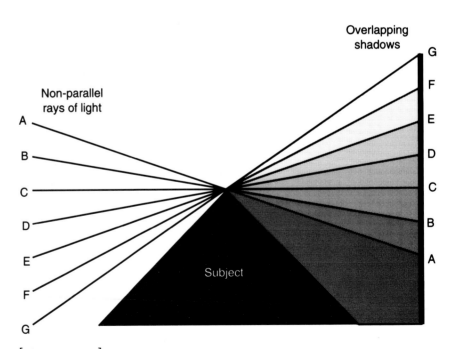

[figure 8.7]

A penumbra results when light rays, traveling in various directions, hit a subject edge forming numerous overlapping shadows on the background. The size of the penumbra is determined by the nature and relative size of the light source. As the light rays striking the subject become less parallel, the size of the penumbra will increase.

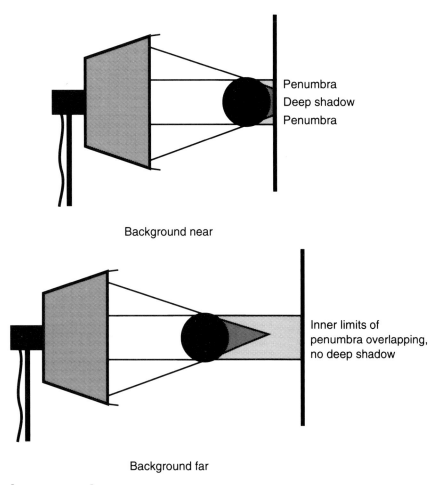

Penumbra
Deep shadow
Penumbra

Background near

Inner limits of
penumbra overlapping,
no deep shadow

Background far

[figure 8.8]

As the distance between the subject and the background increases, the size of any penumbra also increases. Deep shadow lies between the inner edges of the penumbra. Eventually, as the light begins to blend around the subject, the inner edges of the penumbra will overlap and deep shadow will disappear.

source and placement, a closer ground maximizes the overlapping of the shadows and minimizes the penumbra. As the ground recedes, the shadows diverge and light eventually begins to fill in behind the object as the inner limits of the penumbra overlap (figure 8.8). The farther away the ground, the more blended will be the penumbra and the less pronounced will be the shadow.

The three variables above are all interactive and, to a degree, similar results may be obtained by changing different variables alone or in concert. To recapitulate, the contrast of a shadow can be altered by changing light sources, by changing the distance between

the light source and the object, or by changing the distance between the object and the ground.

Obviously, the direction, size, and shape of shadows may be altered by shifting the angle of the illumination. The size of shadows may also be changed by altering the distance between the light and the object or the object and the background. Generally, the closer an object is to the light or the farther it is from the background the larger will be the shadow. Remember, either of these movements will also affect the contrast of the shadow.

Controlling the shape of shadows can be extremely important to the reading of a

photograph. Much can be learned about the direction of a light source and the depth of a scene by studying the shadows. Shadows are not only indicators of direction and depth but also of contour and orientation. Shadows are perceived to be of generally the same outline or shape as, and attached to, the object that casts them. If an object rests on a flat, level ground, a shadow will pivot around the base of the object relative to the direction of the light source, and the size of the shadow will be controlled by the vertical angle of the light source to the object (figure 8.9). Certain distortions of shadows, such as foreshortening and lengthening on such a ground, are easily accommodated. Other distortions due to altering the contour of or tilting the ground can be confusing and disorienting. If the ground is not flat, the shape of the shadow may be radically distorted (figure 8.10). If the ground is not level, the size and the perceived direction of the shadow may be altered (figure 8.11). Shadows with no apparent origin or detached from their obvious source also require interpretation (figure 8.12). As recognizable shapes, shadows can play an active role in the understanding of an image (figure 8.13). In combination, manipulations of light, object, and ground give the photographer almost infinite control over the contrast, direction, size, and shape of shadows in a photograph.

Shading, as defined in this text, occurs across surfaces in a photograph. From a given viewpoint, variation in shading is a function of the orientation of a surface to a light source. It varies with the curving or bending of the surface relative to the direction of the illumination. Shading defines volume. Though shadow may reveal the depth of a scene, it

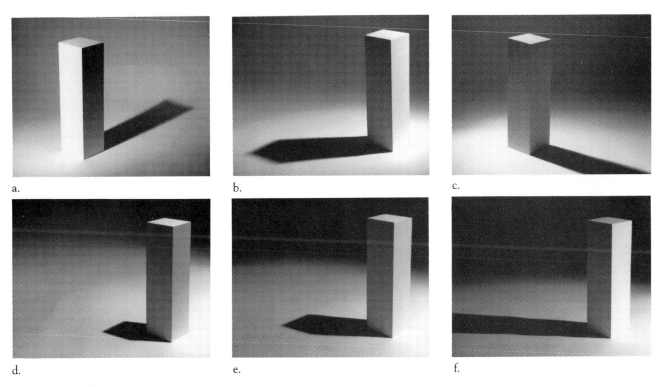

a.   b.   c.

d.   e.   f.

[f i g u r e 8 . 9]

The direction and length of a shadow are controlled by the placement of the light source relative to the subject. The photographs above show variations of front (a.), side (b.), and back light (c.), as well as high (d.), middle (e.), and low (f.) angles of illumination.

[f i g u r e 8 . 1 0]

On a contoured ground, the shape of a shadow is distorted.

[f i g u r e 8 . 1 1]

On an inclined ground, the size, direction, and relationship of a shadow to its origin may be confused.

[figure 8.12]

In this photograph by Michael Datoli, the shadow and the subject do not match. This creates a visual paradox for the viewer to unravel and hints at a presence outside of the frame (original in color).

Photograph by Michael Datoli © 1992.

[figure 8.13]

In her photograph "Leaving the Scene," Olivia Parker utilizes shadow as a narrative image element to hint at meaning. The running figure strongly connotes departure, abandonment, and perhaps guilt.

Photograph by Olivia Parker, "Leaving the Scene"

does not effectively define volumes within a scene. The former perception relies on graphic information, while the latter relies on tonal information. Shadows, particularly contrasty shadows, can actually reduce volume. A gray area exists between shadow and shading. As the change of light over a surface occurs more quickly, the gradient of shading becomes more pronounced, and shading becomes shadow. The exact point at which this transition occurs is subjective. Softer illumination yields a less pronounced gradient of shading

and, to a point, more effective definition of volume. Extremely flat illumination can reduce volume by altogether eliminating shading. Dependent upon the requirements of each image, a balance of lighting must be achieved that effectively defines both space and volume.

A third word that is related to shadow and shading is shade. For the photographer, shade differs from shadow in that it has no important, definable form in the photograph. It differs from shading in that it is not integral to a surface and is often completely

even over a large area. Shade is, in effect, a kind of light. It is totally reflected light, highly diffuse, and possibly colored depending upon the hue of the reflector or light reflected. Open shade is one of the softest forms of natural or studio light.

Shadows and shading can be contrived. Surfaces can be painted to resemble shadows and gradations of tone. This technique is often employed in theater set design. Shadows can also be projected onto diffusion material from behind. The visible difference between a cast shadow, a projected shadow, and a painted shadow may be negligible; however, their potentials for creative manipulation vary significantly (figure 8.14). Daily experience and knowledge of illumination lead to certain expectations about the behavior of light and shadow. When expectations are channeled, an illusion may be experienced; when they are contradicted, confusion may be experienced; and, when they are challenged, interest may be piqued.

Reflections

Reflections can be broadly divided into diffuse and specular reflection. As discussed in previous chapters, diffuse reflection is light having undergone absorption and scattering by a surface, and specular reflection is reflected light from the source that remains relatively unchanged. These two types of reflection must both be taken into consideration in creating a lighting design. Though each may be critical in delineating the image, they perform significantly different functions, behave in different manners, and are controlled with different techniques. Diffuse reflection carries the tonal and color information from a subject; specular reflection forms bright highlights and can be useful in defining edges and delineating surfaces. Diffuse reflection is inherently depolarized and scattered, while specular reflection, except from metals, is polarized to some degree and directional. Diffuse reflection can be reduced by decreasing light intensity falling on a surface or by altering exposure levels, and specular reflection can often be controlled with a polarizing filter. This is not an exclusive or complete list of differences and

[figure 8.14]

James Wojcik has fused cast and painted shadows to confuse our reading of space in this photograph from his series "Wire and Pigment."

Photograph by James Wojcik

characteristics, but it does include important points for consideration.

As detailed earlier, diffuse reflection does not strictly obey the law regarding angles of incidence and reflection. Because diffuse reflection is scattered, it reflects at relatively equal intensities regardless of angle. There will be some differences, with most light reflecting opposite the angle of incidence; however, with highly diffuse reflection these variations may be extremely small. Conversely, specular reflection is highly directional in nature and reflects almost entirely equal and opposite the angle of incidence. Most surfaces yield a combination of diffuse and specular reflection at all angles. If, at a given angle, the proportion of specular to diffuse reflection from a surface is high, the tonal detail and/or color of the surface will be obscured. Such specular reflection from surfaces is often called glare and can be useful or distracting in an image. Glare can obscure desired information or, sometimes, help to clarify the character of a surface such as polished wood, glass, or plastic.

A diffuse reflection changes with the reflectivity of various surfaces, hence, a white surface reflecting a great deal of light and a black surface reflecting very little. A specular reflection remains constant on any shiny surface, regardless of tone or color. This explains the observation that shiny black objects seem to yield more specular reflection than shiny white objects. Actually, it is only the proportion of diffuse to specular reflection that differs, making the specular reflections from shiny black surfaces proportionately more apparent. Fortunately, specular reflection, or glare, is highly predictable and controllable. Controlling and using diffuse reflection is bound up with general lighting and exposure techniques and is covered throughout the text. The following will investigate controlling and using specular reflection which involves understanding the basic mechanics of light and optics.

Selective reflection, first mentioned in chapters 2 and 7, is specular reflection from metals and is different from ordinary specular reflection in two important ways. First, it is not polarized unless the light source is, and second, it can be changed in terms of its spectral composition. For example, selective reflections from gold will appear yellow, and those from copper will appear orange. In all other respects, selective reflection and specular reflection are identical. These differences have critical practical implications. The

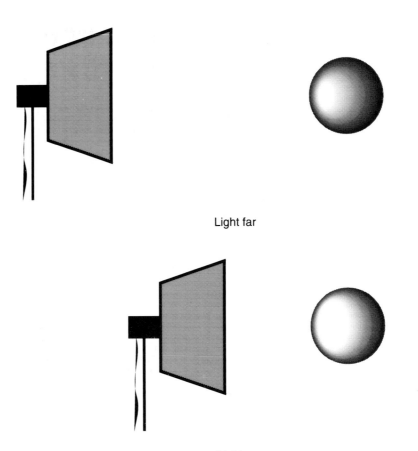

Light far

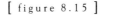
Light near

[f i g u r e 8 . 1 5]

As a light source is moved in distance relative to a highly reflective object, the reflected highlights on the surface of the object will change in size, not in brightness.

most important of these to the present discussion is that ordinary specular reflections are more or less polarized and can be controlled to a degree with a polarizing filter; most selective reflections cannot. Incidentally, one unexpected source of selective reflection is mirrors constructed from a silvered glass. In practice, most specular reflections are mixed with some diffuse reflection, are not completely polarized, and cannot be entirely eliminated with a polarizing filter. Specular reflections of polarized light sources, however, will be almost completely polarized and are an exception to the general rule.

The ordinary specular reflection of a light source will be considerably less bright than the source itself. A substantial amount of light is lost because of the blocking effect of polarization. Conversely, the selective reflection of a light source may be nearly as bright as the source itself because no light is lost to polarization. In both cases some brightness will be lost, as, depending on the surface, more or less of the energy will be converted to diffuse reflection and then scattered. In neither case does the brightness of the reflection depend upon the distance of the light source from the reflecting surface. As the light source is moved in relation to the reflecting surface, the size of the reflection changes resulting in the same amount of light being distributed over a larger or smaller area and the brightness of the reflection remaining constant, while the inverse square law is preserved (figure 8.15).

For this discussion, and throughout the remainder of the text, both specular and selective reflections will be termed "reflected highlights." It is to be understood that these highlights can be either polarized or nonpolarized depending upon whether they are ordinary specular reflections or selective reflections. Other than this, and the brightness difference mentioned above, both reflections are subject to the same laws of optics and the same methods of control. The reflected highlights in a scene are caused by direct reflections of a light source.

A basic knowledge of the physics of light and reflection allows photographers to either eliminate or create reflected highlights. Often both operations are undertaken in a single image. Reflected highlights can play an important shaping and defining role in an image and are not always a problem to be eliminated. In fact, as mentioned earlier, images with no reflected highlights often appear dead and flat (figure 8.16). In certain images, reflected highlights can carry the entire weight of forming and defining content; like shadows, they can also become shapes in their own right. The photographer should control the placement, size, and intensity of reflected highlights rather than be at their mercy.

The primary means of controlling reflected highlights lie in positioning the camera and choosing and positioning the light source. Obviously, the angle of the camera will be determined by choices regarding composition, framing, and intent. As discussed in chapter 4, the distance of the camera from the subject will determine the perspective of a photograph. If the requirements of the image define the perspective precisely, then camera distance may not be a matter of choice. In

[figure 8.16]

The reflected highlights on the pearls in Raymond Meier's photograph provide a sense of rich brilliance on the black surfaces as well as help to model the subject's volumes (original in color).

Photograph by Raymond Meier, "Black Pearls"

such a case, the photographer will have to rely upon manipulation of the light source to control reflected highlights. However, if camera distance can be altered, sometimes this will help to control or create these highlights.

Using a longer lens on a camera will allow greater distance from the subject yet maintain image size. As a camera is moved farther from a subject, the relative size of any light source creating a reflected highlight will increase because of the change in

perspective between subject and light (figure 8.17). This allows for more flexible positioning of light source and subject as well as more control over the relative brightness of diffuse versus specular reflection as the light can be moved in both position and distance while still reflecting properly to the camera (figure 8.18). If, given considerations of image perspective, a greater camera distance is acceptable, it will facilitate lighting.

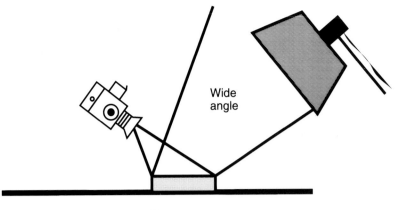

Wide
angle

Camera near

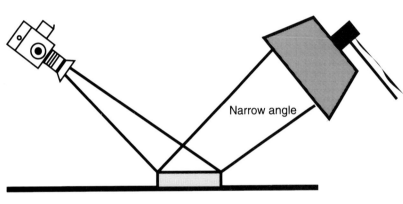

Narrow angle

Camera far

[figure 8.17]

Camera to subject distance affects the relative size of any given light source; the farther away the camera, the larger the relative size of the light source. This knowledge can be useful in creating large reflected highlights on a shiny surface.

For controlling the placement and size of reflected highlights, two basic manipulations of the light source are possible. First, the angle of the light source can be changed relative to the subject. Second, the size of the light source can be changed or the light source can be moved relative to the subject. Actually, any subject plane is composed of a collection of points at various angles to the light and camera. Because both light sources and reflective surfaces have area, there is never simply one angle at which a reflected highlight is visible. The angle of the light source to the surfaces of the subject will largely define the placement of reflected highlights seen by the camera. With flat surfaces, this placement is relatively easy to predict by referring to the angle of incidence rule (figure 8.19). With curving surfaces, this angle is constantly changing and predictions become more difficult.

Increasing the size of the light source provides a greater area of illumination relative to the subject and increases the size of reflected highlights. It also decreases image contrast by softening shadows. Obviously, changing from a spotlight to a large soft box will have a dramatic effect upon

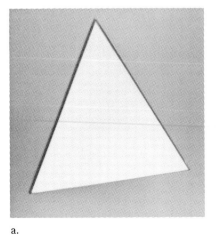

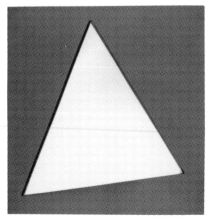

a.   b.

[figure 8.18]

a. With subjects yielding both diffuse and specular reflection, the distance of the light from the scene can control the rendering of surfaces in the image. If the light is placed close to the subject, all surfaces will be rendered high on the tonal scale.
b. If the light is moved back, the surfaces yielding diffuse reflection will darken, while those yielding specular reflection will remain unchanged in brightness.

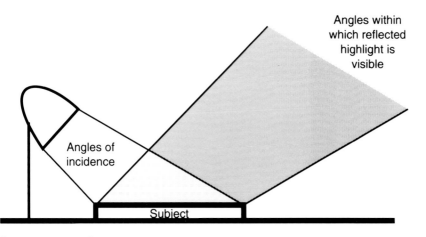

Angles within which reflected highlight is visible

Angles of incidence

Subject

[f i g u r e 8 . 1 9]

A reflected highlight will be visible from a range of angles determined by the size, distance, and angle of the light source to the subject.

reflected highlights. Simply moving a light source closer to the subject in order to increase its effective size can also have a marked effect. A spotlight at a close distance will still be a relatively harsh light source with brilliant specular reflections of fairly small size, but moving a softlight in and out changes the reflected highlights dramatically. This effect will be more or less pronounced depending on the contours of the subject which define the angles and reflected area involved.

The brightness of reflected highlights can be controlled by either reducing the brightness of the light source itself or using polarizing filters. Because the brightness of a reflected highlight is not relative to the distance between the light source and subject, moving the light farther away will not diminish the intensity of the reflection. This can be accomplished instead by reducing the intensity of the light source, which is done in numerous ways. If a large diffusion panel is being used, the light source can be moved farther away from the panel thus reducing the relative brightness of the diffuser's surface. Conversely, the light source itself could be dimmed with a neutral density filter.

Polarizing the light source allows for the control of all specular reflections in a scene. Remember, diffuse reflection is by its nature depolarized regardless of the illumination. As pointed out above, with nonpolarized light, purely polarized reflections rarely exist. In such a case, a polarizer on the camera will not eliminate all specular reflection let alone nonpolarized selective reflection. Illuminating the subject with polarized light produces nearly perfectly polarized specular and selective reflections allowing a polarizer on the camera to almost completely control these reflected highlights. The key word here is control. The polarizer is a creative, not simply a corrective tool.

Once all reflected highlights are polarized, a photographer can make decisions as to how prominent they should be in the image. If the camera-mounted polarizer is rotated at right angles to the polarized light, the reflections will be eliminated. In an odd twist, the polarizer can actually be used to increase the prominence of reflected highlights. This is accomplished by rotating the camera-mounted polarizer to the same orientation as the polarizers on the lights. In this position, the polarizer acts as a neutral density filter for

nonpolarized, diffuse reflection but allows polarized, specular reflection through. The reflected highlights actually increase proportionately in brightness to the rest of the image (figure 8.20). This is an interesting example of using a simple tool in a creative manner that contradicts its normally expected application.

Multiple Lights

An old lighting dictum says, "Keep it simple." Use as few lights as necessary to produce the desired result. This philosophy grows out of the belief that multiple lights introduce multiple complications. While this is true, it is equally apparent that all lighting problems may not be solved with one light source. In addition, multiple lights extend creative flexibility, offering opportunities that a single light source cannot provide.

Noted still life photographer Henry Sandbank discovered, in attempting to duplicate the lighting found in renaissance paintings, that painters took a great deal of liberty with light. Painters were not constrained by the physical laws governing the manner in which light falls-off, creates shadows, reflects, etc.; photographers are. Sandbank found that in order to duplicate many of those lighting schemes, he had to resort to using multiple lights. Whenever photographers want light to behave in a manner inconsistent with physical laws, they must make use of multiple lights or special techniques. Images with numerous discrete areas of illumination, images with strong multidirectional light, images in which the look of a single light source is important but the application is impossible, images that require fine-tuning in the balance of reflections or shadows, all of these may require multiple lights.

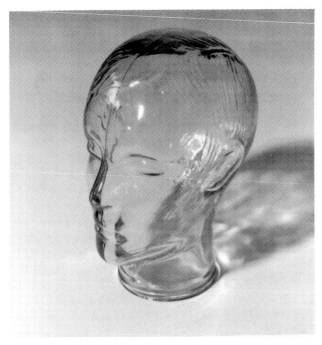

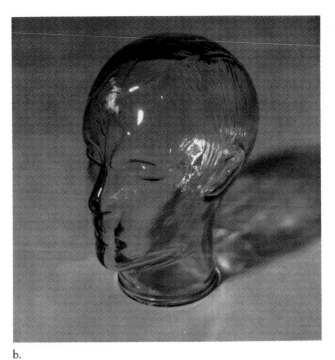

a.   b.

[f i g u r e 8 . 2 0]

In an odd twist, a polarizer can actually be used to increase the proportion of specular to diffuse reflection by acting as a neutral density filter for the latter. Figure a. was shot with no polarizer; in figure b. a polarizer was placed on the lens and adjusted to pass specular reflection. No exposure increase was given; therefore, the rest of the scene was proportionately darkened.

In addition to finding a need for more than one light source, Sandbank found that to preserve the feeling of the ambient illumination it had to appear as though only one light source had been employed. This points to one of the basic rules of lighting; when using multiple lights, make it look as though one light was employed. Going back to the beginning of this chapter and the single, pervasive light source, the sun, some guidelines can be established. A single light source casts only one set of shadows; these shadows all have the same character, and all of them go in the same direction. Combinations of sharp and soft shadows, multiple shadows, shadows within shadows, and crossed shadows are all signs of more than one light source that the viewer may recognize immediately as

contradicting common experience (figure 8.21). A similar case could be made for reflections occurring at specific angles and being of a constant nature.

The problems associated with multiple lights stem from these basic observations. The following suggestions will help guide practice. First, a hierarchy should be established that clearly defines the main light. This light should be positioned to define the dominant form of the image. Second, supplementary lights should not contradict or overpower the main light. These lights should either be less powerful, carefully angled, tightly confined, or softer than the main light. Third, additional shadows should not confuse or distract the viewer. Shadows cast by supplementary lights can be filled in by the main light, directed out

of the scene, or softened to mask their form. Finally, additional reflections should not obscure important forms or create annoying reflected highlights. Supplementary lights can sometimes create reflected highlights that must be eliminated for the sake of clarity or simplicity.

Two different methods guide the use of multiple lights. Though these can both be used in one image, it is useful to make the distinction. First, multiple lights can be used independently to illuminate discrete areas or surfaces within a scene. Second, they can be overlapped to illuminate and balance the entire scene. In the first instance, the lights are essentially acting as individual main light sources and can be treated accordingly (figure 8.22). If the lights are illuminating discrete but adjoining

a.

b.

d.

c.

[figure 8.21]

Various shadow problems with multiple light sources. Clockwise from upper left: hard and soft shadows combined (a.); multiple shadows cast in more than one direction (b.); shadows within shadows (c.); and, crossed shadows (d.). These effects generally tend to be disruptive and distracting in an image, making us notice the lighting instead of the subject.

surfaces, then one light should be identified as the main light. The main light will create the overall design of the image and be brighter than the other lights, which may be used to mold volumes, create depth, and add subtlety to the dominant forms in the image (figure 8.23).

In the second instance, lights are usually divided into a main light and fill lights. The main light defines dominant forms in the image and is usually elevated and to the side. The fill lights illuminate and soften shadows cast by the main light thereby lowering contrast and controlling lighting ratios. Fill lights are either the same intensity as or dimmer than the main light. They can be relatively small, hard lights placed near the axis of the camera lens to provide frontal fill; such light placement will create few new shadows and fill in those cast by a main light (figure 8.24). Alternatively, they can be larger, softer lights placed to the opposite side from the main light, creating soft shadows of their own, and filling in shadows cast by the main light (figure 8.25). The larger and softer the fill light is, the less critical will be its placement. In general, when using fill lights it is best to use too little rather than too much. Too much fill light will flatten the forms shaped by the main light and destroy the initial lighting design.

[f i g u r e   8 . 2 2]

Two lights working to illuminate separate areas of a scene essentially function as independent main light sources. Here a spotlight and a broadlight illuminate two separate subjects.

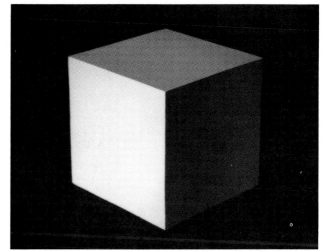

[f i g u r e   8 . 2 3]

Each side of this cube is illuminated by a separate light source. Volume is achieved through independently controlling the brightness of each individual light source and surface.

[f i g u r e   8 . 2 4]

A small, hard light placed on axis with the camera will fill in the shadows cast by the main light. The main light should provide the dominant illumination; the fill light should be of equal or less intensity. Here, the main light is placed to the upper left of the camera.

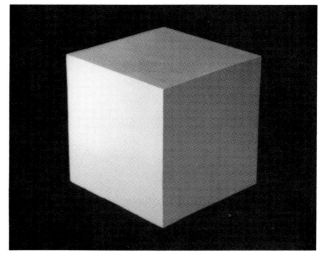

[f i g u r e   8 . 2 5]

A large, soft light placed to the side opposite the main light has substantially the same effect as a small, hard light placed on axis with the camera. The placement of the soft light is not absolutely critical as its illumination is fairly nondirectional and the shadows it forms are often completely overpowered by the main light. Often, however, the softlight will not be as evenly matched in intensity to the main light as a hard, on-axis fill might be. This results in somewhat more contrast in the lighting.

By changing the relative distance or intensity of a fill light to a main light, lighting ratios can be adjusted. With two lights of equal intensity, placed an equal distance from the subject, one acting as a main light and one as an on-axis fill, the lighting ratio will be 2 to 1. The areas illuminated by both main and fill will receive 2 units of light, while the rest of the subject will receive 1 unit of light. As the fill light is moved back farther, the lighting ratio increases rapidly. Because light falls off with the square of the distance, at $3\times$ the distance of the main light, the fill light would be only 1/9th as bright, giving a lighting ratio of 10 to 1. The areas illuminated by the main and fill lights would receive

a.

b.

[figure 8.26]
Lighting ratios of 2:1 (a.) and 10:1 (b.) on a cube

1 1/9th units of light and those illuminated by the fill would receive only 1/9th unit of light. The brightness of the highlights decreases but the overall contrast increases (figure 8.26).

Acceptable lighting ratios depend upon the photographer's intention and the eventual use for the images. Certain aesthetics or applications require specific lighting ratios not be exceeded. For example, most portrait photographers rarely exceed a 4-to-1 lighting ratio (2 f-stops) on the face and often prefer less contrast; lighting ratios for color are generally less than those for black and white; and, for images that will appear in print, overall lighting ratios of more than 16 to 1 (4 f-stops) should be avoided. Of course, as pointed out earlier, a lighting ratio does not always give a good indication of overall subject contrast range. Even flat lighting can appear contrasty if the subject is composed of blacks and whites.

In practice, when setting lights it is best to work with each light individually so that placement of shadows and reflections can be predicted and controlled. When working with tungsten lights or strobe heads of the same rating plugged into a symmetrical power pack, it is also possible to visually observe the effect of each light in terms of balance and lighting ratio. Remember, with ratioed strobe heads, the modeling lamps may give a false sense of the lighting, and actual exposure tests may need to be made on Polaroid materials to confirm lighting balance.

The main light should be placed first to establish the overall sense of the design. Next, the major supplementary lights should be positioned individually. The main light is turned off and the light being positioned turned on to observe its effects in the scene. Close attention to the direction

and angle of the supplementary lights will be necessary. Once the supplementary light is positioned correctly, the main light is again turned on, and the overall effect is carefully observed. Additional accent lights can be used to illuminate small but important areas of a scene or to create reflected highlights for added modeling and brilliance— sometimes these are concentrated and brighter than the main light. Each light must be carefully positioned and controlled to interact with, not disrupt, the overall lighting design. This process is repeated until all of the lights have been positioned; each light should be observed independently and in conjunction with all previously positioned lights (figure 8.27).

Gobos may need to be positioned to block light from various areas of the scene or the camera. In addition, reflectors and diffusers can be added to redirect

a.

b.

c.   d.

[figure 8.27]

A simple still life illuminated with three lights. The main light (a.) is from the rear; a fill light is place opposite the main light at the front of the set (b.); a second fill light is placed above the subject (c.); the four lights work separately and in concert (d.) to define form and detail in the final photograph.

and soften light. Finally, some dark, absorptive panels may need to be positioned to absorb stray light. The final set may be quite intricate if all of the above tools are used; however, the photograph should appear effortless with a clear sense of purpose and control in the lighting. Overlighting a set or lack of control will often result in a flat or confusing image with little sense of direction or purpose in the lighting. In the spirit of this observation, less is often better than more.

LIGHTING FOR SOLUTIONS

Lighting deals with surface and content, with space and environment, and with form and meaning. This discussion will use five specific aspects of form to explore lighting design and to suggest how content and environment can be manipulated with light to create various interpretations. The aspects of form and light to be explored are: lighting for surface, lighting for reflection, lighting for depth, lighting for volume, and lighting for transparency. Lighting for the portrait will also be investigated. The last of these is content specific; however, the portrait has been the most important and enduring subject in the history of visual art and deserves special attention.

The examples that follow must be understood to represent the specific embodiment of classes of problems, solutions, and information. Each will involve details that must be generalized in creative application. They also represent different aspects of form and lighting design that often

overlap. Conceivably, the first five could all occur in one image. The integration of the information provided is far more important than any particular application. The reader is urged to experiment.

Lighting for Surface

The simplest example of lighting for surface is the photographic copy of a two-dimensional subject. The seemingly mundane chore of copy work entails some interesting problems and demonstrates much useful information that can be translated to any flat surface. It has been said that producing an even tone all across a smooth, undifferentiated surface is one of the most difficult tasks in photography. Indeed, absolutely even lighting is difficult to attain. Combine this with the vagaries of photographic materials and the acute sensitivity of the visual system to tonal change, and the problem is magnified to significant proportions.

When considering two-dimensional surfaces, shadow and shading are not of significance. The most important factors in lighting design become evenness of illumination and control of reflections. In most copying situations, it is diffuse reflection that photographers are interested in capturing, as this carries the tonal, color, and shape information, while specular reflection carries only information about the light source. Exceptions to this arise when the surface has a texture that is important to the rendering, making the additional consideration of defining relief an added concern, or when the reflected highlights on a surface are integral to the description of the subject.

To achieve evenness of illumination, photographers must consider the distribution, intensity, and fall-off of light across a surface. Obviously the best light source will itself be even in character with no hot spots. It must also be sufficiently bright to allow workable exposure settings;

for example, color shifts that might occur from reciprocity failure could be deadly in copying a painting. Large softlights could be employed, but, more normally, broadlights or bulbs in spherical reflectors provide a good starting point. There are two basic techniques for lighting depending on whether one or two lights will be employed.

With one light, unless the light is placed directly on axis with the camera lens, fall-off of the illumination can be a problem as distance from the light source changes from one side to the other side of the surface. If the surface is smooth, small, and yields only diffuse reflection, then a ringlight or a single lamp placed close to the lens may provide even illumination. If the surface is large, highly reflective, or textured, this technique will not suffice. The frontal light may fall off at the edges, will form a reflected highlight on the surface, and/or mask any textural pattern. In this case, the light must be positioned off-axis from the lens.

The proper distance of the angled lamp to the surface illuminated will depend on the size of the surface, and the camera lens employed. However, in any case, the closer the lamp, the greater will be the fall-off across the surface. In general, with one light at an angle to the subject, the lamp-to-subject distance should be at least 3× as far as the camera-to-subject distance, assuming a normal focal length lens is employed. If the lens is wide-angle or telephoto, then the lamp-to-subject distance should be at least 3× the largest dimension of the subject (figure 9.1). This will minimize fall-off from one side of the surface to the other. Likewise, the light should be aimed slightly off center toward the opposite side of the subject to help compensate for distance changes. In practice, a gray card or incident meter reading at the

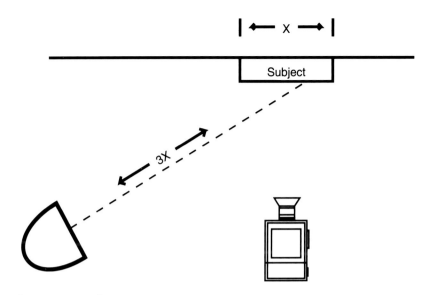

[figure 9.1]

A good rule of thumb for lighting two-dimensional subjects with one light source is to place the light at a distance at least 3× the largest horizontal or vertical dimension of the subject. Also, the light should be directed off center, about one-third of the way in from the opposite side of the subject, to minimize the effect of fall-off in illumination.

center and at all four corners of the subject, or a quick check with a Polaroid, will provide more accurate verification than the eyes.

The proper lamp-to-subject angle is determined by a number of factors including: the distance of the camera to the subject, the nature of the surface, and the degree of polarization desired. The camera-to-subject distance will not determine perspective relationships in a two-dimensional subject and is therefore dictated by the size of the subject and/or the available working space. The selection of lens is based upon the interaction of these two factors. If space is restricted or distance is proscribed, then a wide-angle or telephoto lens may be necessary. As described in the last chapter, increasing the distance between the subject and the camera and using a longer than normal lens to maintain image size will lend flexibility in the placement of the light. This can be important. Once the camera has been placed, the angle of the light may be adjusted.

Formula lighting dictates an angle of 45°; however, this may not always be appropriate. If reflected highlights are a problem, the lamp must be placed outside of the angle where it will reflect from the surface into the camera lens. As mentioned above, this is partly determined by the camera-to-subject distance (figure 9.2). If textural elements of surface must be emphasized, the lamp will need to be placed at an angle sufficiently shallow to create shadows from the subject detail. This angle will depend upon the degree of textural relief on the surface.

Polarization, as detailed in chapters 7 and 8, can be a great aid in controlling reflections on two-dimensional surfaces where the angles of light, surface, and camera can be precisely controlled. Remember, the specular reflection of a light source from a nonmetallic surface will be polarized to some degree, and polarization will be at its maximum when the angle of illumination is 34° to the surface.

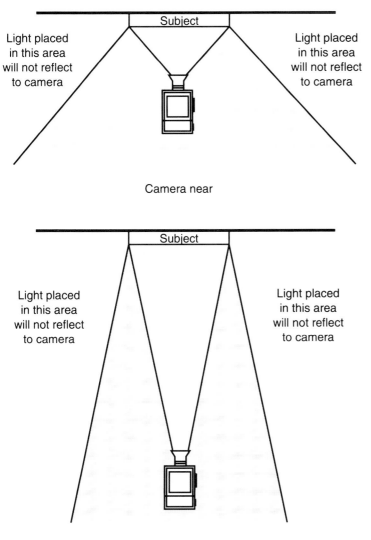

Camera near

Camera far

[f i g u r e   9 . 2]

Camera-to-subject distance will proscribe possible light placement when photographing highly reflective surfaces. The closer the camera, the more limited will be the choices for the placement of lights.

By placing the lights correctly and using a polarizing filter on the camera, most reflected highlights and reflections of camera, tripod, background, etc., can be eliminated. If the lights cannot be positioned to minimize specular reflection, then polarizers on both the lights and the camera can be used to control or totally eliminate reflection. This is most effective when all other ambient light, such as room or window light that is not polarized and might strike the subject at odd angles, is eliminated.

Utilizing totally polarized light might seem an ideal solution to all copying situations. However, as previously mentioned, the removal of all specular reflections can be visually detrimental. For example, an oil painting with a highly textured and reflective surface might be more accurately depicted with some degree of reflected highlight left intact. Diffuse reflection and shadow alone would not yield as accurate a rendering of such a surface. Likewise, if the smooth, glossy quality of a surface is integral to

the description of a subject, then it is important to maintain that information. A highly polished surface may be best rendered as a combination of specular and diffuse reflection as each plays a role in defining the character of the subject.

With two lights, all of the above information applies to both light sources. In this case, the lights should be placed at equal distances and equal angles to the subject. They should be at a distance at least $3\times$ the largest dimension of the subject. Each light should be directed at a point about one-third of the way in from the opposite side of the subject (figure 9.3). This will, again, help insure even light distribution. Using two lights will do a great deal to even out illumination; large pieces may require more than two lights to cover height and width evenly. To provide totally even illumination, some photographers use large circles of lights in which subjects can be positioned. The principles for the placement of the lights remain generally the same for one or twenty lamps.

Lighting for surface may, of course, involve more than evenly illuminating and copying an original. The lessons learned in flat copying can be extrapolated to other subjects but may need to be adjusted in light of new concerns. Shortly, the discussion of surface lighting will be expanded to include three-dimensional subjects. At this point, the additional factors that photographers must take into consideration when lighting surfaces include tonal separation, gloss, texture or pattern, and contour.

Tonal separation of adjoining areas of different color may be an important consideration when lighting surfaces. Without volume, the clues the photographer must give the viewer for separating

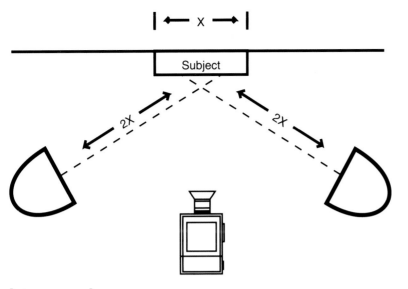

[f i g u r e 9 . 3]

When lighting two-dimensional subjects with two lights, the lights should be equidistant and at least twice as far away as the largest dimension of the subject. The lights should be directed off center about one-third of the way in from the opposite side of the subject.

contours change, the angle of the surface to the camera and the light source changes resulting in varied levels of brightness. These brightness changes are translated to tonal modeling by the camera and perceived as shading or surface undulations in the photograph. Again, the direction of the light can have a great effect upon the rendering of surface contours (figure 9.5). The concepts involved in lighting surface contour blend into lighting for depth and volume.

Lighting for Reflection

With highly glossy surfaces, reflection becomes a useful tool to utilize rather than a problem to be eliminated. In many cases, shading of such surfaces is not an option. They return such a high proportion of specular to diffuse reflection that no tonal rendition is possible. These reflections are either black or white or, if polarized and controlled, an even shade of gray. Two prime examples of such surfaces are shiny metals and glossy, black ceramics. Neither one of these surfaces yields appreciable diffuse reflection, and each of them relies on reflected highlights to define its visual character.

Tonal variation is no longer useful for defining such surfaces. The absence or presence of specular reflection defines their shape, while the distortion of reflection is responsible for defining their three-dimensional qualities (figure 9.6). In some instances, glossy surfaces comprise only a portion of the image and are combined with surfaces yielding diffuse reflection. In such instances, a balance must be struck between diffuse and specular reflection. In either case, to light such scenes photographers

shapes reside in the two-dimensional surface. With color materials, the separation of areas of varied hue will be automatic, though it may be shifted through filtration. However, with black-and-white materials there can be a wide range of potential renderings. Decisions must be made as to the importance of clearly defining shape as opposed to precisely recording tonal relationships. In certain cases, a "correct" rendering of values can obscure important forms. Tonal separation in black and white can also be increased or decreased by using standard exposure and development controls to shift the values and contrast of a negative. This will inherently give a false rendering of the subject values but may be necessary for the photographic translation of a low- or high-contrast subject.

The characterization of a surface is not complete without a reference to its gloss. A high-gloss surface and a smooth, matte surface can be rendered exactly the same in a photograph. For an

accurate description of surface, photographers must employ diffuse and specular reflection in an appropriate balance.

Surface texture ventures into the realm of the third dimension. However, it is endemic to surface and will be considered here. Texture is similarity and proximity of shape—it is pattern. However, the rendering of texture in a photograph is dependent upon light and shadow. Soft frontal light will practically eliminate texture while strong side light will exaggerate it. The entire nature of a texture can also be changed by altering the direction of the light (figure 9.4). Light can also be used to visually separate shapes and surfaces in a scene that varies in tactile terms. Though texture is rarely associated with gloss, it is possible to have a highly textured, highly glossy surface. The reflections from such a surface will be brilliant but may radiate in many directions.

Contour is dimensional shape or relief. As mentioned in the previous chapter, when surface

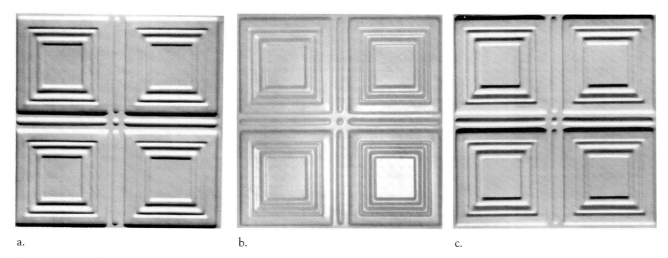

a.   b.   c.

[figure 9.4]

The nature of texture or a relief pattern can be changed dramatically as a light source is moved around the subject. When viewed from directly overhead and lighted from behind (a.), this pattern appears to be raised above the surface; lighted from above (b.), the pattern almost disappears; and lighted from the front (c.), the pattern appears to be recessed below the surface.

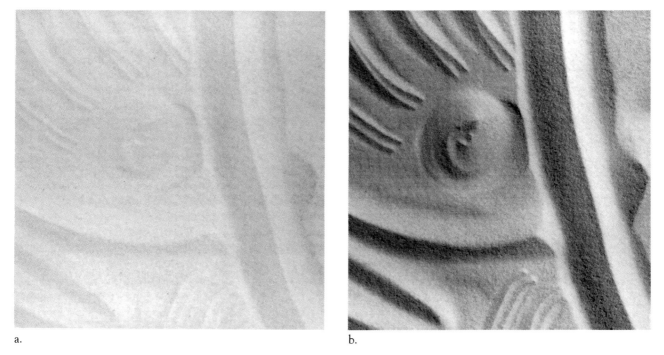

a.   b.

[figure 9.5]

The contours of a surface are defined by changes in tonality. Lighted from overhead (a.), the contours of the sandscape above are difficult to clearly discern; when the light is moved to the side (b.), the contours become well defined.

[figure 9.6]

Specular reflections define the basic shapes and volumes of the chrome teapot in this George Grigus photograph (original in color).

Photograph by George Grigus

must rely on reflected highlights to form important components of the image. The main factors to be considered in lighting such surfaces are the position, size, and relative brightness of the reflections; these factors will be controlled by the direction, distance, and brightness of the light source as well as the contours of the surfaces.

As mentioned earlier, with such surfaces, the direction and angling of the light source to the subject require attention; only a certain placement will reflect light to the lens, and this will be dependent upon the angle and distance of the camera to the subject. This placement can be accurately predicted by applying the rule of incidence and reflection encountered in chapters 2 and 8. A light source must be placed at or close to this angle to be visible in the photograph.

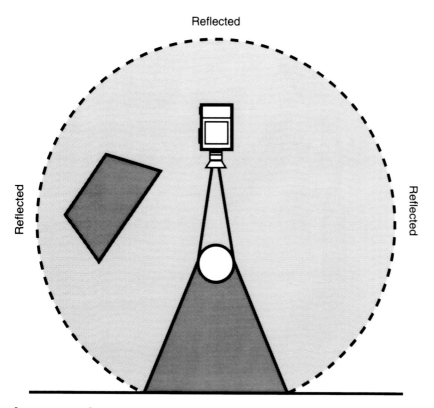

Reflected

Reflected

Reflected

[figure 9.7]

At a given distance, the reflected highlight of a light source on a flat surface may be quite large compared to the same reflected highlight on a curved surface. The curved surface reflects much more of the surrounding environment and effectively reduces the size of the light source.

As pointed out in the last chapter, the relative size of the light source is related to its actual size and its distance from the subject. Not as obvious is the relationship between the curvature of the subject's surface and the relative size of the light source. If the subject's surface is curved, it will reflect a larger surrounding area than if it is flat. This may be true of both concave and convex curvatures. As this area increases, the portion of it filled by a given light source decreases thus resulting in a smaller reflected image of the light source on the surface (figure 9.7). To produce broad reflected highlights on a curved surface, the light source must be significantly larger than the subject. As noted in chapter 8, the distance of the camera to the subject also has an impact on the relative size of the light

source. As the camera is moved farther away, the relative size of the light source increases.

Finally, the brightness of reflected highlights in a scene is directly proportional to the brightness of the light source and will remain constant regardless of the distance of the light source, while the brightness of the diffuse reflections can change radically as the light is moved in and out of the scene. As seen in chapter 8, when lighting for reflection, this brightness differential between specular and diffuse highlights can be critical to shape definition.

When dealing with surfaces that simultaneously generate both specular and diffuse reflection it is often necessary to represent both qualities in order to describe the surface accurately. For example, lacquered wood surfaces must be represented as possessing a glossy

sheen, yet, if the surface is to be distinguished from glass or metal, the grain of the underlying wood and/or any painted design must be apparent. This can be achieved in two ways. First, a reflected highlight covering the entire surface could be created and then controlled with polarizers to allow the diffuse reflection to appear. However, such a rendition could be confusing in its undifferentiated appearance. A better solution might be to position the light so as to cause a reflected highlight covering part of the surface and to allow the rest of the subject to be rendered by diffuse reflection (figure 9.8). This does not always produce satisfactory results but can be a good compromise.

When dealing with surfaces composed of varying materials, each adjacent and competing material can require different types or angles of light to properly define its qualities. One material might require diffuse reflection to reveal color and tonal values residing below the surface, while adjacent material might require specular reflection to define shape, surface gloss, or texture. Sometimes, one of the reflections can be sacrificed to the other enabling the photographer to light for diffuse or specular reflection alone. If this is not desirable, a number of different methods can be utilized in controlling the proportion of specular to diffuse reflection. An attempt to use one type of light or another to render the scene may, in some cases, be effective, in others, abysmal. Polarizers could be used to control the specular reflections off of certain surfaces and thereby extend the versatility of one light. Or, a larger light source that would produce a great deal of diffuse reflection compared to specular reflection could be utilized. These techniques all

a.

b.

[f i g u r e 9 . 8]

*An undifferentiated blending of specular and diffuse reflection (a.) may not be as
effective in conveying all the characteristics of a subject as a selective combination that
involves the discrete use of both specular and diffuse reflection (b.) in adjoining areas.*

represent compromise, attempting
to use one light to perform an
inherently impossible task.

More acceptable results might
be attained by using multiple
lights—each light used
independently to create different
reflections on the surface. One
light could be positioned to create
totally diffuse reflections, all
specular reflection being directed
away from the camera, while
another light could be used to
create reflected highlights, etc.
(figure 9.9). This is a more
flexible compromise as it permits
individual control over the
direction and brightness of each
light thereby allowing proportional
control over the amount of
diffuse-versus-specular reflection.
However, as noted in chapter 8,
multiple lights often produce
unwanted complications, and in
essence, both types of reflection
will always be present everywhere

in the scene; they will simply be
more closely balanced to an ideal
compromise.

Another solution would be to
use one light with light
modulators. A light can be
positioned to create both diffuse
and specular reflection, and the
specular reflection can then be
eliminated from certain areas of
the scene through the use of
gobos. As mentioned in chapter 7,
a gobo cut to a specific size and
shape and positioned correctly
with regard to a light source and
surface will cut the light that
produces specular reflection from
a very specific area of that surface
while not substantively affecting
the light that produces diffuse
reflection (figure 9.10). This
technique allows one light source
to be utilized for producing both
diffuse and specular reflection and
modulates the light in the scene
to block certain specular

reflections. Remember, the larger
the relative size of the light
source, the more effective is this
technique as overlapping light and
a large penumbra will mask the
edge of the gobo's shadow.

In addition to lighting for
reflection, it is possible to light by
reflection. This does not mean the
use of reflected light to illuminate
a scene but rather the redirection
of light within a scene to
illuminate various surfaces.
Because glossy surfaces in a scene
can only be lighted through the
use of specular reflection, if this
reflection is directed away from
the camera, the surface itself may
appear dark while throwing light
into another area of the scene.
The light reflected will be
identical in nature to the light
from the original source. However,
the reflected light will be traveling
in a different direction than the
direct light (figure 9.11).

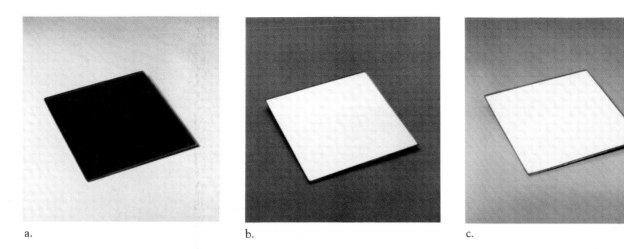

a.   b.   c.

[figure 9.9]

Lighting surfaces that generate both specular and diffuse reflection involves choices. Frontal light directs all specular reflection away from the camera leaving shiny surfaces dark (a.). Back light exaggerates specular reflection causing shiny surfaces to be bright compared to the rest of the subject (b.). A combination of front and back light can be used, with each light ratioed to yield a particular balance of exposure (c.).

[figure 9.10]

In this case, a large soft light and a gobo made from a neutral density gel have been employed to create a balanced rendering. The half-shadow of the gobo reflects in the shiny surface and cuts its brightness while not affecting the diffuse reflection from the rest of the subject. This method of lighting has the advantages of simplicity in employing one light source and of flexibility by allowing for control over the brightness of each individual type of surface.

[figure 9.11]

Light reflected from the shiny black surface illuminates the front of the subject but remains invisible to the camera; a polarizer eliminates any reflection from the black surface.

[figure 9.12]
Charles Purvis has used strong shadows to create depth and to characterize his subjects
in this simple still life.
Photograph by Charles Purvis. Accessories: Study of use of light to create depth and dimension. 1986.

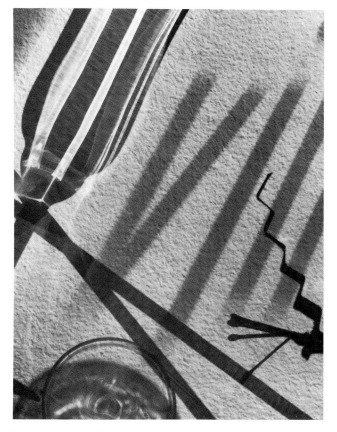

[figure 9.14]

Adjoining areas of light, dark, shadow, and tone create an ambiguous series of shifts in dimensional depth in this photograph by Ken Coplan.

Photograph by Ken Coplan

[figure 9.13]

In this image Purvis has pushed the use of the shadow to the point where it actually flattens space through its graphic character. Interestingly, some of the shadows in this scene were formed by objects placed inside of the 8″ × 10″ view camera itself, between the lens and the film plane.

Photograph by Charles Purvis. Vin: Still life, objects in camera. 1986.

Lighting for Depth

As noted earlier, shadows are an excellent indicator of depth and direction. Taken together these two qualities can shape an image's space. Depth can also be indicated by tonal variation in adjoining planes in an image or by the gradual transition in space from light to dark on one plane. Each of these techniques creates a dynamic relationship or movement in the image between foreground and background based upon the language of light.

Strong directional light tends to shape the subject more than be conditioned by it, thus creating strong boundaries and depth but minimal volumes (figure 9.12).

The nature of shadows in a scene can have an affect upon depth perception. In general, sharp-edged shadows are more easily distinguished than soft-edged shadows and, therefore function as more effective indicators of depth and direction. However, sharp-edged shadows become shapes in an image and can distract from the main subject. Also, sharp-edged shadows tend to be extremely graphic in character and can sometimes flatten an image by eliminating or suppressing tonal information thus negating their effectiveness at creating depth (figure 9.13).

Not only the apparent depth, but also the feeling of an image can be altered by manipulating

the shadows in a scene. Shadows projecting forward tend to involve a viewer more actively in an image while at the same time projecting space out from the photograph in front of the subject. Shadows cast back tend to create deep space behind the subject, allowing a viewer more distance and a more detached relationship to an image.

Tonal variation of adjoining planes in an image can create a feeling of apparent depth. Because the photograph reduces space to two dimensions, interactions of tone can become a playful element of illusion in an image. As lighter tones tend to advance and darker tones recede, tonal juxtaposition alone can create strong figure-ground relationships that powerfully suggest depth. These tonal variations can be created with light. In these instances, careful attention to the set or subject as a light modulator is required (figure 9.14). The

[figure 9.15]
*Ruth Bernhard posed her model behind a painted canvas, lit her from behind, and
allowed the projected shadow to interact with the painted image confusing our sense of
figure and ground. As our attention shifts between "figures," the interaction of the forms
suggests a comparison of traditional styles of representation of women's bodies in art. The
shadow is a stylized African form in silhouette, contrasting the classical European form
of the painted figure. The intersecting lips and breasts suggest a focus on woman as
sexual objects in both styles.*

Photograph by Ruth Bernhard, "Configuration," 1962

[figure 9.16]

As the background fades to black, the left side of Steve Nozicka's image recedes, projecting the subject and creating a powerful sense of depth in the photograph (original in color).

Photograph by Steve Nozicka

content conditions the light which shapes the depth and space of the image. Reversals of commonly interpreted relationships between light and dark can also create unexpected and graphically active images (figure 9.15).

The gradual transition from light to dark can also be effective in creating an image's space. This transition usually occurs in the ground of the image where light tends to visually advance while dark recedes (figure 9.16). This kind of transition on the ground can be produced by angling the light source relative to the ground or vice versa and by allowing fall-off in light intensity to control the gradual darkening. It can create a suggestion of infinitely deep space. It is this same gradual transition from light to dark that helps photographers define contour and volume.

Lighting for Volume

Lighting for volume requires new considerations as the shading on three-dimensional surfaces becomes important to the character of the image. As noted in the section on lighting for reflection, volume may also be defined in terms of specular reflection, and that will be discussed in the next section. Now consider lighting a subject that yields diffuse reflection. Having considered overall depth above, volume may now be considered as confined to the description of the surface contours of various objects within an image. The two most basic considerations in lighting for volume are the nature and direction of the light source. For the perception of volume, an image must achieve tonal variation, or shading, across surfaces.

Strong light and contrasting shadow are not enough to create rich volume. It is the transition between the two and the proportion of one to the other that are most critical. This is why a soft light that wraps around a subject and creates soft-edged shadows and broad areas of tonal transition is usually quite effective in defining volume. The same principle explains why front light, which produces few shadows, and back light, which produces only silhouette and shadows, are both poor at creating volume. Likewise, direct sidelight can be confusing in its emphasis on edges and equal areas of shadow and highlight—equal areas of figure and ground become difficult to interpret.

Essentially, a large light source, used close up, lights a subject from many different angles at once with evenly bright illumination thus creating a wrapping effect. This allows the contours of the subject to condition the light reflecting to the camera and creates shading and volume. The most effective type of light for creating volume will be a soft light from a relatively hard direction. That is a light somewhere between back light and front light that gives a

distinct but not equal proportion of highlight and shadow (figure 9.17).

Some subjects can be modeled effectively with one light alone, but many will require the addition of light modulators or multiple lights. In keeping with the dictum of simplicity, one light with light modulators is a preferable solution to multiple lights, which, as indicated in chapter 8, often imply multiple problems. With one light alone, the photographer's options are limited to changes in direction and distance. Many renderings can be achieved, but all may leave important subject information either in shadow or poorly modeled in volume. With the addition of a fill card to reflect light back onto the subject, we may achieve a more pleasing and accurate rendition.

Lighting for Transparency

Transparency is absence. Specifically, it is absence of diffuse reflection. When lighting for transparency, photographers must utilize qualities of the subject that will produce a visible effect in the image. Because color, surface texture, and shading are not present, photographers must rely on transmission, refraction, and specular reflection to delineate the subject. The most common transparent subject encountered

in the studio is glassware. Two basic approaches are possible— lighting for edge definition and lighting for surface reflection; these may be combined to produce a well-modeled form in an image.

Lighting for edge definition will give viewers a clear idea of the shape of a subject. Obviously, the standard approach of using tonal separation to define figure/ground will not work with a transparent subject. Equally obvious is the fact that transmission alone is not capable of defining the subject. Photographers must usually rely on transmission and reflection working together to define the forms in these images. As we have seen, with curved surfaces many angles will reflect light directly to the lens. This knowledge can be utilized to produce two basic types of edge delineation on three-dimensional glass subjects. The glass can be rendered with dark edges against light backgrounds or with light edges against dark backgrounds. In either case, the same principles apply; the light or dark backgrounds show through the subject while the juxtaposed dark or light edges are actually reflecting the surrounding environment (figure 9.18).

A background that just fills the camera's field of view is ideal in actual size. Because the direct view of the camera is limited in comparison to the area that will reflect to the lens off the curved

[figure 9.17]

Gary Abatelli's still life of eggs uses a soft light from a relatively harsh direction. The light is positioned overhead and somewhat behind the subject yielding strong volumes fading to deep shadows as the rounded shapes curve away from the light source (original in color).

Gary Abatelli Studio

a.

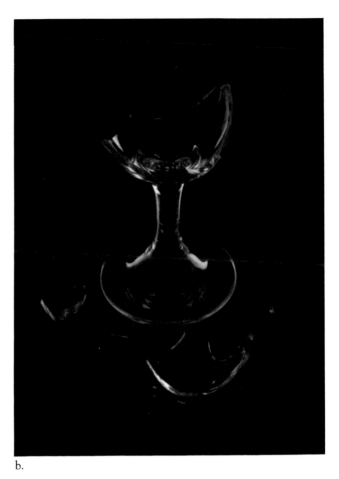

b.

[figure 9.18]

*Both light (a.) and dark (b.) ground illumination allow for strong edge delineation of
transparent subjects. The background shows through the subject, while the edges reflect
the surrounding, contrasting environment. The smaller the ground and the larger the
surrounding area of contrasting tone, the stronger will be the edge delineation.*

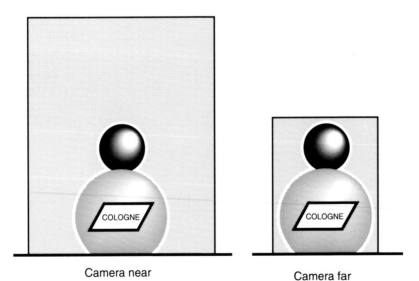

Camera near   Camera far

[figure 9.19]

*As the camera is moved toward the subject, the relative size of the background decreases.
As discussed in chapter 4, camera distance determines perspective.*

glass edges, a minimal background
will maximize the effect of
surrounding reflection. The
relative size of the background to
the subject can be altered by
changing the perspective of the
image through varying the camera-
to-subject distance, thus
increasing or decreasing the edge
delineation (figure 9.19). The
larger the contrasting light or dark
area around the background, the
more pronounced will be the edge
delineation. Both opaque and
translucent materials can be useful
in constructing suitable
backgrounds (figure 9.20).

The light and dark ground
techniques can be combined in a
single image as long as they are

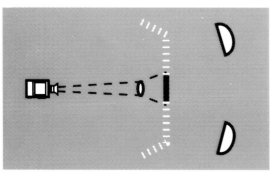

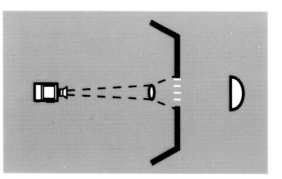

Dark ground
Translucent background

Light ground
Translucent background

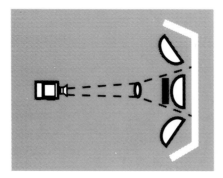

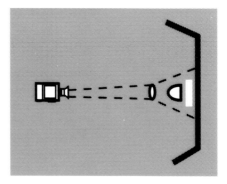

Dark ground
Opaque background

Light ground
Opaque background

[figure 9.20]

Various designs for constructing light and dark ground sets for illuminating transparent subjects. Both translucent and opaque materials can be employed.

applied to distinct areas and do not overlap significantly, yielding dark-on-dark or light-on-light combinations. In any of these techniques, particularly if the scene is illuminated from behind with diffused light, care must be taken to block stray light from the camera lens with a compendium lens shade and/or gobos.

The delineation of the volumes of transparent subjects may require additional techniques. As previously noted, volume is based on surface contour rather than on the outline of edges. In order to reveal the surface contour of transparent subjects, photographers must rely upon broad, reflected highlights. As with glossy, opaque surfaces discussed above, transparent surfaces cannot be shaded, but they will modulate and distort reflected highlights in relation to

surface contours. The same rules that apply to lighting for reflection apply to creating reflected highlights on glass. One potential difference is that glass always creates at least partially polarized specular reflection which can be controlled effectively with polarizers. The most important factors to control in lighting transparent subjects for reflection are the size, placement, and brightness of the reflected highlights (figure 9.21). Reflected highlights alone, though often not as visually dramatic as edge definition, can define both shape and contour.

Glass has the unique ability to "pipe" light through its structure from edge to edge—essentially similar to the principle behind fiber optics technologies. Photographers can utilize this characteristic to add brilliance and

definition to glass by lighting from below. Cutting a small opening under the base of a glass object and illuminating from underneath with diffused light will often provide unique effects along the edges and in the volumes of glass vessels. The piped light will tend to reflect from any facets, rims, or truncated edges of the glass and to produce a sense of brilliance and internal glow (figure 9.22). Also, as previously mentioned, transparency allows for illumination to be redirected back to the camera from behind an object. This is often useful when photographing liquid filled or translucent glass vessels. As described earlier, it is accomplished by placing a small reflective card, strip of metal, or mirror behind the subject. This reflector is then illuminated with the main light, or by a separate

[figure 9.21]

Reflected highlights, as opposed to edge delineation, create a sense of volume with transparent subjects. The distortion and modeling of these reflections is often our clue to the contours of the subject's surface.

[figure 9.22]

Illumination from below is piped through glass until it encounters a truncated edge or facet causing scattering and refraction. The glass itself, viewed from most angles, remains transparent as the light flows through its structure.

light, so as to redirect specular reflection through the subject toward the camera lens. Reflective card material designed for this purpose can be cut to exact shapes to match the required area. The sense of internal light helps to define the nature of the subject and give an overall sense of life to the image (figure 9.23).

A final useful technique in lighting for transparency is to utilize refraction—the bending of light rays as they pass from a less dense to a more dense material such as air to glass to water, etc. Refraction causes distortion of background objects or surfaces seen through the transparent subject. This can be useful in

defining both shape and contour; though by itself, refraction is usually not enough to provide adequate delineation of form. When multiple surfaces are involved, refraction can have complex effects and actually, in the case of liquid-filled glass for example, act as a lens within the image (figure 9.24). This secondary lens can transform backgrounds in surprising ways. In an interesting reversal of the general rules of perspective, the closer the camera is placed to the lens-like subject, the larger will be the relative size of any background; if perspective considerations permit, this can be valuable in controlling what the secondary lens "sees."

Scenes involving both transparent and opaque subjects can be difficult lighting challenges. Like combinations of various surfaces detailed in the previous section, these situations often require compromise or selective control of the light source through modulation. Additional lights, gobos, and careful attention to positioning can be helpful. The same techniques discussed earlier can be applied to controlling lighting of scenes involving opaque surfaces and transparency. Additional attention should be paid to the unique properties, including transmission and refraction, of such subjects.

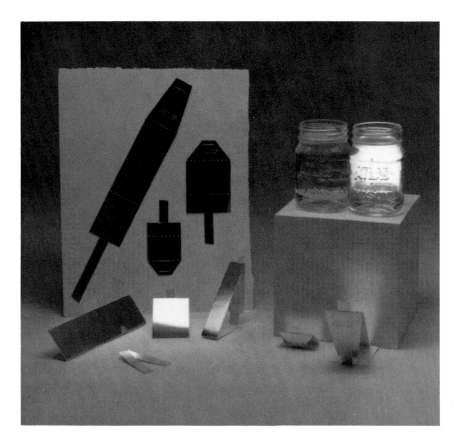

[figure 9.23]

Small reflectors can be shaped and placed behind glass vessels to become sources of radiant light directed toward the camera. Many reflective materials with various surface qualities can be employed, and these range from white or colored card stocks to shiny, foil-surfaced reflector cards and mirrors. Here, a commercially available reflector kit is shown along with two glass vessels, one with and the other without a reflector in place behind the subject.

[figure 9.24]

The liquid-filled glass, acting as a secondary lens, actually reverses the background tones in this Chris Hawker still life (original in color).

Photograph by Chris Hawker

[figure 9.25]

The overall dark setting of this Paul Elledge portrait gives the image a sense of mystery
and a foreboding presence. The subject resides in the deep, dark space of the frame, cut
off from light and distanced from the viewer.

Photograph by Paul Elledge

 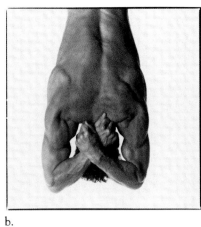 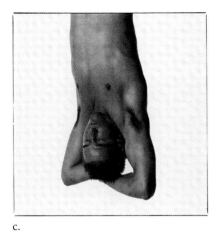

a.   b.   c.

[figure 9.26]

Joe Ziolkowski chose a high-key, light environment to emphasize the feeling of suspension or floating in these portraits for his "Numbered Series." The series deals with the emotional trauma of taking the test for HIV. The state of abeyance between testing and knowing the results creates feelings of anxiety and loss of control. The subjects in these portraits are literally suspended upside down in the white space—isolated, helpless, and self-absorbed.

Photographs by Joe Ziolkowski, from "The Numbered Series" left to right: "#567," "#718," "#524"

Lighting the Portrait

Lighting the portrait is perhaps one of the most complex of undertakings in photography. Viewers' intimate familiarity with the form and the complexity and plasticity of the form itself contribute to this difficulty. Many formulas have been developed for portrait lighting. However, it is the creative application of lighting technique in confirmation or violation of rules that produces interesting portraiture. Basic portrait lighting technique will be reviewed and, through illustrations, some alternatives will be suggested.

In lighting a portrait, the face must be viewed as a sculptural form. As such, it is composed of certain characteristic planes and features, the definition of which is important to a portrait. One possible approach emphasizes the triangle created by the nose, eye, and cheek; another emphasizes the five cardinal, or high, points— the forehead, nose, two cheeks, and chin. Portrait lighting is often thought of as low-key or high-key.

This refers to the basic character of the illumination. Low-key images often employ shadow and texture as dramatic elements in an overall dark setting (figure 9.25), while high-key illumination involves little contrast and elevated tonalities in an overall light setting (figure 9.26). A number of classic portrait lighting techniques exist, and most involve the use of one or more of the following lights.

The main, or key, light will define the overall direction of illumination and delineation of form in the final image. This light is normally placed high and to the side of the subject. It is usually the brightest light used. The shadows cast by the main light must be carefully controlled so as to not obscure important facial features (figure 9.27). The harsher this light, the more defined and deeper will be any shadows it casts. A second light used is the fill light. It is used to soften the shadows cast by the main light. It does not define direction or form; it simply controls lighting contrast. If the fill light is too

strong, shadows cast by the main light will disappear resulting in unattractive, flat lighting.

In order to minimize shadows, the fill light is normally positioned close to the camera, near the optical axis of the lens. Alternatively, the fill light may be placed opposite the main light; any shadows cast by the fill light should be overwhelmed by the main illumination. As discussed in chapter 8, the respective distances of the main and fill lights will create the overall lighting ratio (figure 9.28). In either case, the larger and softer the fill light, the less likely it will cast shadows contradicting the main light, and the more flexible will be its placement.

In place of a fill light, many photographers utilize a reflector to redirect light from the key light into the shadows it forms. These two tools produce different results. The illumination from a fill light often creates its own shadows that overlap and do not completely soften the key shadows, while a reflector normally softens all

a.   b.

c.   d.

[figure 9.27]

In traditional portrait lighting, shadows cast by the main light must be carefully positioned to shape the primary planes of the subject's face (a.). If the light is too high (b.), too much to the side (c.), or too much to the front (d.), the shadows may become distracting shapes in the final image, hiding important detail, or the light may flatten the contours of the face.

a.

b.

[figure 9.28]

Lighting ratios in portraiture rarely exceed 3 to 1 (a.), with less contrast being more common (b.), particularly with color materials. The relationship between the main and the fill light controls the lighting ratio. A hard fill light must be carefully positioned on axis as it can create its own shadows and sometimes emphasize certain shadows cast by the main light.

shadows and creates none (figure 9.29). The reason for this is that a reflector can often be a larger, and therefore softer, source of illumination than an available fill light. It follows that the larger the fill light, the more its effect will approach that of a reflector. Some reflectors may not direct enough light back into the shadows, particularly when they must be placed at a distance from the subject. The brightness of a fill light can be adjusted to suit the circumstances of the image. The key and fill lights are the two standard lights employed in most portrait lighting. In addition, three other lights are often used.

A background light may be employed to illuminate, and to help separate the subject from the background. This light is often placed low and behind the subject, but it can be placed off-camera to one side. It illuminates only the background and can be adjusted in size, shape, and brightness to produce a wide range of effects (figure 9.30). A hair light may be used to give brilliance and luster to the subject's hair and to help delineate form (figure 9.31). Hair lights are usually placed quite high and behind the subject or on a boom almost directly overhead. They aid in separating the subject from the background and can be particularly useful when working with dark-haired subjects and dark backdrops. They should be closely controlled to light only the intended area. Because a hair light often comes from behind, gobos may be needed to block stray light from the lens. An additional accent light can be added to bring out a particular highlight such as on the side of a face (figure 9.32). Any or all of these additional lights can be used in combination with the main and fill lights. These five lights comprise the elements of most traditional portrait lighting; they do not, however, proscribe the possibilities.

No one "correct" formula is prevalently used for lighting all portraits. Lighting should be a creative decision based upon the subject and the photographer's intentions. Many portrait photographers have developed their own unique styles of lighting. These styles are not formulas, and as such they actually violate many of the standard rules of formula lighting in pursuit of a unique statement (figure 9.33).

[f i g u r e   9 . 2 9]

In place of a fill light, some photographers prefer to use a large reflector to redirect the main light back onto the subject to fill in its own shadows. Though reflectors cast few and soft shadows, they are only efficient at close distances and will not soften shadows as much as a fill light.

[f i g u r e   9 . 3 0]

A background light helps to separate the subject from the background and create a sense of dimensional depth in the portrait.

[f i g u r e   9 . 3 1]

A hair light can add reflective brilliance and luster to the hair and/or help delineate the form of the subject.

a.   b.

[figure 9.32]

Additional accent lights may be placed to emphasize particular features or facets of the subject's face (a.). All of these lights together (b.) create a balanced, dimensional illumination.

a.   b.   c.

[figure 9.33]

Lighting the portrait should not proceed according to a formula. Many different styles can be effective. Marc Hauser's soft, enveloping light (a.), Scott Raffe's dark, moody rendering (b.), and Ken Coplan's self-portrait illuminated by reflected light from a mirror (c.) all break traditional rules to the benefit of the individual portrait.

Photograph © Sandy Skoglund, 1991 "Gathering Paradise"

[part]

THE STUDIO ENVIRONMENT

[chapter]

⑩

The Studio as Environment

[chapter]

⑪

Set Building

[chapter]

⑫

On Location in the World

THE STUDIO AS ENVIRONMENT

Three separate and equally important elements exist in every studio photograph: the subject, the light, and the environment. This book has, to this point, been largely concentrating on the light. Subject is content and is sometimes defined by external circumstance. However, in many instances the photographer will have the opportunity to choose the subject or to select the supporting props for an image. This can be a critical decision. A noted still life photographer once commented that, "Lighting is simple, you just find a few good tools that work and stick with them. Ninety percent of the picture is what you put in front of the camera."

This statement reflects an attitude that relegates lighting to a primarily descriptive role and places emphasis on the ability of the photograph to describe the subject in exacting detail. Photography is good at this. As pointed out in chapter 4, the large format image particularly can

convey a sense of the reality of a subject that carries an almost physical presence. In such an image, the integrity and look of the original subject can be extremely important, whether it is a found object or a live model. Subjects can be selected for their surface appearance or for their significance as cultural artifacts or stereotypes. Their message may be clearly defined or obscure. They can embody the meaning of a photograph or simply point toward it. Many photographers employ stylists to help them in locating the "ideal" subject or prop for a particular image. Modeling agencies aid in casting the proper character for a photograph. Whatever the image, it is certain that thoughtful consideration in the selection of subjects will greatly simplify the photographer's role as communicator.

Equally important to lighting and subject is the environment in which the subject is placed. This can range from a simple

background sweep to an elaborately constructed set. Figure, or subject, cannot exist without ground, or set. Whenever one is considered, photographers must consider the other. These two elements work together to create the Gestalt figure/ground relationships that are so important to perception. The construction of a set often involves the propagation of illusion. To create illusion, photographers must understand perception. Photographers can directly employ many of the principles discovered by perceptual theorists in the construction of studio environments, particularly in the structuring of figure/ground relationships to create clearly readable photographs.

A subject's environment can be thought of as a blank slate upon which the subject is presented. Conversely, it can be significant as content and carry meaning in itself that supports or affects the meaning inherent in the subject. In the first instance, the environment is minimal; it functions as a ground and its purpose is mainly formal—it surrounds and supports the subject that carries all of the meaning and emphasis in the image. In the latter case, the environment may be complex; it functions as ground as well as subordinate subject and its purpose is to shape meaning as well as to support form—it provides a "place" in which the event of the photograph occurs. In any case, the hierarchy of an image should be clear in its formal structure. A set should never overwhelm subject to the extent of obscuring meaning, unless of course this is intentional.

Computers have been described as virtual machines; that is, they can be virtually anything depending upon how they are programmed—typewriter, calculator, drawing tool, etc. The studio is a virtual space. It can also be virtually anything, depending upon the intentions and skill of the photographer. Perhaps the greatest challenge that the studio photographer faces is the empty frame of the camera. The necessity to create and populate an environment within those confines, rather than use the frame to edit from an existing world, is the singular province of studio photography.

Two Types of Image

Photographers can broadly and artificially separate studio photography into two types of images—those that reference subjects and those that reference ideas. In an image that references a subject, the physical content and surfaces making up the photograph carry the meaning of the image. In an image that references ideas, the content and

surfaces only point to or serve as the visible foundation for an invisible meaning. Subjects can be seen and photographed, ideas cannot. Photographs are ideal vehicles for the description of subjects, and if this is their main intent, then they function as primary constructs. Ideas are second order constructs derived from the photograph. In this context, the content of a photograph serves only as a code to be interpreted by a viewer.

Though a purely denotative image may not exist, the focus of emphasis in an image can be on description. Such an image might be called what theorist Terry Barret has referred to as an "aesthetic evaluation." This type of photograph may also be called an observation or an appreciation. The intent of images of this sort is to communicate as directly as possible about the appearance of a subject. Meaning arises from the viewer's recognition of and response to that appearance as rendered in the image. Sometimes, this exacting description rouses a meaning derived from the viewer's recognition of the identity of and relationship between various objects in the frame. For their complete meaning, such images rely not only on the description of subject but also on the viewer's knowledge and cultural heritage. Finally, in some images subject is minimally important, providing only a basis from which the viewer must proceed to construct meaning via abstract associations based upon knowledge. These image categories are not absolute—they overlap and coexist; however, the first could be thought of as being rooted in emotional and sensual response, the second in a combination of emotional and sensual response with intellect, and the last in intellectual response.

In an image that references a subject, the entire structure of the photograph serves only one purpose—to formally project that subject. The requirements of such an image dictate that the set be subordinate to the subject. The set should not distract the viewer with graphically assertive pattern or shape, and it should not confuse the viewer by introducing irrelevant information into the image. In this context, the set, or ground, that supports but is not noticed functions most effectively. The image is seen as a whole, but all attention is focused on the subject, or figure. This does not necessarily mean that the photograph must be made on a plain sweep. It simply indicates that whatever the set is, it must not be perceived as competing with the subject for the viewer's attention.

Three basic strategies could be employed here. The first would be to utilize a set that acts as a textural pattern or field in which no strong graphic elements compete for attention. This is similar to the strategy in creating a field image, in which each part of the photograph is of equal visual weight and significance. Referring to chapter 1, proximity and similarity of shape are the Gestalt principles involved in pattern or texture. A totally random field would function in a similar manner, denying the viewer an element of graphic emphasis on which to focus attention. A second strategy would be to utilize a set that logically and unobtrusively becomes an extension of the subject, a simulation of a surface or environment that creates a "natural" or expected environment for the subject. Such a setting functions in a conceptual as well as a visual manner to reinforce the meaning of the photograph while not demanding attention from the viewer. The key here is to understand the viewer's expectations and to structure the set to cater to them. The Gestalt principles of continuity and closure are at work in this strategy. The third strategy would be to construct a set that obviously functions to aggressively project the subject. The meaning of the environment is unimportant; as long as its function is clear it can remain unobtrusive, like a pedestal upon which a sculpture sits. This strategy uses strong graphic elements and all of the Gestalt principles to direct attention at the subject.

In an image that references an idea, the content of the image needs to be tightly controlled. Ideas, being intangible, are difficult to visualize. Making the translation from mind to image and vice versa is challenging. Because the photographer cannot totally control interpretation by the viewer, the image must be tightly structured and effectively coded to communicate the idea clearly. In such an image, not only the form but also the content and meaning of the set become important. Every element of the image must be utilized to direct the viewer to the proper conclusion. Distracting or confusing elements in the image will only serve to make a difficult task more so. Because ideas exist only in time, these images are essentially narrative and rely for their meaning on a life outside of the frame. Subjects can be appreciated in the instant now of the senses; ideas must be constructed over time by the action of the mind. Symbolic objects or designs, meaningful gestures or expressions, light, subject, and set must all function to create a readable statement in

the context of its intended audience. This implies a familiarity with the myths, stereotypes, expectations, desires, and visual heritage of that audience.

The choice of subject, design of set, and selection of props may all be influenced by the intentions of the photographer regarding the role and significance of content in the image. The seductive description of content embodied in the beautiful photographic image can sometimes distract from or contradict a photographer's intended message. On the other hand, that seductive description may be the intention. Photographers' understanding of what they are attempting to communicate from the beginning will help them achieve a clear visualization.

Visualizing Environments

In chapter 2, in the discussion of light and intent, three terms that could also be applied to environment were encountered: fact, fiction, and fantasy. Each of these terms could proscribe a point of view toward the set. Depending upon the intentions of the photographer, the set can portray any real or imagined environment. Many of the same considerations that were mentioned in regard to lighting design also apply to set design. If the set is to represent a factual place, that is a recognizable, real space, then it is critical that great attention be paid to detail. Photography is extremely well suited for recording detail and, unfortunately, flaws. Flaws in the set will create a discontinuity that viewers will perceive and recognize. The fabric of reality is often extremely complex and re-creation of this intricacy can be

difficult (figure 10.1). Sometimes, though not always, this is a sufficient reason for moving out of the studio and shooting on location. With a factual set, the viewer of the final image is encouraged to accept what is given as real and definitive. Little is open to interpretation, and viewer participation is not necessary to complete the environment.

Fictional environments, like fictional lighting, are often synthesized realities in which elements are combined to create a believable, though not specific, space. As with fictional lighting, the environment created must have the visual trappings of reality, but it is not necessary to re-create a recognizable place, just a plausible one. Plausible realities are much broader and looser constructions than specific places; they are defined by the same physical rules that govern real space but their characterization can be fanciful and their appearance may be highly contrived (figure 10.2). Suggestion can often replace delineation of form or surface and economical design can replace the complex layering of reality. The viewer may be asked to complete details and make connections that the set builder has left open-ended for interpretation. These environments might be best compared to skeletons which the viewer fleshes out with the complex overlay of life. Many theater sets fall into this category—they nudge the viewer toward belief without restricting imagination. Their location between fact and fantasy lends them the authority of the real world and the freedom of the inventive mind.

Fantastic environments, like fantastic lighting, can conform to their own internal rules. They

[figure 10.1]

Jeff Wall re-created this 1947 environment as part of his narrative fantasy depicting the arts of ventriloquism and storytelling as interpersonal entertainment prior to the age of television (original in color).

Photograph by Jeff Wall: "A Ventriloquist at a Birthday Party in October, 1947" (1990). Collection Dumont-Wautier, Brussels.

need not re-create a given reality as they have no reference in the world. However, if they are to be perceived as actual spaces by a viewer, they must at least be understandable. This may mean that they conform in some ways to the rules governing perspective rendering or it may mean that the viewer is given sufficient information to decode an entirely new representation of space. Again, as with fantastic lighting, all considerations of space in such an environment function to support the concept of the image. It is the image concept that defines the logic of spatial

relationships. The viewer of the image is asked to suspend disbelief and participate in an imaginative voyage (figure 10.3).

Whatever the nature of the set, its purpose is often narrative in that it is designed to transport the viewer or the subject outside of the confines of the studio. Even the plain, white sweep is designed to create a void. It draws attention away from the studio environment and provides a neutral space in which to view the subject. The exception to this may be when the camera pulls back and the studio itself, along with the lights and props, becomes the set and the narrative device.

Principles Underlying Design

As noted above, many studio sets re-create reality rather than trade in illusion. A room setting, for example, can be built full size, with standard materials and methods, within the confines of a studio bay. Elaborate design and great expense are sometimes undertaken in constructing a real world environment in the studio. The control and predictability of working in a studio environment often justify the expense and outweigh any advantages of finding a location in the world that matches the requirements of the photograph.

[figure 10.2]

Janis Tracy created a fictional, narrative environment for this stylized studio photograph. The set has plausible elements arranged in an improbable interaction accented by dramatic lighting design (original in color).

© Janis Tracy Photography, Inc. 1991

Conversely, from the restricted confines of the tabletop to the great expanses of large studio cycloramas, photographers have created illusionistic space (figure 10.4). Sometimes these creations, both representational and abstract, must actually distort the viewer's perception of scale, depth, and/or spatial relationships; these sets only appear "real" when seen from the particular angle and perspective of the camera or in the photograph (figure 10.5). Like magic, all of these visual illusions rely upon the expectations of the viewer as to the nature of reality. Unlike magic, they also rely upon the viewer's expectations as to the

nature of a photograph. Combine these powerful perceptual forces with control over what will be seen and how it will be rendered and the image becomes a visual theater of opportunity for the knowledgeable photographer.

In creating illusion, photographers must pay careful attention to the visual clues they use to establish a sense of space. Close observation of the real world is the illusionist's best method for collecting tools and learning techniques. In addition, the photographer must intimately understand the theories of optics and perspective, the technical aspects of available materials and equipment, and the possible

manipulation of materials through extended techniques. The viewer, fortunately, only sees the final image, not the studio or the techniques used in production. The photograph is a wonderful masking device. It eliminates information not within the field of view of the lens. It also conceals sleight of hand through the viewer's own assumptions about the nature of the photographic process, which include: it produces an accurate picture of what was in front of the camera, it occurs instantaneously in one exposure, and it renders scenes as the eye would see them. It is easy to be fooled when the truth is viewed as self-evident.

[figure 10.3]

This Bob Forrest photograph places a computer in a surreal environment, perhaps
suggesting the powerful creative and imaginative tools inherent in the machine (original
in color).

[figure 10.4]
*Arthur Tress created this miniature proscenium and fantasy environment for his series of
photographs "The Teapot Opera" (original in color).*
Photograph by Arthur Tress

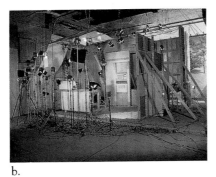

[figure 10.5]
*The reality of many photographic sets is
based in a two-dimensional image space
with one point of view and a fixed
perspective (a.). Seen from another angle
and distance, the illusionistic space of this
Barbara Karant set is unmasked (b.)
(originals in color).*

Photograph by Barbara Karant

a.   b.

As noted earlier, the principles of Gestalt psychology directly apply to the construction of environments in the studio. When Gestalt principles are applied in tandem with the rules for perspective rendering, convincing, illusionistic spaces can be created. In chapter 1, some of these principles and rules were explored as they apply to visual perception and the photographic image. This chapter will suggest how they can be applied in the design of an environment. Once a decision has been made as to the function of the environment, how it should interact with the subject, and its basic character, then some thought must be given to the visual structure of the image space. Considerations include: dimension—will it be shallow or deep, what will be its scale in relationship to the subject, what perspective relationships will define the image; surface—what tones and/or colors will be most effective, will pattern and/or texture be important, what role will shadows and reflections play; and, level of detail—will the environment be sharply delineated or suggested, what will the viewer's role in completing the space entail. Logistically, photographers must ask if various requirements of the set necessitate distortion.

Once these, and perhaps other, questions are answered, the photographer can proceed to designing the environment with specific goals in mind. The rules for perspective rendering define the view of the lens, the principles of Gestalt can predict visual response, and the viewer's experience and culture shape interpretation. The rules of perspective rendering, which will define the overall spatial relationships in the photograph, can be used to design the physical structure of the environment.

Predicting the visual response of a viewer will suggest how intricate photographers must make their environment; photographers can omit details the viewer will supply or ignore. It will also imply the structure of visual dialogue within the frame. Finally, a viewer's life experience can be relied upon to supply certain underlying assumptions about various observed phenomena. Photographers may choose to reinforce or contradict these assumptions creating continuity, ambiguity, or disorientation.

Perspective rendering creates a scale by which photographers measure relative distance, size, and orientation. Of course, in the space of the image, everything is internally relative; photographers don't concern themselves with the world outside of the frame. As long as the internal structure of the image represents certain visual relationships according to familiar rules, that rendering will be accepted as an accurate representation of a real space. The rules of perspective rendering have been in use for centuries and its visual code has become ingrained in society. People have learned to quickly translate from a perspective rendering to the real world; photographs, by their nature, encourage this translation.

However, this same fluid relationship between two- and three-dimensional space can be confused and utilized to create an illusion. The convergence of lines, texture gradients, the direction and shape of shadows, comparative scaling, the resolution of detail, and surface shading can all be manipulated to create or destroy dimension, depth, and volume. The lined ground glass of the view camera becomes the logical grid upon which the world is projected and the image is constructed. Manipulation of the internal

picture elements rebuilds the "real" space of the image. Questions about reality, as well as alternative explanations of space, can result when the logic of single-point perspective rendering is challenged by the creative application of its own rules (figure 10.6).

As indicated in chapter 1, Gestalt principles suggest that viewers across a wide spectrum tend to perceive information in a manner consistent with specific visual processes. These include the physical processes, dictated by the structure of the eye and brain, and the mental processes, synthesized in the thinking mind. Not only proximity, similarity, continuity, and closure but also shape detection, spatial transposition, brightness and/or color perception, time/motion perception, and other processes can be considered in predicting perceptual response. Application of Gestalt principles aids in establishing the appropriate figure/ground relationships, creating connections between various planes of space or objects in an image, defining patterns, suggesting scale, directing eye movement, and encouraging viewer participation. In order to control a viewer's perception photographers must use its basic functioning to their advantage (figure 10.7).

A viewer's knowledge about the visual world can be used to a photographer's advantage. This knowledge is both physical and cultural. Space and time are continuous. Size decreases with distance. Shadows are cast by, and related to, objects in specific ways. Objects do not float in midair. These assumptions are based on physical experience of the world and form the basis for the interpretation of the photograph. On the other hand, the visual portrayal of specific character or

[figure 10.6]

Barbara Kasten used the rules of single-point perspective rendering and her viewers'
expectations to confuse rather than clarify spatial relationships in her photograph
"Construct VIII-A" (original in color).

Photograph by Barbara Kasten

[figure 10.7]

Applying simple Gestalt principles and perspective distortions, Barbara Karant created this illusionistic, visually dynamic space (original in color).

Photograph by Barbara Karant

meaning is almost always rooted in cultural stereotypes regarding people and places or in the culturally defined, symbolic value of content. A broadly based liberal arts education, a thorough knowledge of art history, and recognition of societal diversity will help a photographer effectively identify and utilize this culturally based knowledge (figure 10.8).

Models as Sets

Some photographers specialize in photographing models or miniatures. Likewise, some individuals specialize in building models to be photographed. Elaborate models are used in many film productions; still photographers sometimes find the model more workable than a life-size or real environment. Models may be facts, fictions, or fantasies.

They represent self-contained worlds with their own miniature scale and spatial relationships. Model building is expensive and time consuming; it must be justified by certain image considerations. These considerations can be logistical or conceptual in nature. The uncertainty of shooting on location or sometimes the unavailability of an acceptable location can prompt a

[figure 10.8]

By placing seemingly meaningless content in a context normally designed to showcase a precious object, James Welling created a dichotomy that speaks to our culturally defined expectations of object value. The image also speaks to the creative possibilities inherent in the most banal of subjects—possibilities discovered by the human mind and crafted by the photographer.

Photograph by James Welling. "The Waterfall." 1981.

[figure 10.9]

David Levinthal's photograph from the series "Hitler Moves East" is a re-creation in miniature of an imagined moment in a historical event. Levinthal's use of models and miniatures makes the event real in the mythological terms of our contemporary fictions. The photograph lends authenticity to the specifics of the imagined scenario.

Courtesy Laurence Miller Gallery, New York. Copyright David Levinthal.

[figure 10.10]
Nick Koudis used a model to make a modern cliché real in his depiction of the subway at rush hour (original in color).
© 1990 Nick Koudis

photographer to choose a model. In the studio, it may be more feasible to construct an imagined environment in miniature than life-size (figure 10.9). Conceptually, a model can provide opportunities that no real environment could ever accommodate (figure 10.10).

A model that is to be photographed for a recognizable reality must be meticulously constructed to withstand comparison with the viewer's experience. The relative scale of materials, the appearance of surfaces, and the complex

randomness of reality must be mirrored for the camera to record. Just as with this type of full-size set, the camera will reveal visible flaws and create discontinuity. Models photographed for fiction or fantasy are, of course, subject to less rigorous comparison. They may embody more liberties with scale and surface, and they may be highly abstract or fantastic creations. However, unless they are being photographed as models, they will still need to create a space that extends beyond the boundaries of their own limitations of size and artifice. As with full-size sets, models often

serve as narrative devices that transport viewers away from their own physical reality.

Limitations of optics, scale, and materials can make it impossible to model certain environments. In the future, these limitations may be overcome by electronic imaging systems that recombine images, create mathematically based visual imagery, and model any three-dimensional reality inside of a computer. Eventually, such equipment may drive the model builder into obsolescence as quickly as the hand retoucher is vanishing.

Props

Essentially, anything in an image that is not subject or set is prop. Props can range from simple, singular items purchased off-the-shelf to elaborate constructions capable of movement and/or special effects. They are sometimes real objects used to "dress" a set, and they are sometimes finely crafted counterfeits taking the place of their real life counterparts. They can be used to lend a sense of texture and realism to a scene, to enhance the formal language of an image, or to replace real objects that might be perishable or nonphotogenic. In photography, they range from simulated ice cubes to real vegetables, from ersatz oranges to live animals, from bogus cereal boxes to actual cars, and etc. Props are not the main subject and should not compete for that emphasis; they can, however, be important to the reading and wholeness of an image. Indeed, if what the photographer puts in front of the camera is ninety percent of the photograph, then the right props can make or break an image.

As real objects used to dress a set, props can lend an air of authenticity to an image. The physical description of objects provided by the photograph often carries along with it the authority of the objects described (figure 10.11). Objects with interest and integrity have unique aspects of form and surface that the camera accurately conveys. Particularly in a photograph that references subjects, a prop can be a critical supporting element. As mentioned earlier, many photographers utilize professional stylists to find and obtain props for images. These individuals' trade involves

[figure 10.11]

The detailed attention to appropriate propping in this Jim White photograph adds an air of authenticity to the scene (original in color).

Jim White Photography, Chicago

knowing where to source almost anything that might be required. Photographers also collect inventories of potentially helpful objects used in previous images. Glasses, chairs, clothes, mannequins, almost anything is a potential prop for future use, and access may sometimes determine whether or not a prop will spring to mind.

Model makers are often prop makers. Many props are in fact models that are constructed to have a certain appearance and to function predictably in the studio. Real ice cubes melt, real oranges can wither or vary in size and color, real boxes are often not perfect enough for the camera; a prop can be the answer for a logistical or visual problem. Polymer-resin ice cubes, rubber oranges, and handmade, individually painted boxes are controllable—they are produced

to "look right." Props replace the inconsistencies and imperfections of real world objects with photogenic perfection. They are also reusable while many real objects are not. Like models, props can be expensive and must be justified by specific image considerations.

Though props, by definition, play a subordinate role, the selection of the wrong prop can detract from the visual and/or conceptual impact of an image. A prop that looks or reads wrong can be particularly disastrous in an image portraying a re-creation of a real activity and/or environment. It is, after all, details that make up and impart life to the fabric of reality. In fact, attention to detail is perhaps the most important factor separating accomplished studio photographers from those whose work is mediocre.

SET BUILDING

Set building is an area of study unto itself. Often, professional set builders construct the sets used by photographers. Much of the same technique used in theater set design and construction is applicable to photographic sets. Occasionally, theater set crews build sets for photographers between productions. Photographers do, however, sometimes construct their own sets. As seen in the previous chapter, these range from simple backgrounds to more elaborate, constructed environments. The level of complexity of these projects ranges with the talents of the photographer. It is valuable for a studio photographer to know a bit of carpentry, electrical, and plumbing technique to aid in studio and set building and design. This chapter will discuss some common backgrounds, detail a backdrop painting technique, and suggest some flexible and easily constructed set elements.

Perhaps the one aspect of photographic set building and design that differs most from theater and film is that the set for a still photograph will only be seen from one angle and distance at a time. The implication here is that only what the camera sees counts, and the camera only sees surfaces. Most photographic sets, with the exception of some special effects sets, do not have to function—only appearance counts. This lends a great deal of flexibility to design and construction. Another aspect of photographic set design is knowing how the camera sees various surfaces, tones, and colors. This relates to the inherent workings of the process—how black-and-white film renders brightnesses as tones, how colors and contrast record on film, etc. Remember that the eye and photographic systems do not see in the same manner; what looks right to the eye may appear wrong

on the film. Taken together, these concerns of viewpoint and rendering define the parameters of set building and design.

Backgrounds

The simplest background is plain, seamless paper. This background paper is available from a number of manufacturers in a wide range of hues and values. It comes in rolls, usually from 10 yards to 50 yards in length and 4-1/2 feet, 9 feet, or 12 feet in width. Various surfaces that reflect light differently are available. Some of the papers have a smoother surface that can yield a high degree of reflection while some have a rougher surface that reflects little specular light and produces a flat, even tone. These rolls of paper can be hung and pulled down to provide flat backgrounds behind a subject or can be rolled out into "sweeps" (figure 11.1). As noted earlier, a sweep is the simplest form of a set. It is a space with no character; a neutral ground on which to place the subject. The only distinction on this ground comes from the subject and any shadows that it might cast on the sweep. Sweeps focus attention on the subject and light by eliminating environment. They can be valuable whenever a plain, unobtrusive ground is desired. They can also support a sense of space and depth created by the interaction of subject, light, and shadow.

Beyond paper sweeps, many other background materials are available and in general use. Two of the most common in recent years have been muslin and canvas. These fabrics can be used in their natural states or can be painted. They can be stretched tight to form a smooth, yet slightly textured background, or they can be draped loosely in folds to form a more dimensional surface. They can also be used in place of sweeps to provide a neutral, yet visually intriguing ground. These fabrics can be dyed to control their brightness or color.

When ordering canvas or muslin backgrounds it is important to specify that they be seamless; otherwise, one might receive a piece with a seam where bolts were spliced together. When shipping the material, be sure it is rolled on a core instead of folded. Folding will leave creases that can be difficult to eliminate. If creases are present, they can sometimes be ironed out, or effectively removed with a professional quality fabric steamer. Both canvas and muslin are available in standard widths up to about 12'. Custom widths of almost any dimension can be specially

[figure 11.1]

A small sweep rolled out in place and surrounded by lighting equipment (lights courtesy of Balcar)

produced. One photographer uses a 30′ × 60′ painted muslin sweep in her studio. It is made from one huge piece of fabric that was specially produced and painted for her at a cost of over $5,000. Generally, a piece of fabric 12′ to 16′ wide and 24′ long should be large enough for most applications. Smaller pieces, 8′ × 10′ or less, can be useful as portrait backdrops or for small still lifes.

Muslin is usually preferred to canvas for backdrop applications as it is far lighter, accepts dye and paint easily, and is cheaper (figure 11.2). One technique used to prepare muslin is to wash it, to dye it in the process if desired, and to tumble dry it in a large

stuff sack. This softens and crinkles the whole sheet of fabric, producing a textural surface with definite character. As wrinkles are not a concern, the stuff sack can be used for permanent storage of the muslin. As an alternative to muslin or canvas, if seams are not a concern, painters' drop cloths or various canvases can make excellent photographic backdrops (figure 11.3).

In addition to the monochromatic backdrops described above, painted backdrops of all varieties are available. These range from soft, randomly mottled patterns to specific scenes painted on the backdrop in a representational style. Architecture, landscapes,

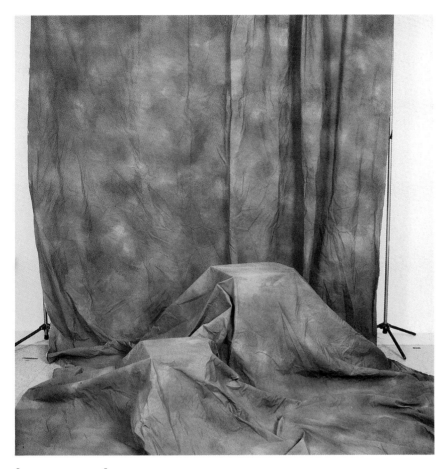

[figure 11.2]

A mottled gray muslin sweep that is available from Denny Manufacturing of Mobile, Alabama. Muslins are available in a wide range of styles and sizes (original in color).

Photograph courtesy of Denny Manufacturing Company

Painting a Muslin Backdrop

Many techniques are used to paint muslin backdrops. In theater, specific painting techniques are used to achieve various effects. These include: wet blending, scumbling, spattering, sponging, stippling, rag rolling, flogging, puddling, dry brushing, stenciling, rolling, and spraying. Though all of these techniques are individually useful for photographic backdrops, this section will describe a process employing a mixture of wet blending, sponging, and puddling to produce a mottled backdrop.

Muslin is easily painted, though evolving a technique may take much experimentation. The following muslin painting technique will serve as a beginning point for future experimentation. The materials needed are plastic sheeting, muslin, paint, a long-handled paint roller, a sponge, some paint trays, a bucket, rubber gloves, and old clothes. The muslin itself should be an unbleached, medium-weight fabric. The paint can be any latex paint but certain other paints specifically designed for painting on fabric and/or used for scene painting in theaters are particularly good. The best alternative to latex paint is casein, which utilizes a different binder than latex paint. Casein will produce a flatter, less reflective surface than latex and, at the same time, can be more vibrant and saturated in color.

Latex paint is available in hundreds of colors. It is available in gloss or flat surfaces. It must be diluted with water for use, so it does not become too thick and crack when the background is rolled up. A ratio of 1 to 1 is a good starting point. It tends to dry darker than the wet paint and to lose some of its brilliance. Casein

interiors, almost any conceivable backdrop can be found. The next section will present a detailed description of how to paint a mottled background on canvas or muslin for general studio use. As for the representational scenes, they provide a strange mixture of real/unreal space in a photograph. Often easily discerned as "false," a representational scenes' very fakery adds a kitsch to images that is often fascinating. Of course, they are also employed to invoke seamless, trompe l'oeil illusions, and they offer a means of readily creating a fictitious setting by simply rolling down a backdrop (figure 11.4).

Backdrops can be rolled on cardboard cores; old carpet cores are ideal and can usually be had for a few dollars. The cores are then hung on rollers or pipes suspended between stands or placed in brackets attached to walls or ceilings. Compound assemblies are available that allow three or four backgrounds to be mounted and rolled up or down individually to quickly change a set. These simple backgrounds and sweeps often make elegant sets by themselves; they are economical, transportable, and extremely useful in the studio or on location. In theater, the comparable item is called a drop.

[figure 11.3]

Marc Hauser employed an unusual, painted canvas from an old circus sideshow tent as a portrait background. The woman's stylized dress, pose, and makeup complement the theatrical backdrop.

Photograph by Marc Hauser, "Circus Lips"

[figure 11.4]

This re-creation of a renaissance painting is propped entirely with painted and dyed backdrops. Note the painted, representational backdrop of the stone wall in the background (original in color).

© *Sajid/Marshall. Creative Director: Sy Sajid, The Backdrop Solution, Chicago. Photographer: Paul Marshall*

comes as a thin paste in several basic colors that must be mixed to produce various hues. Again, it should be diluted with water for use. It can be diluted, more or less, according to the desired saturation of color and can range from a saturated, opaque color to a light wash. Water soluble dyes may be added to casein in order to change its value or saturation. Casein dries lighter than the wet paint and with a flat surface. In saturated applications it tends to have more brilliance than latex paint.

The color of the paint is a matter of choice. Does the photographer want a light or a dark background? Will it be used with black-and-white or color films, or both? Does the image call for a soft mottling or a fairly contrasty tonal differentiation? Remember, the camera will likely see more contrast than the eyes will. This is particularly true with smaller f-stops or when the subject is closer to the background. Also, colors and tones, when they are lighted and photographed, may not appear as first assumed. As a rule, begin with a rather neutral color that is medium in value and saturation for the base coat. Earth tones, blues, greens, and grays work most effectively, but there really are no rules and only experience will determine the best choices. In addition to the base-coat color, the photographer will want white, perhaps black, and maybe small amounts of a few closely related colors. The simplest technique involves only the base color and white. Usually, the idea is to start with the darkest color and work toward the lightest. Exceptions are possible and darker shades can be applied over lighter for a particular effect.

Many theater-scene shops tack the muslin to a vertical frame to facilitate painting; however, photographers do not normally have access to such facilities and usually work on the floor. The plastic sheeting, which should be several feet larger than the muslin, is laid out flat, with no wrinkles, on a smooth surface. A clean concrete floor with no seams or holes is ideal for this purpose. Any dirt, seams, wrinkles, or depressions in the floor or plastic sheeting under the painting surface can cause the paint to pool or settle in patterns on the surface of the fabric, creating lines or spots in the random design. The edges of the plastic are taped down to keep it flat.

The clean, wrinkle-free muslin is spread flat on top of the plastic and taped down around the edges to keep it smooth but not taut. The first step is to wet the muslin thoroughly with water. This can be done with a sponge or a garden sprayer. The muslin can be primer-coated with gesso before the base coat is applied. This is not necessary, but does help seal the cloth, so that the base coat flows on more easily. The base coat, which can also serve as a sizing, is laid down on the wet muslin with a long-handled paint roller. It should be thoroughly worked into the fabric with several passes and a good deal of pressure. Some workers allow this base coat to dry before proceeding, others continue to work after the coat has set up but remains tacky. This second method seems to allow for a more subtle blending of pattern.

The subsequent coats of paint are all laid down with a sponge. Many workers feel that natural sponges are best for this process as they have a random shape and

texture; however, they are soft and tend to be a bit sloppy. A hard, synthetic sponge with one flat and an opposing curved surface can be useful. Though it will leave a more definite pattern of shapes to be worked out on the muslin, it can make the application of paint more controllable. Paint of the base color is poured into a tray of white and then some closely related color can be added to alter the hue slightly. The amount of base color added to the white will control the saturation of the mixture. As a starting point, more base color is probably better than less. Anywhere from four to six coats of paint will be laid down, each successively less saturated and perhaps of a different hue than the last. The range of tone and color from first to last coat will determine the overall contrast of the background. The steps in between should progress in subtle shifts of saturation and color.

The sponge is dipped into the paint, soaked fully, and squeezed out. Then, beginning in the center of the muslin and working in a random distribution out toward the edges, splotches of paint are applied. The sponge is pressed or rocked onto the fabric, and the splotch is worked out in all directions till it blends softly with the ground. The splotches must be applied randomly, avoiding the appearance of any order. They should occupy fairly distinct areas, as subsequent coats will overlap and blend between each other. After this second coat is finished, the sponge is rinsed out thoroughly, and the third coat follows in the same manner with a slightly different mixture of paint. Again, working while the sponged-on paint is still tacky facilitates blending. The subsequent coats are all laid down in random fashion using the method described. A general pattern can be established on the muslin that will, for example, work from a light center to dark edges, thus giving the background a specific focus. Many portrait backgrounds are painted in this fashion to create a lighter area around the subject in the center of the image.

When the painting is finished, the sponge is rinsed and the final blending process begins. The bucket is filled with water, and the sponge is saturated. A light coat of water is spread over the entire surface of the fabric, and the painted splotches are blended with the sponge. Alternatively, the water can be sprayed on with a garden sprayer, and the blending can be done with a string mop or some other contrivance. It is important to use sufficient water to allow for easy and smooth blending while at the same time not totally losing differentiation and mottling on the surface. Overblending will result in a muddy, even color. After the painting is finished, the muslin is allowed to dry thoroughly and then rolled onto a core for storage. The finished muslin provides a random, yet visually stimulating background for many uses (figure 11.5).

Pigment must be closely monitored during painting. If too much accumulates, the muslin may become brittle and could crack when the fabric dries. Also, weight is a consideration. A large muslin can require 2-to-3 gallons of paint, which is both expensive and heavy; it can weigh 40 lbs or more. Some photographers paint over old backdrops many times; these can become loaded with pigment and crack. This in itself might provide an interesting look. Experimentation will reveal many

variations on the general method just described. Using different methods of application, ranging from brushes to foam applicators, from rags to sprayers, will result in numerous appearances. A visit to a theater-scene painting shop will suggest many possibilities.

Basic Modules

Many sets are assembled from varied configurations of the same basic elements. These elements can sometimes be constructed in a modular fashion, providing flexibility and ease of handling as well as recycling of continuously more expensive materials. The basic modular unit that this discussion will refer to is the flat. Flat is a descriptive term borrowed from theater. The flat provides a surface that can serve as a stand-alone element in a set or become a foundation element for a wall. Flats are inexpensive to construct, easy to store, and are reusable.

The flat is basically a wall segment. In its simplest form it is constructed of a wood frame and a piece of canvas or drywall. Flats covered with canvas have the advantage of being lightweight, but drywall is less expensive and can be used when a more substantial structure is necessary. Canvas, as noted above, is available in a wide range of sizes; drywall is limited to 4′ × 8′ or 4′ × 12′ sheets. This basic element can be used as a reflector panel, a design element creating space within a set, or as a part of a larger wall assembly. A number of flats can be joined together to form a long, straight wall, a corner, or an entire room. The joints between the flats can be covered with fabric and painted over, or taped, mudded, and

painted as in standard drywall technique. Alternatively, canvas can be stretched tight over a multiflat wall then painted to create a smooth surface hiding any joints.

The surface of a flat can be treated in a number of ways. For example, canvas can be painted a single color for a smooth wall; it can also be painted in either abstract or representational styles. Drywall can be mudded and textured with joint compound and then painted to produce an adobelike effect. Flats with windows and doorways can be constructed and used when appropriate. After a shot is finished, flats can be disassembled and stored in a minimal amount of space. They can be reconfigured and repainted when needed. The following is a suggested design for a simple flat.

A flat basically comprises two vertical stiles and a number of horizontal rails. In theater, the standard calls for 1″ × 3″ wood to be used for framing. The stiles and the rails are laid flat and fastened together. Many types of wood joinery can be used to build the flat; however, the simplest technique is to use corner blocks and keystones made from 1/4″ or 3/8″ plywood. Corner blocks are triangular and keystones are trapezoidal—slightly wider at one end than the other. The corner blocks are used to join the top and bottom rails to the stiles, while the keystones are used to fasten the center, or toggle, rails in place. The triangles should be positioned so that their wood grain runs vertically, while the grain of the keystones should run lengthwise. The assembly can be nailed or screwed together. After this basic assembly is framed-up,

[figure 11.5]

Various steps in painting a mottled, muslin backdrop. First, the primer is applied. Next, a layer of darker paint provides a basic color ground (a.) on which lighter colors (b.) are worked out to a random pattern. The whole is blended with sponges and water (c.) to form a softly mottled final product (d.).

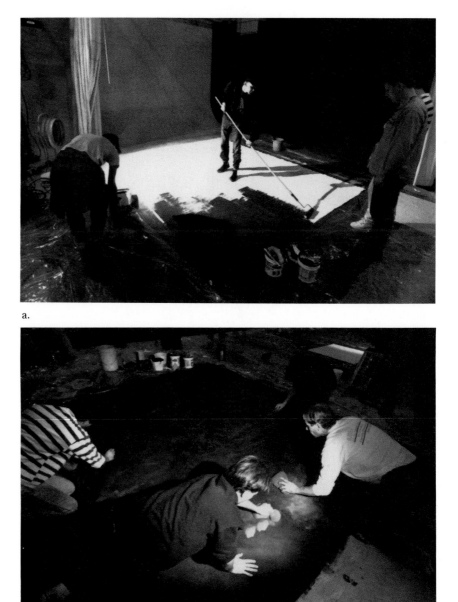

a.

b.

corner braces can be added to increase stability and assure squareness (figure 11.6).

If the flat is to be freestanding, then a floor brace must be added to support the structure. This can be a simple triangular brace attached to the stiles, or a more complex folding brace can be constructed. After framing is complete, the flat is covered. Canvas is stretched over the frame and tacked down every few inches about two inches in from the edges. Canvas-stretching pliers help in this task. The canvas is then trimmed to the size of the flat, and the loose edges are glued down with a white glue which is diluted with water. Drywall can be nailed or screwed to a flat, mudded, and sanded smooth. These basic flats can be painted or have various surface treatments applied as necessary. A few variations on this basic design will suffice for window and door flats (figure 11.7).

Flats can be used in many creative ways. They will not, however, always suffice for

c.

d.

detailed or exotic sets. Beyond the flat, virtually anything can be constructed in a studio. As noted in the last chapter, actual room settings and complex environments, as complete as in a real home or landscape, are sometimes built for photographs. The only thing that separates many of these elaborate sets from real world environments is that they are comprised only of surface. In other words, their appearance is perfect. This is sufficient for photographic reality. For architectural environments, interiors or exteriors, the construction techniques used in these sets for rough framing and finishing work are not so different from those used in real buildings. For more complex, artificial environments many specialized building and set-dressing techniques and materials are employed. Creating a realistic garden or forest in a studio requires a skilled craftsperson. These elaborate projects are best left to professional set builders.

[f i g u r e 1 1 . 6]
A design for a simple flat

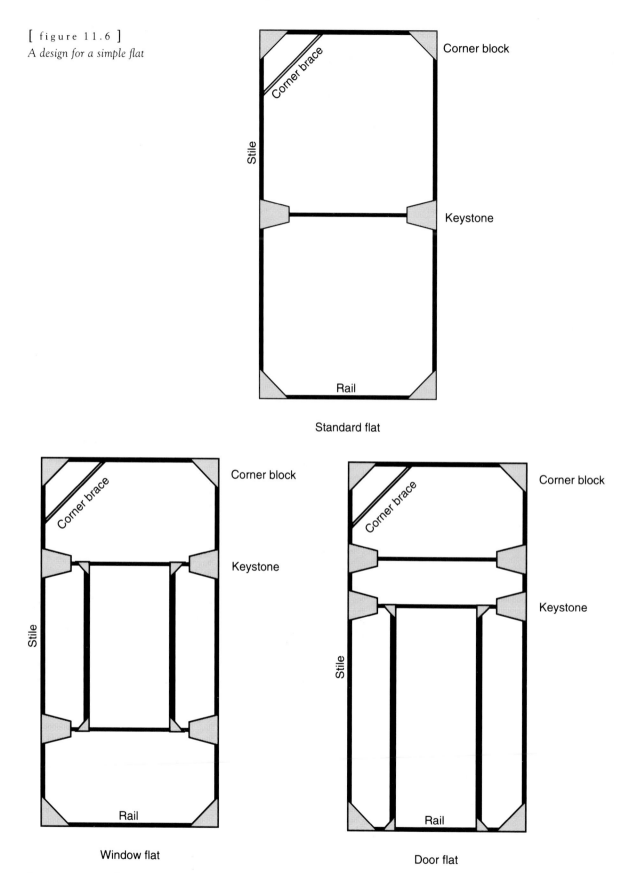

[f i g u r e 1 1 . 7]
Some possible variations on the basic module for window and door flats

ON LOCATION IN THE WORLD

The control that exists in the studio environment can be extended to the world outside. Moving from the studio to a location entails a great deal of planning, preparation, and, often, site work. Many photographers prefer to remain in the studio rather than incur the risks associated with going on location. In the studio, light, environment, and subject can be easily and effectively controlled, work days are predictable, and all potentially necessary tools are at hand. On location, unpredictable weather, random events, and lack of equipment may complicate a shoot. While studio expenses for the construction of elaborate sets may be quite high, they can be accurately estimated; location expenses can mount quickly because of unforeseen problems. However, there are times when the requirements of an image necessitate leaving the studio and finding a suitable location in the world. These include: sets that are too large or complex to re-create

in the studio in life-size or miniature; images in which the nature of a specific place or space is critical to the meaning of the photograph; images that must be made on location, such as architectural photographs and photographs about a particular place; images in which the subject cannot be brought into the studio; and, environmental portraits in which the subject's own space informs the meaning of the image.

The primary problem to overcome in moving out of the studio is finding the right location for an image. Many photographers employ location scouts whose job it is to find appropriate places for location shoots. This may necessitate advance planning to accommodate travel to and research at various locales. Finding just the right location for an image in the complex world of a large city or regional environment can require a great deal of searching. In planning for a complex location shoot, geographical areas are selected, a

location scout is sent ahead to find and photograph potential locations, and the resulting "visual notes" are assessed by the photographer to select the most well-suited place. This process can require weeks. Good location scouts, like good stylists, assemble mental files of potential photographic locations and develop techniques for researching specific needs.

The same tools explored for use in the studio environment can be utilized to alter and/or control a location set. Lighting equipment and camera equipment must be transported to the location giving rise to concerns about weight and portability. Another potential problem is electrical power for lighting equipment. If power is not available or if circuits are not of adequate capacity, portable generators may be necessary. Much contemporary studio lighting equipment is designed with these factors in mind. In addition, many other tools may be necessary for cleaning, controlling, and shaping the location set. A location that appears perfect to the eye may not appear perfect on film. The translation between reality and image often reveals or emphasizes details and flaws that direct visual experience suppresses. A great deal of site preparation may be necessary before the first film is exposed.

Once the location is found, the equipment is transported, necessary personnel assembled, and the site prepared, the photograph can be made. If preparation and planning have been thorough, and if factors beyond the control of the photographer do not interfere, the shoot will proceed smoothly. A photographer who does a great deal of location work commented that, "At least three-fourths of the photograph is the preparation you do before the shoot. If you've been thorough, then you can waltz in, make it look easy, and come away with the image you want. If you aren't prepared, then you're courting disaster." Again, attention to detail and planning are the keys to success.

The Location

Once it has been determined to leave the studio and to go on location, certain decisions must be made as to the relationship of the location to the meaning of the image. As location becomes set, the photographer might again think of the distinctions between photographs that reference subjects and photographs that reference ideas. Is the location a visual or a conceptual device in the image? Of course, these categories often overlap and must be balanced in the photographer's considerations. If a location is to serve as a visual arena in which the event of a photograph is to take place, then its specific

appearance may not be as critical as its visual potential. In this type of image, location becomes a device for projecting subject and may play little role in contriving meaning; hence, it may be treated as an array of formal possibilities. If the location is playing a narrative role in the image, then its appearance may be the single most important aspect to be considered in selection. In such an image, location plays either a primary or supporting role in creating meaning. The information and consequent meaning that a photograph conveys are based in the appearance of the surfaces recorded. The authenticity or particular character of a location may add a great deal of depth and breadth to the meaning of an image (figure 12.1).

The answer to the above question may determine the photographer's attitude toward preparing the site for photographing. If the location is simply a visual or formal opportunity, then it may be treated in a formalist manner. It may be added to, taken from, transformed, or distorted (figure 12.2). If the specific, factual appearance of the location is important to the meaning of the photograph, then careful attention must be paid to preserving its original character. This may not be the same as preserving its found state. Visual character is dependent upon the clear presentation of certain information, and a found location may require alteration to emphasize or suppress certain details. In either case, the photograph freezes detail for inspection. From a small piece of trash to an intruding tree limb to the messy clutter of an office desktop, the camera will faithfully record the scene. Often site preparation involves the exact opposite of set construction—

things must be deleted from rather than added to the space of the frame. On location, photographers are once again faced with editing from the world.

Often a location serves as a raw set space for a photographic fiction or fantasy. Manipulation of the environment to fit the narrative style of the image can increase the location's impact as a communicative element in the photograph (figure 12.3). In altering the location, the photographer may consider the same principles and techniques encountered in set design. Single-point perspective rendering, Gestalt principles, and the knowledge of the audience can all play a role in the photographer's decisions.

Wilderness, opulent mansion, city street, or crowded store, all of these places have their characteristic stereotypes that the photographer can utilize in selecting and preparing a location. Awareness of how an audience will read a location is critical to a narrative image. A subject may be placed in an expected environment, creating a seamless conceptual whole or, in a bizarre environment, creating an exotic or visually disruptive contradiction within the image (figure 12.4).

Location Lighting Equipment

Taking lighting equipment on location can be arduous and can introduce new concerns for the studio photographer. Three major areas of concern are weight and/or portability, power consumption, and safety. In some ways, these are interrelated, as each choice carries certain implications. In addition to these concerns, photographers must consider the various types of lights available and the use of light modulators on location.

[figure 12.1]
Working on an annual report for Wichita State University, Dan Overturf shot this basketball player in the University arena. The location provides a dramatic and conceptually integrated environment to highlight the University's sports programs.

Photograph by Daniel Overturf

Much older tungsten lighting equipment is extremely heavy and bulky. The tungsten bulbs in this equipment increase dramatically in size with wattage, and the housings, designed to dissipate heat, can be quite large. This equipment is designed to take great abuse and is constructed of heavy-gauge materials that withstand punishment in the field. However, transporting these lights can be logistically difficult or impossible.

Many studio photographers choose comparatively lightweight strobe or quartz lighting equipment for location use. Though these lighting systems can still represent a good deal of weight and bulk, they are much

[figure 12.2]

On a portrait assignment, photographer Greg Gillis discovered his subject's hobby of making his own furniture. They subsequently moved a handmade bed out into the woods adjoining the house to create an unlikely setting for an unusual portrait of both craftsman and handiwork.

Photograph by Greg Gillis

more easily transported. A complete strobe system including power packs, light heads, cables, stands, and accessories can fit in the trunk of a midsize car and provide enough light for most applications. Many strobe systems are designed with portability in mind. They have built-in handles, molded carrying cases, and are easily assembled. Contemporary tungsten-halogen quartz lighting equipment is also compact, lightweight, and efficient, producing a great deal of illumination from a small source. It is often available in kits, designed to travel easily and to fill a wide range of applications.

Of course, the amount of equipment taken on any location shoot will be dictated by a balance between the requirements of the image and the logistics of

[figure 12.3]

John Divola transformed the interior of a burned-out and vandalized beach house
through the addition of his own painted designs. Divola's painting functions as a kind of
formal "graffiti" playing off of the found location in his "Zuma Beach" series.

Photograph © John Divola, "Zuma Beach #29," 1978

transport. Once on location, a photographer is limited to the equipment on hand. If the necessary tool is back in the studio, the image may suffer. Conversely, nobody will want to carry three-hundred pounds of lighting gear five miles into the wilderness when a small hand-held strobe will suffice. Careful planning and knowledge of the availability and capability of equipment is essential to location lighting. Most photographers who frequently work on location develop a basic kit that adapts to different on-location situations. This kit will include a wide range of tools and will provide maximum flexibility with the minimum amount of equipment— the rule for most location lighting kits.

All lighting equipment operates on electricity. Power requirements are a major concern when working on location. Three major sources of electrical power for lighting equipment are used. First, and most obvious, there are existing power outlets; second, there are portable electrical generators; finally, there are batteries. Each of these power sources has unique capabilities and associated safety concerns. As noted in chapter 6, while on location, it is often necessary for the photographer to become an electrician. A basic knowledge of electricity, wiring, and equipment is essential.

[figure 12.4]

Guy Hurka employed natural, ambient light to preserve the feeling of the location in this portrait of the retired mayor of Jonesboro, Illinois.

Photograph by Guy Hurka

Available power outlets on location will usually be of two types. They will be either 220-volt circuits, rated between 30 and 50 amperes, or, more commonly, 110-volt circuits, rated at either 15 or 20 amperes. Outlets used for studio lighting equipment should be grounded. Many lights utilize a great deal of power, and safety devices often rely on the electrical system ground for their effectiveness. The carrying capacity of a circuit, as noted in chapter 6, will determine the total wattage that can safely be plugged into that circuit. Note that there

may be many receptacles on each circuit. Exceeding the power-carrying capacity of a circuit can be extremely dangerous and result in equipment failure or fire. Wattage adds up quickly in situations where high levels of illumination are required. For this reason, many photographers prefer to use electronic strobes on location. Strobe equipment normally requires less power than equivalent tungsten equipment.

Portable electric generators can supply sufficient current to operate much lighting equipment. The photographer has a number

of options for power generation. Independent, gasoline-powered AC generators are available that output enough electricity to power a number of strobe systems or tungsten lights. These generators are fairly small, easily transported, and require little fuel. Also available are generators that can be added onto automobile engines. These generators are powered off of the car's engine and, again, produce sufficient 110-volt AC current to power a number of strobes or lights. In addition, power inverters are available that will convert the regular 12-volt DC power from an automobile's own electrical system to 110-volt AC current. Many of these inverters are limited in their capacity and will support only modest power demands.

Some studio strobe systems designed with location work in mind incorporate a system accessory that allows for conversion to a 12-volt automobile power source. Other strobe systems are designed specifically for location work and are powered off of their own rechargeable, internal batteries. These are usually relatively low-power units compared to standard studio-based strobes; however, they are small, integrated light/ power sources, they are easily transported to even remote locations, and they produce enough illumination for many applications.

It is not always necessary to transport studio lighting equipment into the field. A series of small "hand-held" strobe units, each with its own battery power and slave trigger, can be an effective way to light a location photograph. These units are compact, can be extremely flexible in placement and control, provide a good deal of light, and are inexpensive. Some strobe units designed for on-camera use are quite powerful and flexible tools with interchangeable light heads, high-powered batteries, and relatively high-light outputs. Combined with light stands and modulators, these units can provide a great range of illumination.

Safety concerns often surface when working on location. Basic concerns about wiring and carrying capacity of circuits were mentioned above. Other commonsense electrical safety precautions should be observed. Remember, working with electricity around water or in damp environments can be

dangerous or fatal. Water amplifies the effect of electrical shock and can also cause equipment shorts and unintentional grounding. Tungsten lights on location can cause additional concerns. They draw a great deal of power and produce a great deal of heat. Bouncing a light off a ceiling may seem like a wonderful idea until the ceiling begins to blacken and burn. Care must be taken to keep flammable materials a safe distance from tungsten or quartz light sources.

Electrical cables and synch cords themselves can be hazardous to people as well as equipment at on-location sets. Cables and cords should be bundled, taped down, and kept clear of pathways where people will be walking. Light stands should be weighted with "shot bags" at the base to provide extra stability and, if possible, positioned out of high-traffic areas. Attention to these and other basic safety procedures can help assure an accident-free location shoot and will also make working more efficient and enjoyable.

Given the above concerns, any studio light can conceivably be taken on location. The choice of which equipment is most appropriate will depend on the image requirements and the accessibility of the location itself. In addition, light modulators can be used on location. Often, existing light from the sun or other sources can be controlled to advantage with light modulators. Diffusers and reflectors can be effectively placed to alter or redirect sunlight. A strong breeze can play havoc with diffusers and reflectors on location. Some diffusion and reflection panels specially designed for location work incorporate a flow-through construction that allows wind to pass through the panels. It may sometimes be necessary to

eliminate extraneous light at a location in order to control illumination; windows and doors can be covered with black plastic sheeting to block out daylight, and large black panels can be used to absorb and control light just as they are employed in the studio.

A photographer can, of course, choose to rely on ambient light when photographing on location. Architectural photographers often consider the sun as their light source and regard clouds as large reflectors and diffusers. The right location lighting may simply be a matter of timing and weather rather than elaborate design. This can be particularly true when the character of place is critical to the image. As previously noted, light does a great deal to define character. Employing ambient light should always be considered as an alternative to transporting studio lighting equipment to a location shoot (figure 12.4).

Techniques for Location Lighting

All of the principles underlying light and lighting design that have been discussed in previous chapters apply to lighting on location. Some specialized techniques can also be used to overcome problems encountered on location. It is the unpredictable variables of space and light that make location lighting a challenge.

Once a location has been selected and its role in the image has been determined, the lighting design can begin. As discussed in chapter 2, light can play either a passive, descriptive role in an image or an active, transformative role. If the location is simply a formal backdrop for the subject, then the lighting can play an active, transformative role in determining the appearance of the final image. If the physical appearance of place is important to the meaning of the image, then the lighting must be designed to embrace and enhance the character of the location. The preservation of the characteristic look of ambient light can be extremely important in creating a strong sense of place. In this section, ambient light will be understood to encompass both natural and artificial light endemic to a location, and artificial light will mean light provided by the photographer.

Three basic approaches are available ranging in order from least to most intrusive. First, the existing ambient light can be employed to make the image, thus totally preserving the character of place. Second, the ambient light can be altered and/or supplemented with gels and artificial light. This approach preserves the original character of place but corrects color balance, raises levels of illumination, and adjusts contrast ranges in the scene. Third, the ambient light can be rejected and eliminated in favor of totally artificial light. In the first instance, straightforward photographic technique with attention to the natural illumination of the location may be sufficient. Attention must be paid to any changes that can occur in the location at different times of day as the angle of the sun changes or other ambient light sources turn on or off. Also the type of day, bright sun or overcast sky, will influence the look of the image. If the shoot is in color, then the color temperature and nature of individual or mixed light sources in the scene must be considered. Occasionally it may be impossible to acceptably balance all light sources in terms of brightness and/or color. Ambient light may

[figure 12.5]

Cheryl Pendleton used four separate exposures in creating this interior photograph for a bed and breakfast. Separate exposures were used for the interior illumination, the light coming in through the door and windows, and the various wall and ceiling lanterns.

Photograph by Cheryl Pendleton

still be the answer, but it can require a special technique to record a balanced scene.

As briefly mentioned in chapter 3, multiple exposure techniques can be used to extend and/or control the usefulness of ambient light. The simplest example of this is a daytime architectural interior that also includes views of the outside through windows. The problem is that the brightness levels outside may require a certain exposure while the brightness levels inside require another exposure. Also, the interior can be illuminated with tungsten or fluorescent lights, while the exterior is illuminated with daylight. The solution is to make two separate exposures. The camera is set up during the day, the inside lights turned out entirely, and an exposure is made for the outside views. If color correction is

necessary, the proper filtration is applied. The camera is left untouched. When darkness falls, the inside lights are turned on, and a second exposure is made on the same piece of film for the interior. Again, any necessary filtration is applied; with color materials, one of the exposures will require filtration depending upon the type of film employed.

This multiple exposure technique can be extended to encompass two, three, four, or more exposures as long as the light sources are functioning fairly independently and not overlapping. Where the light sources overlap, brightness and color blending will take place that can influence the exposure and/or color balance of the image. In many instances, this blending will occur gradually over detailed areas of the image and be unnoticed (figure 12.5). It will be most apparent on flat, even-toned surfaces. This technique maintains the appearance of ambient light throughout the scene allowing the photographic process to mask the sleight of hand.

If multiple exposure techniques are not possible or will not solve the problems, but the feeling of ambient light is still critical to the image statement, then the ambient light can be altered or supplemented with artificial light. A number of different possibilities exist here. Light fixtures can be modified to give more light. Diffusers and reflectors can be employed to alter off-camera light. Light sources can be gelled to match color temperatures to one standard. Finally, artificial lights may be employed along with ambient light sources to adjust the illumination.

Existing light fixtures in the scene can have standard tungsten bulbs replaced with photoflood bulbs to increase levels of illumination. The maximum allowable wattage for the fixtures must be checked to insure safety, but most lamps and many overhead tungsten light fixtures will accommodate at least a No. 1, 250-watt photoflood bulb. Some will accommodate a No. 2, 500-watt photoflood. These bulbs are significantly brighter than standard light bulbs and are balanced correctly for tungsten color films. Diffusers and reflectors can be used on location to soften and redirect ambient light in much the same way as they are employed in the studio. For example, a diffuser can transform the harsh sun into a large softlight.

If varying types of light sources are present, some may need to be gelled to match a specific color temperature. Color correction gels are available in large sheets that can be cut to fit lighting fixtures. Though gelling lights can be time consuming, it

does provide for consistent illumination and allows the use of a single exposure. In situations where light sources of various color temperatures are all on the same electrical circuit, gelling may be a necessity.

Alternatively, artificial light sources can be added to reinforce the ambient illumination of a scene, to alter contrast, or to increase overall levels of illumination. In this case, it is usually important that these new light sources either blend with or succumb to the existing ambient light. They must also match ambient light in color temperature or be appropriately filtered. Shadows can be filled, new areas of emphasis in terms of lighting can be established, and the subject can be enhanced as long as the character of place is maintained. If the additional illumination blends seamlessly with the ambient light and/or plays a subordinate role, it will appear integral to the scene (figure 12.6). The simplest example of this technique is the use of a flash to fill in shadows or to raise overall levels of illumination in all or part of a scene. The flash is adjusted to a level 1 to 2 f-stops below the ambient illumination and allowed to raise the level of brightness in the shadows in order to reduce the overall contrast of the scene. Conversely, if the flash is set above the ambient light level, areas of dynamic emphasis can be created that visibly contradict the existent illumination of the scene (figure 12.7). The addition of artificial illumination to a location can be combined and balanced with the multiple exposure technique previously described to create an intricate layering of effects.

In contrast to the above techniques, the photographer may decide to block out all ambient

illumination and supply totally artificial light. This does not necessarily mean that the character of the place will be sacrificed; it does, however, require the same kind of attention as lighting in the studio. If the character of place is to be preserved, then careful attention must be paid to the character of light. If the character of place is to be sacrificed to emphasize form or concept, then the light must function in service of those goals. When totally artificial illumination is employed, the location becomes an elaborate studio set, with the lighting controlled by the photographer (figure 12.8).

Preparation for Photographing

Site preparation can range from minimal to extensive. Even if the appearance and character of the location are to be preserved as closely as possible, preparation will likely be necessary. As mentioned above, the camera freezes all detail. Anything that might distract a viewer, interrupt the continuity of a location, or detract from the intended meaning of an image must be considered as extraneous. Sometimes simply cleaning and organizing a location can affect the appearance of a photograph. This is often the case with architectural interiors. The normal clutter of day-to-day activity appears chaotic on film. Dust and finger marks on surfaces become distracting flaws, a crooked picture on a wall throws off compositional harmonies, and dirty windows become glaring annoyances. Unless the original state of the location is part of the message, these photographs must be preceded by a thorough housekeeping.

[figure 12.6]

Kevin Mooney utilized electronic strobe to light the subject in the foreground but also integrated the extraordinary ambient light of the location into this dramatic portrait. Four types of light sources illuminate this photograph: strobe light, daylight, mercury vapor lights, and tungsten lights.

Photograph by Kevin O. Mooney

[figure 12.7]

In this portrait of his grandmother, Kevin Mooney employed an on-camera fill flash to isolate the subject from her environment with a wash of light. In this case the flash was set to slightly, but not completely, overpower the ambient light; at a lower setting, its effect would have been noticeable only in the shadows.

Photograph by Kevin O. Mooney

If the location is simply serving as raw material in and from which a set will be developed, preparation may be more elaborate. Sometimes it involves bringing large props, painting crews, carpenters, electricians, and a production team together for rebuilding, dressing, and lighting the final set. Fortunately, it is only what the camera sees that will be transmitted to the viewer, so cosmetic repairs often suffice. In the preparation of a location, all of the studio set design and building principles and techniques that have been described can be applied in the field. Spatial relationships, color combinations, and illusions can be employed to

[figure 12.8]

*Barbara Kasten used totally artificial illumination to transform this architectural location
into a nocturnal fantasy of color and abstract space.*

Photograph by Barbara Kasten

restructure the raw location into a calculated and contrived set .

Once the work of preparation is completed, photographing may begin. Unlike in the studio, where the photographer will often have the luxury of leaving a shot set up until the images are processed and studied, and where reshooting is possible, location work often involves onetime opportunities. Success must be assured on the first attempt. This requires careful attention to all technical and visual aspects of the image. Shooting tests on Polaroid

materials, bracketing, and shooting backup film can help insure acceptable results. Again, much of the key to success lies in adequate preparation for the shoot. With this in mind, it should be obvious that whenever there is a possibility of visiting a location before a shoot, assessing the problems and potentials of the site, and preparing for specific needs, the photographer should take advantage of this opportunity. It may make the difference between triumph and failure.

When On Location Is Not

Sometimes going on location is actually the search for subject, not environment. If a subject cannot be reasonably brought into the confines of the studio photographer's world, then the photographer may have to take the studio to the subject. In truth this happens regularly with, for example, school portraits. On a more sophisticated level, a studio backdrop, lighting equipment, and cameras can be transported

[figure 12.9]

Marc Hauser, with a backdrop and lighting equipment, went on location to a neighborhood tavern where the motorcycle riders he was photographing congregated. The location provided the opportunity to have many of Hauser's subjects together in one place at the same time, allowing him to complete this photograph and dozens of other portraits all in one day.

Photograph by Marc Hauser, "Bear"

anywhere and used as a studio on location. With portraits, this may be necessary when one is forced to travel a great distance to the subject's own home ground, when the subject refuses to or cannot come to the studio, or when the subject's ease in their own territory is important to the image.

In a sense, these photographs surgically remove the subject from environment and place them in a neutral space for the photographer to study. The control and precision of the studio are imposed on the subject whose relationship with personal space is severed. This technique has often been employed when the photographer has left the studio in search of the visually exotic. Criticism has pointed to the fact that such photographs appropriate, commodify, reduce, and exploit the subject for the intentions of the photographer. Often, the more culturally distant the subject is from the photographer and the viewer, the truer this becomes.

Elaborate sets can be constructed on location, but the simplest of backdrops hung between supports is often enough to neutralize environment. Many materials have been used for such backdrops; some of the more popular contemporary materials are again, canvas and muslin. Combined with standard studio lighting techniques, these portable backdrops produce self-contained fields, suspending the subject in a space designed for the camera (figure 12.9).

Photograph by Charles Shotwell

POLAROID

Polaroid films have been widely used in studio photography for many years. They have been used as a tool for confirming exposure and composition—yielding a visual checkpoint along the road to a final photograph on traditional black-and-white or color materials. They have also been used as an original medium to produce negatives, finished prints, and transparencies. Polaroid materials are unique in their instant, on-the-spot processing. These materials are also unique in their flexibility, range of color, and manipulative potential. In this chapter, some of the applications of Polaroid films and techniques of contemporary studio photographers utilizing this distinctive and significant medium will be explored.

The immediate accessibility to the photographic image offered by Polaroid materials has proven attractive to many photographers for varied reasons. For the 1960's family snapshooter with the Swinger camera, the ability to

possess the recorded moment in the now of its happening was seductive. For the 1970's artist with an SX-70, the chance to respond to and manipulate the image as it was forming was challenging and creatively stimulating. Finally, for the contemporary studio photographer with the 8″ × 10″ Polaroid color system, the ability to view a finished print while a shoot is still in progress saves time, materials, and money.

Though immediacy is the characteristic most often associated with Polaroid, it is not its only asset. When properly handled, Polaroid black-and-white materials can produce rich, full-scale prints and have been employed as an original print medium by a number of photographers. The palette of Polaroid color materials is singular in its departure from expected photographic renderings, yielding subtle and beautiful prints. Manipulation of Polaroid materials can include alterations

of surface and color during development, transferring the image to alternative supports, and separation of the emulsion from its support for use as a transparency. As the process has matured and the product line has expanded, the applications for Polaroid in the studio environment have also diversified.

Polaroid materials are available in black and white and color as well as in specialized films for particular uses such as radiography, video image recording, and high-contrast graphic arts applications. Formats range from 35mm to 20″ × 24″ and produce black-and-white negatives and prints as well as color transparencies and prints. This discussion will be limited to the standard panchromatic and color materials. In studio applications, the most common Polaroid films used are the black-and-white and color medium format pack-films, 4″ × 5″, and 8″ × 10″ materials. These can be divided into three major categories: black-and-white print films, black-and-white positive/negative film, and color print films. The particular properties of the films in these categories can vary considerably, but each category is distinguished by specific characteristics. Some Polaroid films are only available in one size, so, occasionally, specific needs may define the format the photographer chooses. All of the Polaroid instant films, black and white and color, are balanced for approximately 5,500° K or average daylight, the same as daylight color transparency films.

Processing of Polaroid films is accomplished by rupturing a pack or pod of chemistry and spreading it evenly across the film surface. This is initiated by rolling the film and chemistry pod between two smooth steel rollers at a controlled rate of speed. As processing progresses, the image is transferred from the negative to the positive receiving support. This support can be a paper base or a transparent base. Some films must be combined before and/or separated after processing while others are integral units. The black-and-white positive/negative films produce both a positive and a negative developed simultaneously and separated after processing is complete.

Exposure Testing

As previously mentioned, many studio photographers employ Polaroid films to test for exposure. Polaroid materials are positive-working. They produce a positive print directly upon processing without additional darkroom steps. Some Polaroid materials also produce a negative along with a positive print. Photographic transparency films are also positive-working. As detailed earlier, exposure for transparency materials must be based upon

highlight rather than shadow readings. The same is true of Polaroid materials when the goal is a positive print. Because of this similarity, the print obtained from Polaroid black-and-white or color materials is ideal for evaluating transparency exposure.

To recapitulate the metering method for highlight exposure control, the important surfaces in the scene are those that will render as bright, textured whites. These surfaces should be metered and, depending on the delicacy of the highlights, placed 2 to 2-1/2 f-stops above middle gray. This produces the proper highlight densities in transparencies and Polaroid materials. If no whites lie within the scene, an incident or a reflected gray card meter reading can be used as a beginning guide for exposure. The only exception to this rule occurs when the shadows of a scene contain important image information that must be readable in the final transparency. In this case, exposure readings of both highlights and shadows must be taken, exposure of the film must be based largely on shadow readings, and lighting contrast must be adjusted to place the highlights in the accordingly correct relationship. After years in the studio, most photographers develop an affinity for a particular style of lighting; they employ similar lights and lighting designs in most of their photographs. With experience, a photographer will be able to judge a starting point for many exposures without the aid of a light meter. A number of studio photographers exclusively use Polaroid materials for checking exposure. Some only use their light meters when they are on location or depart from their standard lighting methods.

The ISOs of Polaroid films range from 50 to 3,000 and accommodate almost any application. In some cases,

Polaroid materials used to check exposure will have ISOs that vary from the film to be used in making the final image. At first, this may seem an insurmountable disadvantage, but two simple techniques can help to make the necessary adjustments. In the first, divide the ISO of the faster-speed film by the ISO of the slower-speed film to yield a factor by which exposure can be multiplied or divided. This method works well within the specified reciprocity range of each film.

If exposure times that can cause reciprocity failure are encountered, this method will not produce satisfactory results unless the exposure adjustments are made with the aperture while the shutter speed remains constant. Aperture adjustments may be prohibited by depth-of-field requirements. In this case, a second method can be used to adjust for film speed. Neutral density filters of the appropriate factor may be used with the faster-speed film. Depending on the ISOs involved, a perfect match may not be produced, but it should be close enough for most applications. This second method avoids the necessity of changing camera settings between exposures, a filter is simply placed or removed as necessary. Exposures causing reciprocity failure can still result in problems as the two films involved may fail at different rates.

As a method of checking exposure, using Polaroid film has advantages in that it yields a visual check on exposure levels, thus providing a positive confirmation of the photographer's projections. Corollary to this advantage, a Polaroid print will also provide information about the lighting contrast, the general composition of the image, reflections, and shadows. It is useful to analyze this information in crafting the final image. This type of concrete visual reference often highlights information that might have been overlooked in direct observation of the scene.

Polaroid color films tend to shift toward the blue and cyan with longer than normal exposures and toward the red and yellow with shorter than normal exposures. Interestingly, with some of the films, this actually results in their being balanced for daylight within the normal reciprocity range and, with no filtration, coming back into balance for tungsten light at a four-second exposure. Contrast of Polaroid color films tends to increase with longer than normal exposures and decrease with shorter than normal exposures.

Black-and-White Polaroid

Polaroid produces numerous black-and-white print films in various formats ranging from 3 1/4″ × 4 1/4″ to 8″ × 10″. This section will center on the black-and-white films most commonly used in the studio, including medium format and 4″ × 5″ print and positive/negative films and 8″ × 10″ print films. Medium format and 4″ × 5″ black-and-white print films are available in film packs of eight exposures each. These print films are designed to fit specially adapted camera backs that are marketed for many small and medium format cameras. Black-and-white 4″ × 5″ and 8″ × 10″ print films are available as individual film packets. They are exposed and processed in special Polaroid film holders and processors (figure 13.1). As previously noted, the ISOs of these films vary greatly. They all produce full-scale black-and-white positive prints, though the tonal scale may change considerably for each type.

[figure 13.1]

Various Polaroid films, camera backs, holders, and processors for 120, 4″ × 5″, and 8″ × 10″ formats

Processing variations are possible with some of these films, others must be processed for recommended times. Basic variations extend or shorten the processing time, thereby affecting the amount of silver transferred to the print during development and producing more or less contrast in the print. The longer the processing, the more silver is transferred, and the more contrasty is the resulting positive. Processing film beyond three minutes can result in print delamination; the positive emulsion will stick to the negative base during separation. Other problems commonly encountered with extended processing times include: developer carry over, print staining, mottling, and curling.

Varying the temperature of processing can have similar contrast effects; the lower the temperature, the lower the contrast. However, varying the processing temperature will also affect the relative ISO of the film, with higher temperatures producing higher ISOs and lower temperatures reducing ISOs.

After processing, some prints must be coated to stabilize and protect their surface. This is accomplished with a coating brush and solution provided with the film. Many of the newer print films are coaterless. The medium format and 4″ × 5″ films must be pulled steadily at a measured speed through the rollers of their holders/processors. Any interruption in the pull will likely leave "hesitation bars" across the image. Too rapid or too slow a pull will result in uneven development. Though hand operated processors are available for the 8″ × 10″ films, they are normally developed in a special processor that is driven by an electric motor.

The above films can be used for exposure, composition, and lighting tests or to create original print statements. In workshop and teaching situations, the instant feedback from Polaroid prints provides for interactive critiquing. Working with clients in commerical studio settings, Polaroid prints can give a better representation of the finished image. They can also yield a monochromatic rendition of the scene for evaluation. This can be useful when an image is to be reproduced in both color and black and white. The black-and-white rendition may reveal problematic tonal renditions of colored surfaces that require adjustments or filtration of the image. Without the monochromatic proof, these problems might escape unnoticed and cause future complications. The black-and-white rendition helps those people who are not as skilled as the photographer in translating from set to photograph. These materials have applications wherever a black-and-white photograph is needed for quick evaluation, documentation, or even publication.

While the positive/negative film offers the same convenience, its unique ability to produce both a positive and a negative accords it a special place in this discussion. This film is available as medium format pack film in eight-exposure packs or as individual 4″ × 5″ packets, is rated at ISO 50, and is exposed and processed in the same special holders. It yields a medium

[figure 13.2]

Rob Shields made this portrait of a boxer on location in a local gym using soft lighting and Polaroid 55 P/N film. The resulting fine print expresses the potential for beautiful, subtle description of surface and light inherent in this emulsion.

Photograph by Rob Shields

contrast black-and-white print and a negative with a long tonal scale. The negatives produce remarkably beautiful black-and-white prints that rival or surpass standard black-and-white negative film (figure 13.2). Metering for positive/negative film exposure is dependent upon the desired product. If the resultant negative will be used for future prints, then shadow measurements become critical. If the film is being used to test for transparency exposure, then highlight measurements, which will yield the best quality positives, are appropriate. The negatives that accompany properly exposed Polaroid prints may be thin in the shadows and not capable of yielding fine enlargements; likewise, the Polaroid prints that accompany properly exposed negatives may well be washed out in the highlights.

Time and temperature processing variations are not possible with the positive/negative film. Underprocessing will result in tonal reversal in the shadow areas of the negative, while overprocessing will have no effect upon the negative contrast or density. Again, greatly extended processing times may result in print and/or negative failures. Following processing, the negatives are separated from the prints. The prints must be coated, and the negatives must be immersed in a sodium sulfite bath for clearing. After clearing, the negatives are washed and treated with a wetting agent before being hung to dry. The negative emulsion is delicate when wet and must be treated carefully to avoid scratching. Excessive washing or warm water can also soften and damage the emulsion. It is best to complete processing through drying on the spot; however, if working on location, the negatives can be cleared and stored in a water bath for later washing and drying. It is best to store such negatives in film hangers and large tanks; when stacked in trays, they will often scratch each other.

Positive/negative film is the only Polaroid film that facilitates multiples and enlargements of the original print. The flexibility of producing a high-quality negative almost instantaneously allows the photographer to check results in the field or while still in front of a set. Reshooting is minimized as negative quality is assessed on the spot. Many photographers employ the border surrounding the 4″ × 5″ negatives as a graphic device in their prints. This calls attention to the photographic process, and, for those who know the medium, to the instantaneous nature of Polaroid. These considerations certainly affect how a viewer perceives and interprets a print (figure 13.3).

[figure 13.3]

The border of the Polaroid 55 P/N negative is here used as a graphic device to echo the rough edges of the content and contradict the neat, white space of the frame. Joe Ziolkowski made this portrait in the Medusa's Juice Bar in Chicago. It is part of a series documenting the cross section of young urban society that frequented the club.

Photograph by Joe Ziolkowski from "The Medusa Series," "Jerry Rodgers, 21 years old, 1987"

Color Polaroid

The Polaroid color print films considered in this section are available as eight-exposure film packs in medium format or 4″ × 5″ and as individual film packets in 4″ × 5″ and 8″ × 10″. These films are exposed and processed in the same holders as the comparable format black-and-white films. As previously noted, all of the Polaroid color films are balanced for 5,500 °K. They yield a full-scale, color print with no negative. All of the films are coaterless.

Polaroid color films are available in normal and extended range emulsions. The extended-range films produce prints that closely duplicate the visual range of a standard color transparency, while the normal color films produce higher contrast, shorter range prints. Processing variations are feasible, though not as flexible as those available with the black-and-white emulsions. Longer than normal processing times or higher than normal temperatures result in prints with higher contrast and a perceivable cyan color shift. Shorter than normal processing times or lower than normal temperatures result in prints with lower contrast, weak blacks, and a perceptible warm-yellow color shift. Processing temperature affects the relative ISO of these films in the same manner as it affects the black-and-white films. As stated earlier, exposure times outside of the recommended range can result in loss of speed and color shifts due to reciprocity failure.

As a visual check on the way to a final image, Polaroid color prints are unsurpassed. They allow not only exposure checking but also a true assessment of composition and lighting as related to color values and combinations. Color proofs are an ideal reference for the nonphotographer-client in the studio. They can be circulated among a number of people for approval, and they can be marked on or tipped into advertising comps. Polaroid recommends a two- or three-stage proofing process using black-and-white films for exposure, focus, and lighting checks, and color print film for final composition and color checks. While this may seem excessive, it can actually conserve time and resources as each step of production is checked and verified before the final image is exposed. Special effects photographers often rely on Polaroid proofing to create elaborate, multiple-exposure images. Such effects

require a great deal of trial and error and would not be possible without Polaroid films.

Polaroid color print films are also utilized as an original print medium (figure 13.4). Photographers have turned to Polaroid color print films for their unique qualities: a subtle and distinctive color palette, a delicate tonal scale, and rich detail. Of course, the immediacy of the image is conducive to the photographer's spontaneity, closing the gap between inspiration and product, and allowing for interactive development of visual ideas.

Unique Formats

By nature, Polaroid has always been a medium of innovation. The first instant films were introduced by Dr. Edwin Land in 1948. The 4″ × 5″ black-and-white sheet film was introduced in 1958 and the positive/negative film in 1961. Polaroid color films were introduced in 1963 with professional format Polacolor 2 becoming available in 1975. The year 1980 saw the introduction of the ER, or extended range, color films, and black-and-white and color instant slide films became available in 1983. In 1988, Polaroid introduced a new line of extended range black-and-white films designed specifically for proofing before exposing color transparencies. Other products intervened in these years; of these, the two most significant for this discussion are the Polaroid SX-70 system, introduced in the early 1970s, and the Polaroid 20″ × 24″ color camera system, introduced in the late 1970s. Both of these products are popular among studio photographers for use in applied and fine arts settings.

The SX-70 fomented a revolution in photography. It was a new technology, combining the appeal of instant photography with an integral format that completely developed before the eyes. It was no longer necessary to wait for the print to develop in contact with the negative and then peel the negative to reveal the image. The format was unique in its manner of presentation; the seductive color square, framed high within a slightly larger white rectangle resembled a matted print. The color palette of the SX-70 print was also unique. It has been likened to an impressionist palette and rendered color in a range of hues that was delicate, yet saturated. Whites were never purely absent, they always retained a sense of substance, and blacks were deep and mysterious (figure 13.5). In addition, the original SX-70 film emulsion remained soft and easily manipulated for many hours after the print was ejected from the camera. This prompted artists to experiment with various alterations of the standard print. The 1970s produced a unique body of SX-70 work that will stand as a distinctive era in photographic imagery. The newer Time-Zero and Spectra films harden almost instantaneously upon development of the image and are not easily manipulated.

SX-70 and Spectra format films are balanced for daylight but can be filtered for use under tungsten illumination; they have ISOs of 150 and 600, respectively. The film, chemistry, and receiving layer are all integrated into one sealed unit. As the image is exposed, the film is ejected from the camera between two steel rollers, the chemical pod is broken and spread across the film, and development begins. During development, the image diffuses

[figure 13.4]

Dan Overturf's moody portrait was executed on Polaroid's 8″ × 10″ Polacolor print film.

Photograph by Daniel Overturf

upward to the transparent-receiving layer at the surface of the final print.

Although not intended for studio use, the SX-70 quickly found its way into the hands of studio photographers. The nearly instant availability of developed images lead to the regular appearance of photographs within photographs (figure 13.6). The visual ambiguity of this double imaging created new potentials for illusion and mystery. The manipulations assertively introduced the hand of the maker into the imaging process. In the studio, the SX-70 became a creative tool for image building.

Perhaps most important to its popularity, the idea of immediacy associated with SX-70 imaging reflected a growing cultural demand for instantaneous gratification. The SX-70 format ideally represented the fast-paced, nonreflective culture of the late twentieth century. It was highly technological, completely self-contained, easily transported, required little skill to operate, and yielded high-quality images. It introduced new levels of interaction and expectation within the photographic process— elements that are today reflected in many facets of electronic photography. The simplified technology of the SX-70 also democratized photography for those with the resources to afford the cameras and materials. Lines between skilled professionals and amateurs began to fade into the rich colors of the instant print.

[figure 13.5]

William Larson was one of the earliest photographers to experiment with Polaroid's SX-70 film in the studio still life genre. Polaroid chose and supplied film to a number of artists, asking only that they experiment with the new material. Larson's playful still life serves as a fanciful "color test" of the SX-70 emulsion.

Photograph by William Larson

[figure 13.6]

Carl Toth employed SX-70 prints as interactive parts of sculptural installations in this series of still life photographs. The picture-within-a-picture becomes a self-referential photographic element, drawing our attention to the process of image making.

Photograph by Carl Toth

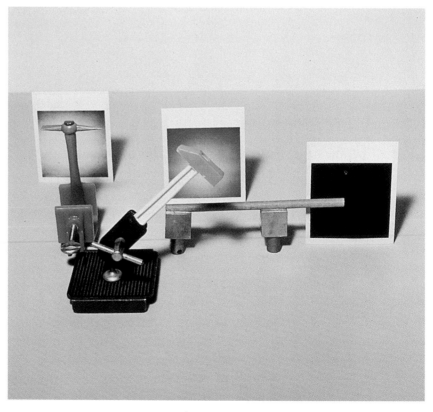

[figure 13.7]

Joyce Tenneson has used the Polaroid 20" × 24" camera at the New York Polaroid studio extensively in her portraiture and commercial illustration assignments. This whimsical image exploits the soft beauty of the Polaroid palette.

Photograph by Joyce Tenneson

The fact that the image was now immediately accessible to a wide audience helped to popularize the growing desire to capture experience which resulted in the explosion of photography in the mid-1970s.

In the late 1970s, the introduction of the 20" × 24" Polaroid camera system again revolutionized photography (figure 13.7). Not since the 20" × 24" glass-plate negatives of the 1800s had such a large format been accessible outside of special applications. The 20" × 24" camera system is not easily transported. A number of special studios with technical staffs have been set up where the cameras are available for rental use and where Polaroid invites photographers to participate in residency programs.

The dimensions of the image coupled with the sharpness and smoothness of the same-size positive print provide a startling visual experience. The direct connection between the final print and the ground glass image of the camera echo the mystique of the contact print that has fascinated photographers and audiences for years. In the introduction to the book *The Contact Print*, James Alinder writes, " . . . the contact print reflects a basic artistic temperament. From the methodical preparation for exposure with the large camera to the considered realization of every nuance and detail . . . the contact process necessitates contemplation." The implications of space within the frame are heightened by the knowledge that the frame is final. Composition, translation, and meaning are all influenced by this direct working relationship (figure 13.8).

Manipulations

As noted earlier, during the 1970s SX-70 film was easily manipulated. As the emulsion layers remained soft for some time, they were easy to rearrange and blend by applying pressure to the surface of the image. Photographers used anything from pencils to fingers to manipulate the SX-70 print. The results were often bizarre and visually entrancing. Detail could be obliterated, forms could be distorted, and abstract shapes could be created. Experimentation revealed that many manipulations were possible (figure 13.9). Photographers cut SX-70s apart and transferred the images to various supports, sometimes montaging them together into large composite pieces. The film could be heated before exposure and development to alter the color and contrast. SX-70s were also used as a print medium under enlargers. The images were painted on, injected with dyes,

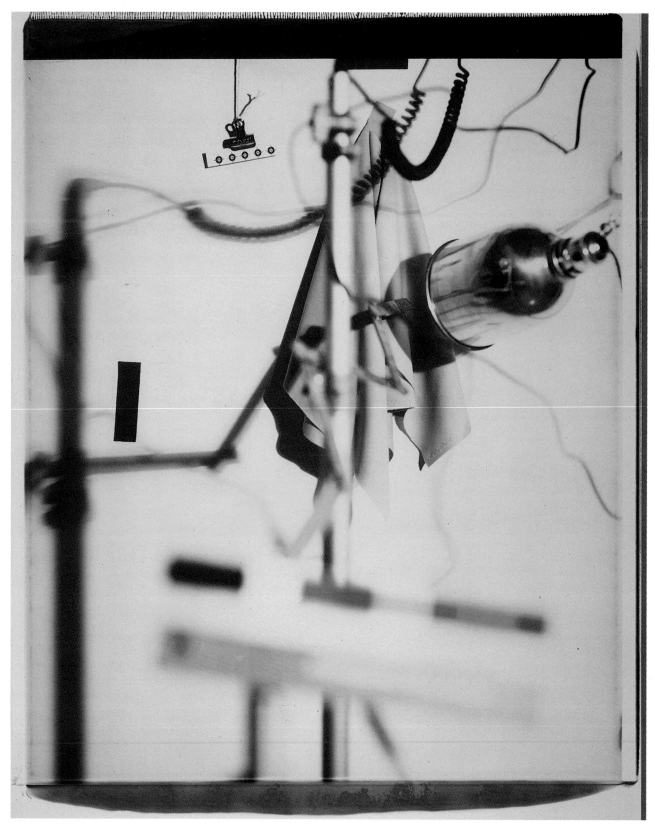

[figure 13.8]

William Larson continued his still life explorations with the Polaroid 20″ × 24″
camera. This image with its references to registration, measurement, and color seems to
be an extension of his earlier SX-70 work.

Photograph by William Larson

[figure 13.9]

John Reuter manipulated the SX-70 emulsion and added acrylic paints before transferring this whole image back onto a blank SX-70 frame. The work was all accomplished from the rear resulting in a final image that appeared to be unmanipulated.

Photograph by John Reuter

[figure 13.10]

The author applied pressure with a blunt stylus to the developing emulsion of this Time Zero photograph to create a graphic manipulation complementing a classic still life subject.

Photograph by Gary Kolb

and put in toasters. Each experiment yielded a panoply of effects from mild distortion to wild abstraction.

Currently, Time Zero and Spectra films are not easily manipulated. Pressure applied during development of the Time Zero image no longer mixes the dye layers effectively, it does leave a dark mark in the image where the dyes have been displaced. Occasionally, the white titanium dioxide undercoating shows through in, or bordering, these areas (figure 13.10). The images from the Time Zero film, which closely resembles the original SX-70 film in construction, can still be transferred to other supports. Once separated from the backing for transfer, the emulsion of the

film lends itself to manipulation. Color can be added to the wet images with watercolors or dyes, and dry, transferred-images can be hand colored. The support for transferred images can be a plain surface or one that has already been drawn or printed upon. Taken together, these techniques suggest a considerable creative flexibility still available with the newer films.

Some of the most exciting work in Polaroid manipulation is being done with transfers of large format Polacolor print images (figure 13.11). The transfer process is accomplished by interrupting the development of the print before the image dyes have transferred from the negative to the positive receiving surface.

The negative is laid in contact with an alternative receiving surface and pressure is applied to force the transfer of the dyes (figure 13.12). Paper and fabric surfaces have been successfully used to receive these images. Color and contrast changes occur during transfer and vary depending upon the support chosen to receive the image. Transferred images are normally lower in contrast and saturation than standard Polaroid prints. They also tend to lose some of their dye density, shifting the image toward cyan and prompting many photographers to use a heavy magenta or red filter during exposure. The transfer process can be utilized with all formats of Polacolor films (figure 13.13).

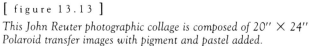

[figure 13.11]

Chuck Shotwell utilizes the Polaroid transfer process extensively
in both his personal work and commercial assignments. The subtle
colors of the transfer palette complement Shotwell's choice and
arrangement of subject matter and create a soft veneer of
nostalgia over the images.

Photograph by Charles Shotwell, "Painter's Cross," 1990

[figure 13.13]

This John Reuter photographic collage is composed of 20″ × 24″
Polaroid transfer images with pigment and pastel added.

[figure 13.12]

This 8″ × 10″ Polaroid transfer was
created as a self-promotional piece by
photographer Dave Jordano. As the
developing emulsion tends to tear and
distort, accomplishing flawless large
format transfers can be an arduous and
film-consuming task.

Photograph by Dave Jordano, "Untitled, 1991"

SPECIAL TECHNIQUES AND EFFECTS

The range of standard photographic processes is open to extension through a number of special techniques. Some of these techniques are relatively straightforward, while others involve elaborate and time-consuming manipulations. This chapter will examine some unique tools and procedures that can provide creative solutions to particular problems. This discussion will also delve into the realm of special effects photography. Special effects images are often defined by their apparent contradictions of real world standards or by their seeming impossibility given the conventional photographic process. At their most extreme, special effects images resemble computer-generated graphics and may indeed represent a visual bridge between silver-based and digital technologies.

The simplest special tools discussed will be special effects filters. Special techniques such as multiple exposure and painting with light will be investigated.

Finally, a foray will be made into in-camera masking, controlled motion, and ray tracing. The combination of these tools and techniques can create an array of special effects that extend the language of photography, create unique realities, and astound viewers.

Unlike illusion, the power of these special effects does not lie in the ability to convey deception, but rather in the novel visual experience that they present to the viewer. As this unique stimulus is integrated with a response to the seamless reality of the photographic image, the viewer accepts the definition of a new reality in which objects float in space, the viewer's eyes see movement, scenes radiate a soft glow, and light leaves a physical trace.

The techniques mentioned in the following are mostly in-camera techniques. It should be noted that most, if not all, of the results obtained could be produced in the darkroom. Many photographers prefer to do their special effects

work in the darkroom or let their lab create the magic. In-camera special effects are time-consuming and tedious; however, they can be spectacular and are more closely related to the spirit of this text.

Filters

Many filters are available for general purpose and special effects photography. The application of some of these filters specifically designed for use with black-and-white and color films has been discussed. This section will consider a few filters available for producing unusual, useful special effects; some of these will be utilized in techniques discussed later in this chapter. Often the least expensive tool a photographer may own, a special effects filter, used creatively, can provide the solution to a difficult problem or simply enhance the impact of an image.

Diffusion filters are useful tools for creating soft-focus and halation in various areas of an

[figure 14.1]

Rob Shields used a Softar diffusion filter to create this enigmatic portrait.

Photograph by Rob Shields

image. Many types of diffusion filters are available. Some diffuse the image without creating halation while others are specifically designed to create glowing, diffuse highlights. Each manufacturer has a unique range of filters available and publishes literature describing their effects. They are usually available in graduated series yielding subtle to extreme diffusion. Some varieties are constructed of single layers of glass that is frosted or rippled on one side; others consist of white or black netting laminated between two layers of glass; still others consist of concentric rings etched into glass. Some soften the entire image while others leave a circular spot of sharp focus in the center surrounded by diffused detail. All produce slightly different effects, and it may require some experimentation to settle upon the right filter (figure 14.1).

Multiple Exposure

Multiple exposure techniques in relationship to specific problems were discussed in previous sections of this book. So many variations on the basic techniques exist that it would be impossible to detail all combinations. These techniques all share the ability of film to accumulate and retain images through numerous exposures. In special effects applications, the photographer benefits from the viewer's assumption that a photograph occurs in one instant and pictures one integrated subject, while the multiple exposure may occur at many times and in different locations. This section will look at two specific types of multiple exposures: fully overlapping, blended images and separately photographed, discrete images assembled on one piece of film. Later, this chapter will combine multiple exposure techniques with other tools and processes.

Because film accumulates exposure, it can also accumulate images. One sheet of film exposed to more than one scene will produce a composite or blended image. A wide range of effects is possible. Unlike any previous medium, photography permits the creation of depth through layering and transparency—a unique characteristic of the medium. The seamless integration of the multiple exposure creates a new reality, often offering a richly textured image embodying spatial ambiguities and temporal mysteries. Once blended together in the camera, the multiple exposure is difficult for the viewer to deconstruct.

When dealing with multiple scenes layered in one image, the photographer must remember the basic workings of the process. As exposure accumulates on film, image densities will tend to block up in the highlights and overall

[figure 14.2]

Al Francekevich used a spectra filter on-camera and darkroom photo composition techniques to create this fanciful composition of balance.

Photograph by Al Francekevich

Star- and spectra-effect filters are available that produce distinct star shapes or spoke-like patterns of radiating, multicolored lines around bright light sources in an image. Star-effect filters are available to produce 4-, 6-, and 8-point stars. Spectra filters are available in a wide array yielding anywhere from 2 to 72 radiating spokes from a central point. These lines will be made up of various colors of the spectrum radiating out and changing hue. Both star- and spectra-effect filters require a small, radiant light source to produce their varied effects (figure 14.2).

Bifocal filters are also available that split the focus of an image along a central line, allowing the camera to focus on two planes at once. These actually function as auxiliary lenses to split the field of the image into near and far areas of focus. Often these filters may be rotated to produce a bilateral split at any given angle in an image.

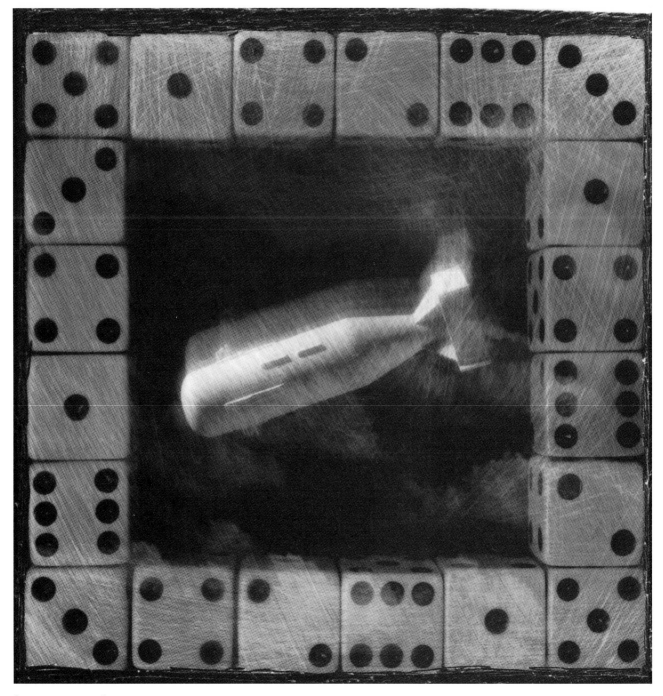

[figure 14.3]

This Paul Elledge photograph is a multiple exposure in a miniature set. The subtle
blending of multiple images creates new and foreboding relationships within the confines
of the single frame.

Photograph by Paul Elledge

contrast will be reduced as shadow densities rise. This can be compensated for by raising the ISO of the film to intentionally underexpose each image, thereby deepening the shadows and holding back the highlights. The amount by which the film speed is raised depends on many variables including the type of film, the type of images being exposed, and taste. To begin experimentation, try increasing the speed by 2/3 of an f-stop $(1.66\times)$ for two overlapping exposures or 1 full f-stop $(2\times)$ for three exposures. With transparency films, the exposure must be carefully calculated and bracketed because no corrective steps can be exercised during printing to bring back lost highlight detail. With negative films, slight underdevelopment may be useful in controlling highlight densities.

It is not necessary to expose each image equally. Exposure levels can be varied, thereby producing a dominant and subordinate image. Careful attention to the scenes and diagrams of image placement will facilitate composition. Obviously, where dark and light areas overlap, one image will blend into the other most noticeably. Dark on dark or light on light will either be unnoticed or blocked up. Overlapping midtones will blend well and create rich areas of composite information. This technique is extremely flexible, and experimentation is the only means of truly understanding the range of controls available (figure 14.3).

Though not normally thought of as a form of multiple exposure, the flash-blur is another technique that creates two overlapping exposures. In the flash-blur, a long ambient light exposure is combined with a brief strobe exposure to create both a blurred and a frozen image on one piece of film. This provides for a range of possibilities as exposure times and flash durations are varied, filtration is applied at different stages, and movement is introduced. The flash-blur is often considered a technique of street photography but can be effectively utilized in the studio to suggest energy and movement (figure 14.4).

Photomontage assemblages can be created in-camera through multiple exposure techniques. In these images, discrete areas of the film or scene are exposed separately, building up an image from individual pieces joined together in the space of the frame. This is accomplished by strictly

[figure 14.4]

Steve Nozicka utilized a long (1/250″) strobe exposure to slightly blur the fast-spinning bicycle tire in this studio photograph. Because the strobe peaks at the beginning of its flash, the tire is actually spinning opposite the apparent direction. The background is a transluminated, enlarged color transparency.

Photograph by Steve Nozicka

controlling the illumination of a scene or the placement of areas of dark and light in the image. Where one exposure is light, others remain dark. If a view camera is used, grease pencil drawings are easily made on acetate or directly on the ground glass to facilitate image composition. The final picture can be assembled from numerous exposures, each occurring in separate sets or all in one set with various areas lighted or darkened. Composite assemblages of this sort can create many special effects (figure 14.5). Various areas of the image can be composed, focused, and exposed separately allowing for individual attention to design and lighting, differential focus in various areas, and the combination of multiple perspectives, places, and events in one image.

Painting with Light

A light source is normally thought of as stationary. However, two techniques in which the light source actually moves during exposure contradict this thought. Both movements can be broadly categorized under painting with light. In one technique, the light source is directed at the camera itself; in the other, the light source is directed at the scene in front of the camera. The former technique is sometimes called tracing with light and is a specialized use of radiant light in an image. In both of these techniques, the light source is moved during exposure to create otherwise impossible effects. Images produced in this manner embody time in their very structure and rely on the unique capability of still photography to

faint blur in the image; if it is moved slowly, it will record as a solid white line of substantial width. Of course, the size and shape of the light source will have a great effect upon the character of the tracing. A pinpoint source can be compared to drawing with a very fine graphic arts pen, while a fluorescent tube or light wand might be equated to painting with a broad brush (figure 14.6).

Exposure of light tracings is controlled by the aperture of the camera, the brightness of the light, and the speed of the light's movement. As the speed increases, the light remains in any one place for a shorter time thereby reducing exposure. Rapid movement of a light source creates tracings with an extremely volumetric appearance as the tonal changes in the lines of light begin to resemble contoured reflective surfaces. Slow movement of the light often produces a two-dimensional traced image that rests in front of the picture plane (figure 14.7). Tracings can be abstract designs, representational drawings, or an actual outlining of complex scenes in front of the camera. Integrating light tracings with another exposure, ambient or flash, can produce surreal special effects images. The most interesting application of any technique occurs when the concept and execution of the image reinforce each other. Tracing as a record of movement allows the photographer the freedom to combine multiple layers of related information in one image; the image speaks of two aspects of the subject, form and function (figure 14.8).

Painting the subject with a continuous light source involves using the source as a brush to selectively or completely cover the surface of the subject with a "coating" of light. It takes place in a dimly illuminated studio or location. The camera shutter is

[figure 14.5]

Neil Molinaro used in-camera, multiple exposure techniques to create this complex assemblage incorporating numerous perspectives.

© 1990 Neil R. Molinaro

translate time into visual form. This holds their apparent magic; they make the ephemeral presence of light permanent.

Light tracings can become extremely complex. As long as the shutter remains open, any light directed at the camera will record on the film. If the light were to remain in one spot, it would simply appear as a bright, halated highlight in the image. However, if the light is moved during exposure, it traces a path on the film that varies in brightness and width as the speed of the movement changes. If the light is moved quickly, it may record as a

[figure 14.6]
Aaron Jones used a light sword attachment for his Hosemaster to create the broad bands of liquid light in this portrait.

Photograph by Aaron Jones "L. D. Burke III"

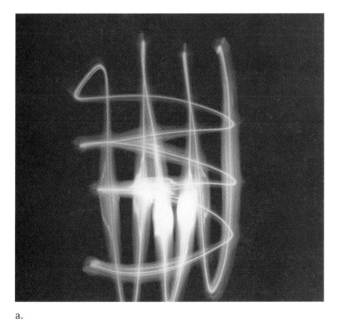

a.

b.

[figure 14.7]
The two abstract designs above were created side by side with the same household flashlight. On the left (a.), the light was moved rapidly to create variation in tone, line, and transparency, while on the right (b.), the light was moved slowly to create a solid line of substantial width and even tone. The design on the left has a three-dimensional character, while the one on the right has a two-dimensional quality.

[figure 14.8]

In this multiple exposure with light tracing, Giorgio Majno asked his subject to trace a design in the air with a lighted bulb and then photographed him contemplating his creation.

Photograph by Giorgio Majno

left open, and the light source is hand-held. During the length of the exposure, the light is continually moved to literally paint light onto the subject. This painting is, of course, only visible to the film on which the build up of light records as exposure. The light can be moved around the entire subject, allowing illumination from many angles in one image. This creates a soft, enveloping bath of light in which the subject resides. Conversely, the illumination can be controlled selectively, being directed at only specific areas of the subject or from only specific angles. This creates a patchwork of mottled light across the image (figure 14.9).

Experimentation with this technique should begin with a number of concerns in mind. Exposure is again controlled by the aperture of the camera and the length of time light is directed at any one spot in the scene. It is best to use a small aperture, so exposure times are longer and more controllable; also, small working apertures allow enough ambient illumination in the studio to facilitate the process. The light must be kept moving to guard against hot spots developing on the subject.

As the "painting" progresses, the photographer should be wary of blocking light from the subject to the camera. The photographer can pass in front of the lens as

long as light is not blocked for a substantial period of time; otherwise, a silhouette of the photographer will form where the exposure was held back. The photographer should also avoid directing the light source into the lens of the camera, thus producing a hot spot of radiant light in the image. Specular reflections of the light source may also produce brilliant highlights. The decision on where and how to move the light should be carefully monitored. Sometimes, photographers use a base exposure to establish an overall dark image on the film and then use light painting to flesh out and highlight the image. This base exposure should be calculated to underexpose the film between 2 and 3 f-stops.

Though the technique involved, particularly exposure calculation, seems formidable and rigorous, experimentation will reveal a great deal of leeway and flexibility in practice. The results can be exciting. Recently, the introduction of fiber optics systems for light painting has prompted a resurgence of the technique. New systems involve the use of highly controllable fiber optics light sources that allow precise direction in an image. These systems provide true exposure control, daylight balanced light sources, and additional flexibility through numerous accessories. Some systems also involve a shutter mechanism that resides in front of the camera and that can function through a button on the photographer-held light source. Additionally, these shutters, when supplemented with filters that can be similarly moved in and out, can produce color or diffusion effects during all or some of the light painting. The range of possible extensions of this technique is immense. It offers control and precision not possible with fixed light sources and can create images that transform light into a fluid substance "brushed" on at the discretion of the photographer (figure 14.10).

In-Camera Masking

In-camera masking that uses Kodalith film to block light from certain areas of an image can produce an array of special effects. This technique is commonly known as photocomposition. It is based on the precise alignment of multiple exposures in-camera and is similar in appearance to many darkroom processes but eliminates the need for time-consuming and expensive postproduction work (figure 14.11). It requires precise registration of a single sheet of film behind various Kodalith masks. Standard view cameras and film holders can accurately accomplish this task. However, special pin-registered film holders assure proper registration. One type of pin-registered, vacuum film holder utilizes a rubber gasket and vacuum pump to hold the film and masks intimately in contact, thus assuring almost perfect registration.

This technique involves a single set and camera or combinations of multiple sets and cameras. In darkroom photo composition, as practiced by photographers such as Jerry Uelsmann, multiple enlargers, each containing a separate negative, are often utilized to create the print. The paper is moved from one enlarger to the next for successive exposures. This proves more effective than using one enlarger and changing negatives, trying to reregister each time. In the case of in-camera photo composition, photographers

[figure 14.9]

Painting with light allows the photographer to control the rendering of detail, color, and reflection throughout a scene. Subtle nuances, blendings, and washes of light not possible with other techniques can be easily achieved with light painting, as in this Aaron Jones photograph.

Photograph by Aaron Jones for Naturalizer Shoes

[figure 14.10]

Aaron Jones selectively used diffusion filters in conjunction with light painting to create the enveloping glow surrounding the subjects in this image.

Photograph by Aaron Jones

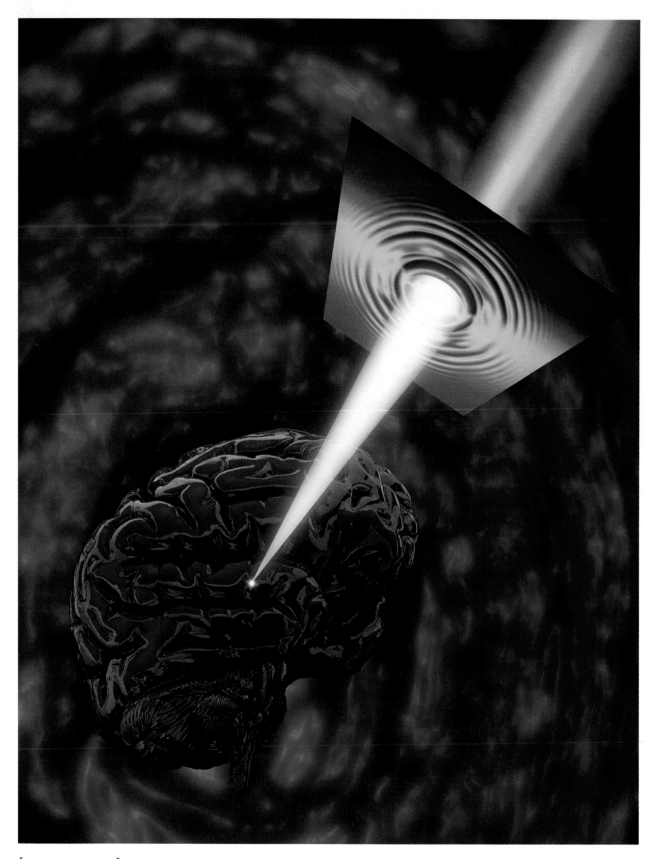

[figure 14.11]

Uldis Saule completed this composite image in-camera through elaborate masking and multiple exposure techniques.

Photograph by Uldis Saule, Evanston, Illinois

often move the film from one camera/set to another instead of trying to change the set in front of a single camera with each new exposure. Photo composition of this sort is effectively accomplished when various parts of the image are separated by areas of black or white, or when edges are concealed by texture and detail; it is difficult when sharply defined shapes of even tone and medium brightness are abutted in the image. In the latter case, any small overlapping of exposures produces a noticeable double image or "halo" effect around the discrete areas involved.

In the case of a single set, the camera is placed in front of the subject and the composition of the frame is established. The camera should remain absolutely stationary throughout the rest of the process—this is critical. As the sheets of Kodalith film are exposed, each receives a different level of exposure, or the lighting of the set can be controlled and altered between successive exposures to produce a variety of masks that record different details of the scene. These films are processed in a litho developer and then touched up with photo opaque to allow only the desired details to show. These primary masks are applied directly and/or used as negatives to produce reversed masks through contact printing in the darkroom. The more precise all registration is kept, the more accurate will be the resulting image. A registration punch and pins will aid in proper alignment during the production of additional negative masks.

The completed masks are sandwiched, one or more at a time, with a piece of film in a film holder and the scene is re-exposed. The original Kodalith negative masks will be black in areas recorded during the masking exposure and will block the image in these areas of the scene. The

reversal negative masks produced in the darkroom will be clear in corresponding areas, thus allowing light through to the underlying film. Various combinations of original and reversal masks can produce a range of effects, or masks, when used one at a time during successive exposures, can build up a complex image on the film. The simplest variation would be to use a primary mask to block the main subject during the first exposure and then a reversal mask to block the background during a second exposure yielding a composite image precisely combining the two masked exposures.

When multiple cameras and sets are being used, precise alignment is difficult. The masks, carefully taped to the ground-glass backs of the various view cameras, can be used to position each camera on set and then inserted in the film holder for use during exposure. Alternatively, the same camera back can be moved from set to set with a grease pencil or pen-on-acetate drawing on the ground glass being used for positioning. If precision view cameras are being used, and care is taken to insert the film holder the same way each time, fairly exact registration is possible with this technique. In any case, each separate exposure requires testing and determination prior to the final composite production. Polaroid film allows careful assessment of each exposure and, to some degree, of the combined masking effects that can be expected. Unfortunately, the individual masks cannot be inserted into the Polaroid holder; however, they can be laid down over the Polaroid prints and used to check sizing and composition.

The most important aspect of in-camera photo composition is rigorous attention to detail. Complex shots of this nature can take days to complete. No real

magic occurs in the production of the image, just a logical, knowledgeable manipulation of the basic processes of photography. The magic lies in viewing the final image, which can be surreal, fantastic, and mysterious (figure 14.12).

Controlled Motion

Movement of the subject or the camera during a long exposure will create a blurred image. The controlled movement of either subject or camera can be utilized to create a number of intriguing special effects such as zooms and wipes. The resulting photograph often does not show whether the movement was in the subject or the camera, and may sometimes imply one while actually embodying the other. Movement of the camera is often more controllable and precise than movement of the subject. Gyroscopic platforms and fluid head tripods are available that will help stabilize and smooth camera movement. However, to avoid jagged inconsistencies in what should appear as smooth transitions, precise control over camera movement can require tolerances as close as a thousandth of an inch. Special equipment designed and built to allow for this degree of control over camera movement helps in many of these situations. If the subject is moved as opposed to the camera, each situation will call for a unique and complex solution, new equipment, experimentation, and additional expense.

Special leveling platforms fitted with precisely machined and mounted tracks can be constructed. Cameras mounted on rolling platforms that ride along these tracks on precision bearings are afforded extremely flat tracking through straight line

motions. These can occur front to back along the lens axis, thus producing a zoom effect, or they can occur laterally across the subject producing a linear movement in space. In-camera masking can combine with these zoom/wipe effects (figure 14.13). The resulting images are complex and intriguing reconstructions of reality (figure 14.14).

Exposures must be of sufficient length to record the desired motion. In single exposures made with tungsten light, the speed and consistency of the movement will determine the appearance of the subject. Combinations of movement and stasis can create images in which a subject is recorded in both blurred and solid form. This can also be

[figure 14.13]
These positive and negative leaf masks formed the basis for the in-camera photo composition in figure 14.14.

Photograph by Uldis Saule, Evanston, Illinois

accomplished with the flash-blur technique described previously. Other multiple exposure techniques in which various parts of the scene are illuminated and exposed separately can result in the movement of specific elements

of an image while the rest of the photograph remains still. This is realized in a single exposure by moving part of the subject rather than the camera. Again, variations and combinations of techniques provide for many possibilities.

Ray Tracings

Some special effects images have what appears to be a line of colored light, like a laser ray, connecting objects or tracing its way through the image. Of course, these are not actual laser beams, but rather they are lines of conventional light exposed onto the film separately from the main image. This technique is rather simple, yet dramatic. The

[figure 14.14]

The positive/negative masks pictured in figure 14.13 were utilized in-camera along with multiple exposures and controlled motion to create this fantasy leaf fall by Uldis Saule, Evanston, Illinois

Photograph by Uldis Saule, Evanston, Illinois

numerous ways to produce such lines of colored light all rely, once again, on logical application of basic photographic principles. The following will detail one method and suggest a few variations.

The photographer might, at first, guess that tracing with light, as described earlier, would be a viable technique for introducing these laserlike effects.

Unfortunately, the level of control, in both exposure and placement available through tracing with light is usually inadequate in producing the clean, precision effect desired in these images. Instead, a multiple exposure technique is utilized that separately exposes the main subject and the rays. This multiple exposure technique does not

always require the aid of masking and can produce remarkably complex images when combined with numerous other techniques.

In its simplest form, ray tracing consists of using two exposures to introduce rays of light in the frame. The first exposure is made for the main subject and the second for the special effect (figure 14.15).

[figure 14.15]

Uldis Saule created this set for the primary exposure in a special effects shot involving laser ray tracings. Note the black velvet used to provide a dark ground for the eventual addition of the rays of light.

Photograph by Uldis Saule, Evanston, Illinois

Because exposure is additive, if the rays of light are to occur in a dark area of the image, then accurate placement and exposure control are the main elements of concern. If the tonalities are lighter and/or significant overlapping of exposures occurs, then additional controls may be necessary.

In the former case, after the exposure for the main subject is completed, the film holder is removed and the desired rays of light traced on the ground glass or a piece of acetate with a sharpened grease pencil; the tracing must be accurate and exact in width and placement. The camera back, or the whole camera, is then moved to another set. This second set consists of a sheet of translucent Plexiglas illuminated from behind. The camera is set up in front of this sheet, and the grease pencil lines on the ground glass are used as a template for marking out the rays with black tape on the front of the Plexiglas. The width, placement, and length of the rays are matched to the ground glass lines.

An interesting trick to facilitate this process is to set a spotlight behind the camera and, with the lens open, project an image of the actual lines onto the Plexiglas sheet (figure 14.16). This allows for extremely exact control in marking. After the edges of the rays are marked, the rest of the Plexiglas can be masked off with black paper thus leaving only the rays open for transmitting light to the camera (figure 14.17). The second exposure is made by using a diffused light behind the Plexiglas to "burn in" the laser rays on the film. White light can be used to make this exposure or filters can be used to produce color effects. Filters placed on the camera or gels used between the light source and the Plexiglas will allow for numerous colors to be used in one exposure. A small hole drilled in the Plexiglas that allows the radiant backlight directly to the lens can be used with a star filter to produce a star-shaped point of emission or impact in the image (figure 14.18). This requires separate exposures for the star and rays, with the rays covered and the hole open for the star exposure and vice versa for the ray exposure.

Individual exposure testing for the main scene and the ray exposure must be done before the composite is attempted. Again, Polaroid film will help with the testing. An interesting variation on this effect is to split the laser exposure into two or three lesser exposures and use diffusion filters for some of the exposures. This produces a soft radiating light around the rays (figure 14.19).

For extremely precise alignment or for instances where overlapping colors of ray and background are not compatible, a masking technique can be used in conjunction with this multiple exposure technique. For example, brilliant blue rays over an orange or yellow background will not record properly and will require a masking procedure similar to that previously described but with a

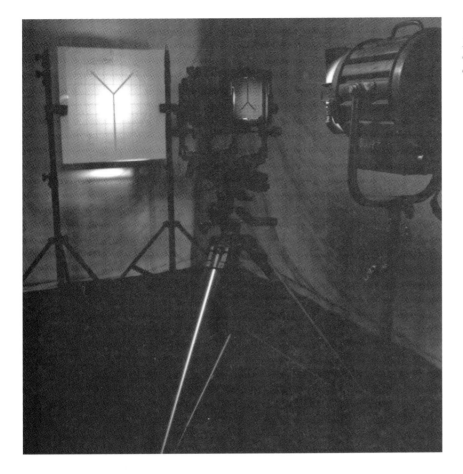

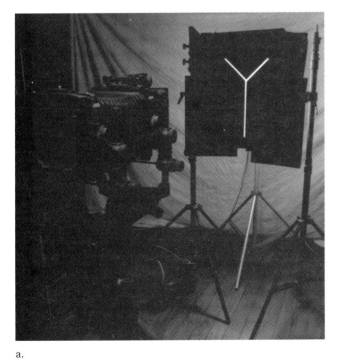

a.

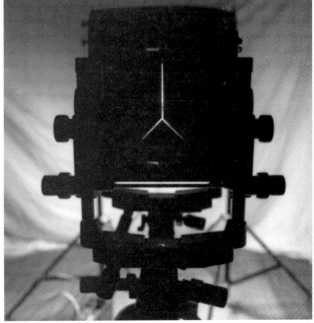

b.

[figure 14.17]
To add lines of light to the original image, a separate exposure is made of the ray template illuminated from behind (a.). Seen through the camera back, the template is brightly outlined (b.).

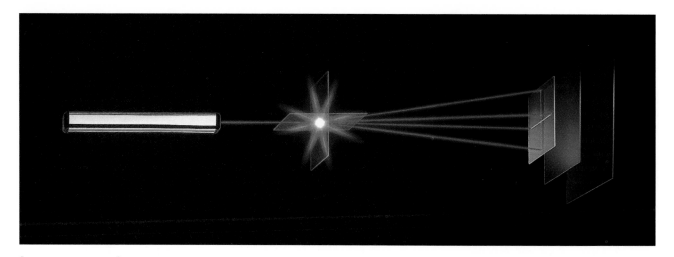

[figure 14.18]

This is the final composite image formed from the exposure of the set in figure 14.15 and the additional exposures for the laser rays and star burst.

Photograph by Uldis Saule, Evanston, Illinois

few additional steps. The rays traced on the Plexiglas are used to create a Kodalith mask that is sandwiched with the film during the main image exposure. This mask prevents any significant overlapping exposure of rays and background; it is removed for the ray exposure, thus allowing the laser light to record and bleed in to fill up any unexposed areas of the film. This works well with the previously described diffusion technique to mask any possible flaws in registration.

As an alternative, a primary mask can be produced from an acetate line drawing or tracing from the camera back and used to create a reversal mask; the two masks are interchanged during the exposures. The second exposure can then be done through the reversal mask eliminating the need for the Plexiglas altogether. This will produce a sharp edged line of light or, if some layers of diffusion material are sandwiched between the second mask and the film, a soft-edged light effect will be produced.

All of the above special tools, techniques, and effects can combine in exciting and creative ways. The essential relationship of all of the processes described is implicit in their foundation in the basic principles underlying the functioning of photographic materials. As a closing note to this chapter, it is interesting to compare the special effects possible in photography with the potential manipulations possible in electronically generated or assisted imagery. It is quite likely that the future of special effects photography will be intimately tied to new technologies that can already achieve all of the aforementioned effects through computer manipulation of photographic images. The overlap between these two different methods of producing the same effects is apparent in much special effects imagery of today that resembles computer-generated imagery in form and detail (figure 14.20). Indeed, the computer-assisted artist may replace the special effects photographer as the reigning visual magician. Curiously though, the standards by which this new work will be evaluated are based in the seamless reality of the photographic image.

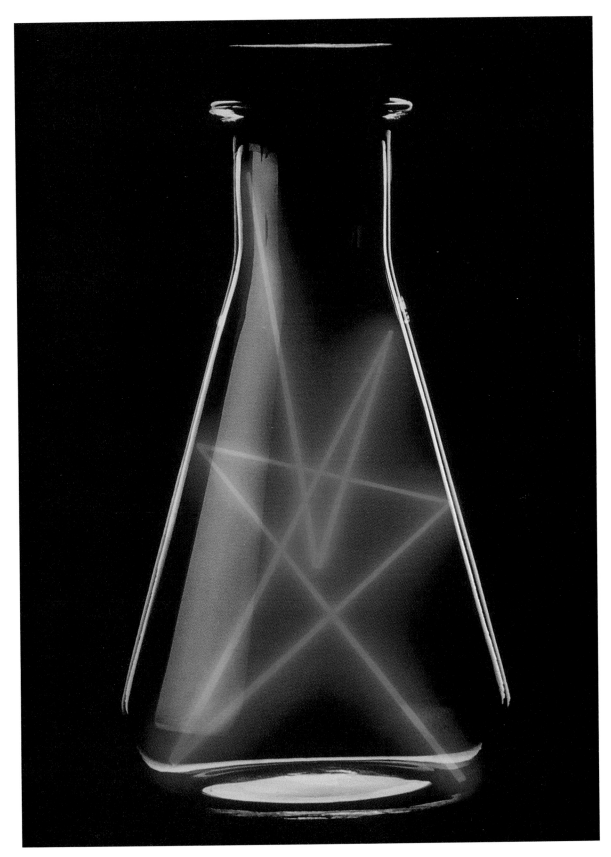

[figure 14.19]
The soft, glowing rays of light trapped in the flask in this Al Francekevich photograph were produced with a diffusion filter.

Photograph by Al Francekevich

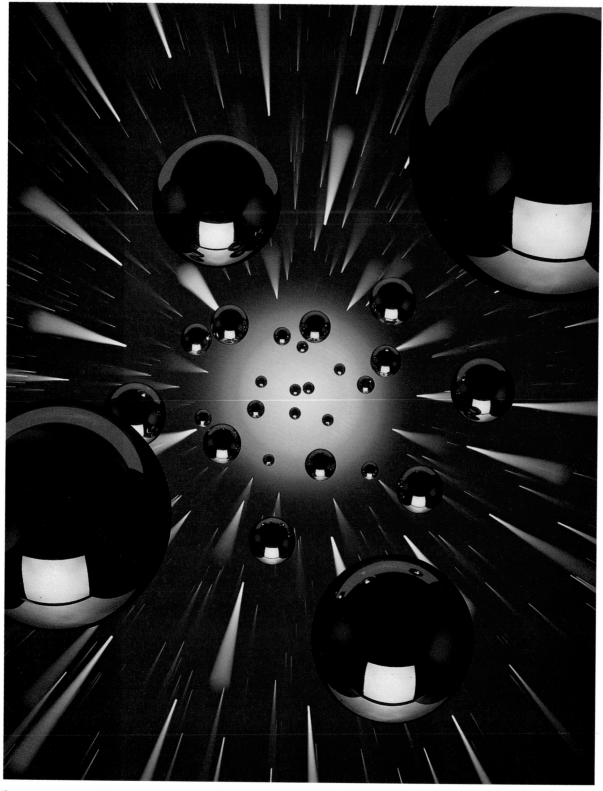

[figure 14.20]

This composite image involving in-camera masking, controlled motion, and multiple exposures is similar in appearance to many of the computer-generated, geometric abstractions of early computer-imaging technologies. Though the processes involved are dramatically different, similar images may result from both silver- and electronically-based technologies.

Photograph by Uldis Saule, Evanston, Illinois

THE ELECTRONIC IMAGING REVOLUTION

Technologies are inherently fleeting. Silver-based photographic imaging is less than two-hundred years old, yet it is apparent that it will eventually be supplanted, some would say soon, by electronically based imaging technologies. Though Kodak and other photographic manufacturers recently projected that silver-based films would have a useful life through the middle of the twenty-first century, it is clear that long before that time the majority of images generated will be electronically based. Electronic imaging in the form of video and computer technologies already occupies a large and growing share of the imaging market.

Major photographic manufacturers are quickly entering the electronic imaging fields, and the thrust of much contemporary research is toward the development of photographic quality in electronic images. Currently, the silver-based photograph lists image quality and cost effectiveness as major advantages over the electronic

image, but the electronic image is rapidly gaining ground. As technologies are perfected and costs decrease, electronic imaging tools will displace silver-based photographic imaging in both the amateur and professional marketplaces. This may leave fine arts photographers as the sole practitioners of what will eventually become an alternative imaging process alongside platinum printing and gum-bichromate.

Though contemporary photographers may find this news distressing, many interesting opportunities exist in electronic imaging and the new technologies will be relatively easy to learn. Image makers will always be needed—creative individuals to utilize new technologies in exciting ways. As traditional photographic appearance seems to be the benchmark for new imaging technologies, much of the adaptation to new tools may prove to be largely a technical rather than an aesthetic challenge. The image-making skills and creativity

of the photographer may simply be transplanted from a physical to an electronic medium.

Electronic imaging will present new possibilities and extend the range of the photographers' creative tools. This is perhaps the most important aspect of the new imaging technologies, they will enlarge and reintegrate picture making. The title "photographer" will eventually become archaic, being replaced by a word more descriptive of an integrated approach to imaging. As this transition takes place, it will be increasingly important for photographers to reassess their medium, to employ new tools as appropriate and to redefine their role as image makers.

Two Systems

Though the thrust of electronic imaging will be toward integration of processes such as drawing, painting, still photography, film, video, and computer imaging, the available electronic tools for photographic imaging fall into two major groups—analog and digital. These categories are not exclusive, and often analog and digital tools are integrated in the same system. They do rely on significantly different technologies, and both offer stiff competition to the traditional photographic technologies.

Most video recording equipment is based on analog technology similar to that employed with analog audio tape. Video tools electronically record images formed by a lens onto a magnetic medium for storage, further processing, and retrieval. Video cameras can also send their electronic signal directly to a monitor or some type of processor. Computer technologies, like compact audio discs, are digitally based. Computer imaging systems can utilize digitized images from video sources; receive images directly from CCD (Charge Coupled Device) sensors used in cameras; or, create photographic-quality images directly from mathematical algorithms, bypassing the camera entirely. Digital images can be stored on magnetic tape or disks, in electronic RAM (Random Access Memory) or ROM (Read Only Memory), and on digital optical media such as CD-ROM (Compact Disk-Read Only Memory) disks. Some still video systems employ digital recording technologies similar to those used in digital audio tape recording. While photographers may feel more comfortable with video systems in which magnetic tape can be imagined to function in a manner similar to film, it is likely that analog video imaging will eventually be displaced by digital imaging technologies that offer higher quality, flexible image manipulation, and transmission advantages.

Analog video images are made up of horizontal scan lines and have the familiar look of television. These images have a relatively low resolution with color and brightness controlled through the continuous modulation of the video signal. Higher-resolution analog images such as S-VHS video or High Definition Television (HDTV) boost the visual quality of the video image and offer renewed life to the technology. Digitally recorded video imagery will further extend the usefulness of that medium and will easily integrate with computer processing systems.

Digital computer imagery is often higher resolution than analog video imagery. It is composed of individual pixels (picture elements), each pixel precisely controlled in terms of brightness and color. Digital imagery is not dependent on the continuous modulation of signal strength as it is composed of discrete units of binary information. This provides advantages in recording, storage and compression, transmission, and longevity over analog imagery.

Both technologies rely on video monitors as their primary output device. Quality computer monitors provide higher resolution and more accurate imaging than normal television monitors. Hard copy output from electronic imaging systems, video or computer, is evolving at a staggering rate. Currently, most of the systems capable of high-quality reproduction prints or transparencies are hybrids that employ traditional photographic technologies as well as digital equipment. In these systems, films are laser scanned and then used as originals for various presentation and printing processes. It is possible to burn printing plates directly with digitally guided equipment, bypassing photographic processes entirely; however, the equipment necessary for such operations is extremely expensive. As technologies and demands develop at an increasing pace, direct digital output will increase in quality.

On a more affordable level, the available options for direct output are myriad. Some of the more common forms of hard copy are the dot matrix print, the ink jet print, the thermal transfer print, and the laser print (figure 15.1). These prints can be black and white or color. Resolution with low-end printers is currently limited to about 300 dots per inch, and color reproduction is relatively limited compared to most film-dependent processes. It should be noted, however, that the quality has increased phenomenally in the past few years; the benchmark of photographic quality at an accessible price may be attained in the near future.

Both analog and digital electronic images can be transmitted rapidly around the globe implying obvious advantages over silver-based photographs for journalism, advertising, manufacturing, science, and the consumer market. Electronically based images, particularly digital images, are relatively permanent compared to traditional photographic media. They do not mold, stain, and fade like negatives, transparencies, and prints. Electronic imagery is not impervious to destruction; however, it is easily duplicated and exact copies can be readily stored in various locations to insure preservation. Huge numbers of high-quality images can be stored in a small space. One digital optical disk the size of a compact audio disc can hold hundreds of high-resolution

[figure 15.1]

This Tom Porrett image was printed with a color ink-jet printer. These printers provide
relatively low-cost, but coarse, image output (original in color).

Image by Thomas Porett, "COUNTERPOINTS"

images. These disks can be easily and quickly cataloged, searched, and accessed with relatively inexpensive equipment requiring no special laboratory environment, chemicals, or technical knowledge of the end user.

In addition, with today's computer technologies, electronically based imagery is easily analyzed, enhanced, manipulated, and combined. The implications of these practices in medicine, science, cartography, and surveillance are apparent. These same options may be equally attractive to the creative image maker, suggesting new horizons for the imagination.

Applications

The application of electronic tools in photographic imaging will impact two distinct phases of production. First, and perhaps most obviously, the way images are produced will change. Cameras will contain light-sensitive electronic components instead of film. Silver and dye negatives, transparencies, and prints will be replaced by other media. Computer terminals with video monitors and printers will replace enlargers. These and other changes will affect the technical specifications of the equipment, the processes of production, and the physical appearance of the

image. Second, and more importantly, the working environment in the studio, postproduction processes, and the distribution of imagery will be radically altered. Individuals at different geographic locations will cooperate on the production of images, significant image manipulation will become economical and commonplace, and rapid transmission of imagery will facilitate access on many levels. These developments will obviously impact the studio photographer. The technology to support these practices is not science fiction; it exists now, and is rapidly becoming widely accessible.

As cameras evolve, electronic imaging sensors will replace film. These devices will capture an image and save it to magnetic or optical media, transmit it to a display terminal or processor, and permit flexible in-camera manipulations. Color balance, exposure level, and tonal distribution will be adjustable along with focus, composition, and shape. Lighting may even be adjustable at the film plane through computer manipulation of selected pixels of exposure information. The implications of these possibilities for the production of images are obvious. The photographer will be able to work quickly and accurately with the ability to instantly check and adjust many variables; lab time and expense will be greatly reduced, or eliminated altogether; and, the ability to quickly experiment with many solutions will enhance creativity.

Technicians at enlargers, graphic arts cameras, and optical printers will be replaced by operators at video display terminals (figure 15.2). Here, images will be enhanced, altered, combined, and fine-tuned before being sent to various printers. Operators will have access to large data bases of imagery and will have the ability to combine numerous images into a seamless final product. Retouching, emulsion stripping, and multiple exposure techniques will become obsolete. Output will range from image proofs to finished "comps" to final copy. When linked with advances in camera technologies, these new imaging processes will predicate a more efficient, more controllable, and highly interactive working environment for the studio photographer. They will allow rapid production and transmission of images.

The mode of operation of many commercial photography studios may undergo a significant

[figure 15.2]

A view of Duggal Color Projects on-line, electronic-image generation lab in New York City

Duggal Computer Imaging/Duggal Color Projects

change as working environments become more interconnected and interactive. Technologies will allow instantaneous communication between clients, art directors, and photographers. Already accessories are available for certain view cameras that replace the film holder, capture an image electronically, and transmit it to a processor. Here the image is digitized. It can then be sent over standard telephone lines to an office across town or across country, viewed on a display terminal or printed out, critiqued, and adjusted before the photograph is ever exposed. Such "video backs" literally allow an art director to be "on set" electronically, seeing through the camera.

Geographic location will soon pose no barrier to the interactive working of individuals or groups. In the commercial world, clients, art directors, and photographers, all at diverse geographic locations, will soon be able to function as cohesive teams in the production of images. This is already a reality

for certain firms and will rapidly become more common; witness the impact of the FAX machine on photographer/art director/ client communications. Artists will be able to access huge data bases of imagery, collaborate on projects, and transmit their finished work over huge, ultrafast computer networks. The extensive time required to transmit the large amounts of data comprising high-quality images has been a barrier to such interactive working; however, advances in transmission rates will soon make "real time" interactive, image creation a reality.

Once a photographic image is translated into digital form it can easily and radically be manipulated. These manipulations can range from simple corrections of color balance or contrast to elaborate alteration or montaging (figure 15.3). The ability to control the individual pixels of a digital image in terms of brightness and color implies the ability to structure the information in the image into any

[figure 15.3]

Duggal can generate photographic quality output with its laser scanners. In years past, this image would have required the building of an elaborate model and photo composition techniques. Duggal produced the image from straight photographs of the actual subjects, creating all manipulations and combinations electronically, and generating a seamless final image (original in color).

Duggal Computer Imaging/Duggal Color Projects

[figure 15.4]

David Haxton used an Iris computer system to create this still life image. The image is similar in concept to his earlier photographically generated studio work (see chapter 3, figure 3.15), yet is totally electronic in origin (original in color).

Computer-generated Iris image by David Haxton

desired form, to add or delete information at will, and to create entirely fantastic "image realities." Any resulting version will carry the seamless look of the original.

In certain cases, computer technologies can assume much of the photographer's role and revolutionize how business functions and art is produced. It is possible to imagine an electronic advertising environment in which a product is designed on a CAD (Computer Aided Design) system, modeled three-dimensionally, electronically pasted into a manufactured digital background, and set into advertising copy for a finished composite before the actual product is ever in existence. Advertising campaigns could be designed and executed while the product was being manufactured, compressing development, engineering, and marketing into a single, coordinated phase of activity. Likewise, in the arts, three-dimensional modeling algorithms allow the creation of photographically "real" images.

These can be composite montages created from many sources blended seamlessly together, or images that are generated mathematically using techniques such as fractal imaging and ray tracing (figure 15.4).

Not only the production but also the distribution of images will be affected by new technological developments. While print media will still hold a significant and useful place in the distribution of available images, electronic distribution of images will become commonplace. Teletext systems, combining text, still imagery, video, and audio, will become a reality as transmission technologies are perfected and popularized. Commercial applications are obvious; news media and advertisers will make wide use of these technologies. Video printers attached to these systems will bring hard copy versions of transmitted imagery into the hands of the viewer. Likewise, through their home telecommunications centers,

viewers will have access to huge image libraries, such as the Library of Congress collection, museums, and the works of individual artists. This access will revolutionize the distribution of imagery in the culture.

The role of photography in the imaging environment of the future will be multifaceted and integral. As the medium has evolved from still images through film to video, photographers have adapted to new technologies. If photographers can surmount their initial cyberphobic fears and think creatively, computer technology and electronic imaging will become enlightened arenas for exploration, productivity, and creativity. Clearly, the possibilities are exciting; the challenge will be to evolve as image makers and to use new technologies creatively to produce powerful images. This will require open-minded investigation of new tools and fresh aesthetics. In addition, new technologies, as always, will be accompanied by new dilemmas.

Possibilities and Problems

Clearly the introduction of electronic imaging systems is going to revolutionize many of the practical aspects of studio photography. The imaging process will be streamlined, the photographer's control over the technical aspects of the image will increase, the studio will become a more interactive environment, and new imaging possibilities will predicate new aesthetic criteria. While these practical, working implications are rich in exciting new creative possibilities, increased control over the specification and form of images implies serious legal, aesthetic, philosophical, and ethical questions. Most of these questions relate more directly to the worlds of commerce and journalism than to the art world where appropriation has become an accepted practice.

If a graphic artist at a computer work station accesses and combines several images from the files of digitized photographs at a large advertising agency and then produces a seamless, new "photographic" image, who holds the copyright? If a photographer's image is digitally manipulated, new information is added and elements of the photograph moved, what becomes of the integrity of the photographer's aesthetic? Is there an ethical problem with reconstructing an image to fit a layout? Should information be deleted or altered electronically to alter meaning? For photographers, the answers to these questions may seem obvious; editors, art directors, clients, and audiences may have different opinions.

The issues involved in these practices are complex, yet they seem to revolve around three areas of concern: first, questions of ownership; second, questions of aesthetics; and third, questions of truth or authenticity. Ownership of the photographic image has been traditionally governed by copyright law. It is generally understood that photographers own the copyright to any image that they create, by whichever techniques they employ. Unless contractually specified, publication of a copyrighted image in any form, including electronic, must be with the consent of the photographer and is usually granted for specific purposes and scopes in exchange for the payment of a fee. However, when an image undergoes substantive or meaningful artistic alteration, its copyright status is open to question. Such altered images can be copyrighted by the individual or group that performs the alteration. In a related field, the colorization of original MGM films purchased by media-mogul Ted Turner was considered to be such a manipulation and the copyright of the colorized versions belongs to Turner.

The appropriation, alteration, and synthesis of photographs threatens to impact the livelihood of photographers. One solution to this problem would be for photographers to charge more for their services, thus insuring against future loss due to unauthorized use and alteration of their original images. This might encourage clients to develop their own image synthesis capabilities and bypass photographers entirely. Another solution would be to effectively extend the copyright law to fragments of images, though this would obviously be difficult or impossible to enforce. Yet, a third solution would be to enact controls over the availability and use of certain technologies capable of image alteration. This solution is most questionable as it would place control over the free flow of information in the hands of a vested minority, surely violating the spirit of free speech. As new imaging technologies proliferate, these questions will become crucial for photographers working in a competitive marketplace. Photographers' associations have begun to vigorously oppose the electronic alteration of original photographs and to lobby for strict control over the use of copyrighted images.

The aesthetic implications of electronic imaging are likely to be as far-reaching, if not as contentious, as the legal questions of ownership. Each new visual medium from oil painting to lithography to photography has been accompanied by changes in aesthetic values. While each medium has, to a degree, developed its own esoteric language of expression and criticism, this level of discourse has traditionally been limited to artists, critics, curators, and collectors. The aesthetic expectations and sensibilities of the general public have to a large degree been shaped by forces of broader, societal scope, rooted in media, technology, and economics.

Certainly, photography has had a great influence upon the aesthetic sensibilities of modern society by creating expectations of realism or authenticity and by confirming people's individual perceptions. The former of these effects is largely a result of mass media distribution of photographic imagery, while the latter rests in the individual use of the photograph to record personal history. As the public has come to be familiar with photographic imagery, the "look" of the photograph has become the accepted standard for visual media. Whether the photographer should take an optimistic or dismal view of this observation is debatable. In the nineteenth century, Baudelaire said that photography, " . . . panders to the public's desire for verisimilitude in art." While, on a more positive note, in the twentieth century, William Ivins felt that, "It is through photography that art and science have had their most striking effect upon the thoughts of the average [citizen]."

Ivins goes on to point out that, "The photograph became the norm for the appearance of everything." As one reviews the development of standards by which the quality or success of electronically generated imagery is judged, this observation rings with renewed truth. The aesthetic standard of photographic appearance is the goal of most electronic imaging technologies. However, an important aspect of photographic appearance lies in the nature of the silver-based photographic print.

As the final print/presentation form of electronically generated imagery matures, the aesthetics of imaging will undergo changes, just as the evolution from the daguerotype to the modern silver print precipitated changes in aesthetic standards. The rendering of detail, contrast, and color may be altered. More importantly, the mode of presentation may metamorphose from print to video or LCD displays. These transformations will in turn affect the way imagery is transmitted, the rapidity with which it is digested, and the standards by which it is judged. While photographers may decry "pop" cultural aesthetics, they cannot deny the influence of such perceptions upon the production and distribution of imagery.

As pointed out previously, photographic representation carries the authority of truth. Though the absurdity of such a belief is manifest, the tendency of most people is to accept, not to question, the veracity of a photograph. This societal assumption lies at the base of photojournalism and documentary photography. The pervasive manipulation of imagery through electronic means may challenge the cultural foundation of this supposition. Journalistic media will be particularly vulnerable and sensitive to the consequences of image manipulation. Reliance on the authenticity of the image may force the mass media to eschew certain technologies; for example, the Associated Press has promised to avoid any digital manipulation of the content of its transmitted imagery. Perhaps the public will change its definition and expectations of truth in media reporting. Likewise, advertisers will be presented with increased potential for altering or creating imagery to suit their intentions. The results may be viewed as elaborate fictions or as acceptable creative license.

The famous photojournalist Robert Capa is quoted as saying that photography in service of the truth is as good as the truth itself. As this kind of truth seems relative to the teller, this is certainly foreign to modern notions of accuracy and honesty in reporting. Yet, the public's thirst for reenactments and schematic stagings of current news events seems to be escalating. As this trend continues, image manipulation may become commonplace and accepted. Biases or inaccuracies in imaging may come to be viewed as editorial slant or interpretive commentary. If such eventualities come about, the public's fundamental understanding of the photographic image will undergo a profound change. The erosion of the link between the photograph and the manifest world will signal the death of William Ivins' observation that photography made possible the profound difference between "pictorial expression and pictorial communication of statements of fact." The photograph will be relegated to the realm of interpretive imagery, reintegrated with the history of picture making, and finally understood as a construction, not a reality.

In the studio environment, where fanciful creation is the rule rather than the exception, the manipulation of photographic imagery will herald new freedom in creative expression. Whether in an applied or an artistic context, the ethical responsibilities associated with this freedom will call upon the photographer to make moral and philosophical judgments as to the importance, limits, and nature of truth.

GLOSSARY

Absorption
The ability of a material to absorb and convert some of the light energy that falls upon it, usually to heat or electricity.

Ambient light
Existing, constant illumination within a scene or at a location.

Angle of incidence
The angle at which light from a source strikes a surface.

Angle of reflection
The angle at which light reflects from a surface; reflection is usually strongest at an angle equal to but opposite from the angle of incidence.

Asymmetrical power pack
An electronic strobe power pack that is capable of providing different, and usually variable, levels of power from each of its power outlets.

Averaging meter
A light meter that measures light from a large arc of angles seen by the meter's light-sensitive cell and produces a reading based on an average of all of the brightnesses within the metered area.

Back light
Light coming from behind the subject; the most contrasty direction from which light can come. Back light is good for defining shapes in the form of silhouettes but not for modeling volumes.

Background light
A light that illuminates only the background in a photograph; a standard light in many portrait lighting designs used to separate the subject from the background.

Barn doors
Folding fins that can be attached to the front of a light and used to control the spread of illumination.

Bottom light
Light coming from below the subject. Bottom light is moderately contrasty and, though unusual to the eye of the viewer, can be effective for modeling volumes. It could be considered a form of side light.

Brightness range
The difference between the lowest and highest brightness values in a scene. Brightness range is a general term that could be measured in many ways and could encompass both lighting contrast and scene contrast.

Broadlight
A light designed to spread illumination over a large area. Broadlights are moderately contrasty.

Candlepower unit
An international standard unit for measuring the brightness of a light source.

Casein
A water-based paint used in theater-scene painting. Casein is useful for set and background painting. It has a different binder and tends to dry with more brilliance and saturation than latex paints. It comes as a paste and must be diluted with water.

Chiaroscuro
The modeling of surfaces with light and shadow; the visual description of the play of light and shadow across surfaces in a two-dimensional image.

Closure
In a photograph, the viewer's act of completing familiar shapes, figures, actions, or ideas that are presented in an incomplete form.

Color-compensating filter
A filter designed to shift the color of light. Color-compensating filters are available in a wide range of hues and densities in gelatin or glass for lights and cameras. They are often used to correct color balance for a particular emulsion of film or to correct for color shifts due to reciprocity failure. These filters can also be used to creatively alter color relationships within a scene.

Color temperature
A descriptive evaluation of the color of illumination present at a given point within a scene. Color temperature is measured in degrees Kelvin.

Color temperature meter
A light meter designed to read the color temperature of illumination and to give a reading expressed in degrees Kelvin. This information can be used to adjust for color balance differentials between various light and film combinations.

Compendium lens shade
A special lens shade comprised of an adjustable bellow that can be extended and manipulated to properly shield various focal length lenses in many different lighting situations. Many compendium lens shades also contain filter holders.

Complementary
Two colors are said to be complementary if they yield gray or neutral density when mixed together or superimposed. Complementary colors are usually located directly across from each other on a color wheel.

Continuity
In a photograph, the viewer's tendency to perceive shapes and lines requiring the fewest possible interruptions in the visual process.

Contour
The undulations of a surface.

Contrast
A general term describing the range of brightnesses or values present within a scene; it can also be applied to light sources. A contrasty light source emits high-intensity beams of light traveling parallel to each other. A high level of contrast is characterized by sharp shadows, extreme brightness differences, and brilliant reflections. See lighting contrast, scene contrast, and subject contrast.

Convergence
The tendency for parallel lines to move closer together as they recede in distance from a viewer or a camera. Convergence is used as a depth clue in perspective rendering.

Cyclorama
A smooth, horizontally and vertically curved wall in a studio that is useful for suspending a subject in a seeming void.

Decamired
Ten Mired units.

Diffuse reflection
Light reflected from a surface after having been absorbed and changed by the surface. The light can be changed in its intensity, contrast, and spectral composition. Diffuse reflection is responsible for defining surface brightness, texture, and color; it enables the visual system and the camera to function.

Diffused light
Light having passed through a diffusing medium. Diffused light is less directional and less intense than direct light. It may also be altered in spectral composition.

Diffuser
A translucent panel or material placed between a light source and subject to soften and reduce the intensity of the light.

Direct light
Light traveling directly from a light source to a subject.

Dispersion
The spreading or distribution of various wavelengths of light, like the separation of white light into its constituent colors upon passing through a prism.

Elliptical reflector
An elliptical reflector concentrates converging rays of light at a spot in front of the light source. The focal length is controlled by the curvature of the reflector.

Exposure value
A measurement of light related to the brightness of the light source, the ISO of the film, and the shutter speed and aperture of the camera.

Figure
In Gestalt, that which is perceived as a whole against the ground of its surroundings; that on which we focus our attention.

Fill card
A small reflective card used to redirect light into or within a scene. Fill cards can be white, silver, or colored depending upon the effect desired.

Fill light
A light used to fill in and soften shadows cast by the main light source. The intensity of the fill light will control the lighting ratio.

Filter factor
The arithmetic factor by which exposure must be increased in order to adjust for the light-absorbing effects of a filter. A filter factor of $2 \times$ requires a doubling of exposure, $3 \times$ requires a tripling of exposure, etc. Filter factors must not be confused with f-stops, which represent a geometric progression.

Flag
Any black card of varying size and shape that is placed between a light source and a camera to shield the lens or that is placed between a light source and a subject to create a shadow. See gobo.

Flare
Internal reflections from the lens and camera system resulting in bright, often geometric patterns of light in the image. Flare is usually caused by a radiant light source.

Flash meter
A light meter designed to read only short, powerful flashes of light from electronic strobes and flash bulbs. A dedicated flash meter will not read ambient light. See strobe meter.

Flash synchronization
The synchronizing of the peak output of light from a flash source with the opening of the camera shutter. With focal plane shutters, there is a maximum speed at which flash can be synchronized. With leaf shutters, flash can usually be synchronized at all speeds. X-synch is for electronic strobes, and M-synch is for flash bulbs.

Flat
A basic element of set construction. A moveable wall partition consisting of a light wood frame covered with canvas or drywall.

Footcandle

A measure of the brightness of a surface related to the intensity of a light source and the distance from the light source to the surface. Footcandles are equal to candlepower divided by distance squared. Footcandles are not to be confused with perceived tonal value, which is dependent upon the reflectivity of a surface. See foot-lambert.

Foot-lambert

A measure of the light reflecting from a surface equal to footcandles multiplied by the reflectivity of the surface. Foot-lamberts are directly related to perceived tonal value.

Fresnel lens

A low-quality, stepped lens used in many lights to focus or spread the beams. The affect of the lens depends upon its distance from the light bulb and the reflector in a light.

Front light

Light coming from in front of the subject. Front light is the least contrasty of all illumination. It is not good for defining volume and may even confuse the rendering of shape as it flattens the subject by eliminating shadows that are clues to depth and form.

Gel

A gelatin filter used in front of a light or a camera lens. Lighting gels are tough and heat resistant; camera gels are thin and do not degrade the optical image. Gels are available in many colors, as light-balancing filters, as polarizers, and in neutral densities.

Gestalt

From Gestalt psychology, gestalt is the wholeness of perception. Rather than analyzing component parts as separate entities, Gestalt psychology focuses on the recognition of the complex yet integrated whole. It postulates that the perceptual process simplifies, organizes, and constructs sensory data to form meaningful visual or intellectual experience.

Glare

Specular reflection in the form of image-degrading light. Glare interferes with the perception of detail, color, and surface. See specular reflection and reflected highlight.

Gobo

A black card that is placed between a light and the camera to shield the lens, or that is placed between a light and a subject to create a shadow or a "black reflection."

Gray card

A neutral gray piece of card of a value that reflects 18 percent of the light that falls on it. A gray card is considered to be "middle gray" and is used as a basis for many systems of film exposure and development. Photographic paper speeds and contrasts are based around the rendering of 18% gray. See middle gray.

Grid spot

A honeycomb-like grid that fits on the front of a light source and restricts the spread of illumination. Grid spots can be varied in density and depth to create a larger or smaller area of illumination. The denser and deeper the grid, the smaller that area will be. Grid spots do not alter the basic character of illumination from the light source. See honeycomb.

Ground

In Gestalt, this term represents that which serves as a background or surround for a figure. The ground is the supporting element that situates the figure in context. It should be noted that while ground may seem of minimal importance, figure cannot exist independently. Therefore, figure and ground are intimately and necessarily intertwined in the whole of perception. In a photograph, attention must be paid to both elements.

Guide number

A number describing the light output of an electronic strobe relative to a specific ISO film speed. Guide numbers are valuable tools in determining exposure and subject distance. Guide numbers also offer a good measure of the actual light output of a strobe system as it affects exposure. Most strobe manufacturers provide guide numbers for ISO 25 and ISO 100 films for comparative purposes.

Hair light

In portraiture, a light used to illuminate only the subject's hair. The hair light is normally placed above and behind the subject to create reflections and highlights on the hair. It helps to separate the subject from the background, to create a sense of depth, and to add brilliance.

Halation

The diffusion of light around bright highlights in a negative. Halation is caused by light penetrating and bouncing back into the film emulsion at varied angles forming a halo around bright spots. The antihalation backing on most films minimizes halation problems. Halation normally occurs around radiant light sources.

Hard copy

In electronic imaging, any form of printed output.

Hard light

Contrasty or harsh illumination creating sharp shadows and small, brilliant reflections.

High key

A style of lighting that floods the entire subject with bright, often shadowless illumination; exposure is adjusted to place values high on the tonal scale. An image in which all of the values are high on the tonal scale.

Highlight

A bright area in an image. Highlights can either be a diffuse reflection or a specular reflection. Though occupying a small area, highlights are often responsible for adding a sense of subtle life and brilliance to an image.

HMI light

Hg medium-arc iodide light. These special purpose continuous light sources are balanced for daylight. HMI lights are valuable for location shooting where daylight and artificial light of a constant nature must be blended seamlessly. They are particularly useful for film and video work or where continuous and strobe illumination are being combined.

Honeycomb

See grid spot.

Hot light

Tungsten, quartz, or HMI light; the name is descriptive of the heat generated by the bulbs.

Hue
The dominant color name—hue is associated with a particular placement on the color wheel or area in the spectrum.

Incident light meter
A light meter designed to measure the intensity of illumination at a given point within a scene. Incident light meters usually incorporate a half-spherical dome over the sensor that gathers and averages the light. In most situations, for accurate readings, the dome must be pointed toward the camera lens.

Interference
The action of various waves of light upon each other that makes holography possible.

Joule
The European equivalent for watt-second. See watt-second.

Kelvin scale
A temperature scale identical in increment to the Celsius scale, with zero degrees Kelvin being equal to absolute zero. Color temperature readings are specified in degrees Kelvin or °K. A black body radiator heated to 3,200 °K would produce light energy of approximately the same spectral distribution as a tungsten bulb.

Kicker
In portrait lighting, a tightly controlled light used to accent or highlight a particular feature such as the side of the face. It "kicks up" the value of the highlighted area.

Light-balancing filter
Light-balancing filters are generally used to adjust light of standard color temperatures to match the response of various films. These include daylight-to-tungsten film, tungsten light-to-daylight film, etc. The color shifts produced are usually quite extreme. Decamired light-balancing filters that provide more subtle control by shifting the light a specified number of Mired units are also available.

Light box
A box with a translucent top surface illuminated from below. A light box provides an even back or bottom light for illuminating subjects from behind or below. It is useful for producing silhouettes, floating objects in a seamless white void, and creating unusual lighting designs.

Light modulator
Anything that comes between the light source and the subject and that changes the spectral distribution, intensity, pattern, or character of the light from the source.

Light tracing
A traced line of light on film created by pointing a moving light source directly at the camera while the shutter is held open.

Lighting contrast
The difference between the brightest and dimmest levels of illumination in a scene often expressed in exposure values or f-stops. Lighting contrast deals only with the intensity of illumination, not with the reflectance of the surfaces being illuminated. See lighting ratio, subject contrast, and scene contrast.

Lighting ratio
The difference between the brightest and dimmest levels of illumination in a scene expressed in terms of an arithmetic factor. A difference of 1 f-stop is a 2-to-1 lighting ratio, a difference of 2 f-stops is a 4-to-1 lighting ratio, etc. See lighting contrast.

Low key
A style of lighting in which the majority of the subject is rendered in values low on the tonal scale. An image in which the tonal values are largely depressed with few areas of light relief.

Lumen
A measure of the quantity of light falling on a subject related to the candlepower of the light source and the area being illuminated. Lumens are equal to footcandles multiplied by the area of illumination in square feet. Lumens are not a measure of specific brightness, but rather of overall quantity of illumination.

Main light
The light responsible for shaping the major shapes, planes, and volumes of a subject. The main light is usually the brightest light in a scene and should remain the dominant force in lighting design.

Mask
A negative or positive reversal image from an original transparency or negative. A selectively exposed, high-contrast film designed to block out exposure in specific areas of an image. Masks can be made and used in-camera or in the darkroom to create a variety of special effects.

Middle gray
A standard reference value adopted by the photographic industry and specified as 18° gray. See gray card.

Mired scale
A scale used to specify color temperature. The Mired value is equal to 1,000,000 divided by the value specified in degrees Kelvin. Therefore, 5,500°K is 182 Mired units and 3,200°K is 313 Mired units. The Mired scale is the inverse of the Kelvin scale with higher values representing warmer colors.

Modeling lamp
A quartz or tungsten lamp incorporated into a strobe head along with the strobe tube. The modeling lamp can be turned on to give an approximation of the light to be expected from the strobe. Some modeling lamps can be ratioed proportionally to match the light output from asymmetrical power packs.

Monoblock
An electronic strobe unit incorporating the power pack, modeling lamp, and strobe head into one compact unit. Monoblocks are usually limited in their power output, but are very flexible and easily transported.

Neutral density filter
A neutral gray filter designed to absorb light evenly across the spectrum thereby decreasing intensity without altering color balance.

Painting with light
A technique in which the light source is constantly moved to "paint" light over the subject while the shutter remains open. As light is painted on, it accumulates on the film as various exposure densities. Exposure level is controlled by the amount of time the light is directed at any one area of the subject.

Parabolic reflector
A reflector designed to emit parallel beams of light. Parabolic reflectors are used in spotlights to create harsh, directional light that casts sharp, deep shadows.

Penumbra
The transition area between light and dark. The area at the edge of a shadow. The size of the penumbra is an indicator of contrast. The smaller the penumbra, the sharper the shadow appears, and the more contrasty is the light.

Perspective
The relationship in the size and position between various objects within an image.

Perspective rendering
A style of representation based on a monocular view of the subject and decreasing size with increasing distance. Perspective rendering reduces the representation of the world to a set of predictable mathematical relationships based upon optical formulas. Cameras produce perspective renderings automatically through the optical workings of the single lens. Sometimes called single-point perspective rendering, referring to the monocular nature of this point of view.

Photo composition
The in-camera or darkroom assemblage of a composite photographic image. Photo composition techniques often involve masking and multiple exposure.

Photoflood
A special type of tungsten bulb sometimes incorporating a reflector in the bulb construction. Photofloods are balanced for either 3,200°K or 3,400°K.

Pin registration
A method of assuring proper registration of various films and masks with the use of holes punched in the films and matching pins on an easel or in a film holder over which the punched holes are placed.

Pixel
An abbreviation for "picture element." The individual dots that make up an image on a computer monitor.

Polarized light
Light that vibrates in only one plane perpendicular to its axis of propagation. Light can be polarized with a polarizing filter or can be naturally polarized to a degree. All specular reflection from nonmetallic surfaces is somewhat naturally polarized.

Polarizing filter
A special filter that polarizes the light passing through it and/or restricts the passage of already polarized light.

Power inverter
An electrical device used for converting current from DC to AC or vice versa. Inverters can be used to convert the DC output of an automobile generator to AC current, which can be used to power lights or strobes.

Power pack
The component of an electronic strobe system that stores and distributes power to the strobe heads. Power packs store their power in large capacitors and operate at high voltages. They act as central control units for the strobe heads and modeling lamps of an entire strobe system.

Prop
Anything in a photograph that is not subject or set. A prop is essentially an embellishment used to create a formal relationship or to aid in creating a sense of realism or a specific meaning within an image.

Proximity
In a photograph, the relationship in space between two discrete visual elements. Elements that are in close proximity may tend to be seen as functioning together to create a single figure, a group, or a pattern.

Pull
To hold back the development of film in order to accommodate for overexposure or high contrast. This term is especially applicable to color transparency films processed in professional labs.

Push
To prolong the development of film in order to compensate for underexposure or low contrast. See pull.

Quartz-halogen
A special, halogen gas-filled tungsten bulb made from quartz glass with a large filament. The bulb burns at a high temperature and when coupled with the halogen gas prevents buildup on the filament stabilizing the light and color output of the quartz bulb.

Radiant light
Light coming from the source directly into the lens of the camera.

Ray tracing
A technique used to create what appears to be rays of laserlike light in a photograph. The technique involves masking and multiple exposure.

Reciprocity failure
The failure of film to respond at the rated ISO when used outside of its recommended exposure time range. One result of reciprocity failure is that film will have a slower than normal response to light, and it can also cause color shifts in color films as the three emulsion layers fail at different rates.

Recycle time
The time required for a power pack to fully recharge its capacitors between firings.

Reflected highlights
Specular reflections of a light source on surfaces in a photograph.

Reflected light
Light reflected from the subject to the camera, or light reflected onto the subject from a remote reflector.

Reflected light meter
A light meter designed to read light reflected from surfaces in a scene. A reflected light meter must be used at a suitable distance and on axis with the camera lens to yield accurate exposure information.

Reflector
Any card or panel used to reflect light into or within a scene. Also a metallic, bowl-shaped component of a light source.

Refraction

The bending of light rays as they pass from a less dense to a more dense medium or vice versa.

Ringlight

A specialized light designed to attach to and encircle the lens of the camera. A ringlight provides the closest possible approximation to on-axis illumination.

Saturation

The intensity or purity of a hue.

Scene contrast

The difference between the brightest and the darkest surfaces in a scene. Scene contrast is a combination of lighting contrast and subject contrast. See lighting contrast and subject contrast.

Scoop

A bowl-shaped reflector designed to hold a bulb. Scoops can be elliptical, parabolic, or spherical, and either shallow or deep.

Scrim

Scrims are wire screens of various meshes designed to fit on the front of lights. They are useful in reducing light intensity and can slightly soften or color the light that they pass through.

Seamless paper

Wide rolls of paper designed for use as backgrounds; they can be rolled out into sweeps.

Secondary

In pigment color, green, orange, and violet are the secondary colors. The secondaries are produced from fifty-fifty mixtures of the primaries red, yellow, and blue.

Selective reflection

A special form of specular reflection from metallic surfaces. Selective reflection will be unpolarized and can be altered in its spectral composition.

Shade

Soft, open, totally reflected illumination.

Shading

The variation of tone or value across a surface. Shading is responsible for the creation of volume in two-dimensional imagery.

Shadow

A specific shape caused by the placement of an object within a light path. Three components are necessary for a shadow to exist: a light source, and object in the light path, and a ground on which the shadow falls.

Side light

Light coming from the side of a subject. Side light is usually good for defining texture, modeling volume, and creating depth. It is a moderately to very contrasty illumination.

Similarity

In a photograph, the likeness of two shapes to each other or of one shape to a recognizable icon or form not included in the image.

Slave trigger

A device used to trigger electronic strobe units in response to a flash of light, a radio signal, an infrared beam, or motion.

Snoot

A device attached to the front of a light source to restrict the spread of illumination. Snoots are tubes of various sizes mounted on flat plates that restrict the light to a circular pattern.

Soft box

A boxlike light with a diffusion panel for its front surface. A light source is mounted inside a soft light, which becomes a large diffuse source of illumination.

Softlight

A light that produces diffused, nondirectional illumination. Softlights incorporate reflectors or diffusers in their construction and no direct light from the bulb leaves the light source.

Spatial transposition

In a photograph, the rotation or reorientation of a figure in space. This can result from movement of the figure itself or from a change in point of view.

Specular reflection

Reflected light from a source that remains unchanged from a surface. Specular reflection from nonmetallic surfaces is polarized to some degree.

Spherical reflector

A reflector designed to spread out rays of light. The degree of spreading is related to the depth and shape of the reflector.

Spotlight

A light incorporating an optical lens and a parabolic reflector designed to focus all of its illumination in a small area. The rays of light leaving a spotlight are traveling nearly parallel. A spotlight is the most contrasty light available to a studio photographer.

Spot meter

A light meter designed to read a very restricted angle of illumination, usually only 1°. Spot meters can either be flash or ambient light meters.

Strobe head

The component of an electronic strobe system containing the strobe tube and modeling lamp. Many strobe heads also incorporate a fan for cooling.

Strobe light

A discontinuous light source delivering a great amount of illumination in a short burst. Studio strobe lights, or electronic flash units, generally have a duration ranging from 1/250 to 1/50,000 of a second.

Strobe meter

A light meter designed to read short bursts of light from electronic strobe systems or flash bulbs. See flash meter.

Strobe tube

A gaseous discharge tube filled with a gas that radiates light as an electrical spark passes through the tube. Strobe tubes are often rated in watt-seconds indicating their power-handling capacity.

Studio stand

A specialized camera support used in the studio. A studio stand consists of a central vertical column with an attached vertically and horizontally adjustable crossbar. The camera is mounted on one end of the crossbar and can easily be positioned at various heights.

Subject contrast

The difference in brightness between the most and the least reflective surfaces in a scene. Subject contrast is based on reflectivity and is not relative to the brightness of illumination in the scene. See lighting contrast and scene contrast.

Sweep
A seamless paper or cloth backdrop suspended at a height and rolled out forward on the floor to form a smooth, arcing background.

Symmetrical power pack
A power pack that distributes its energy equally to each of its outlets dependent upon the number of strobe heads plugged in. One head gets all of the power, two heads each get one-half power, four heads each get one-quarter power, etc.

Symmetry
A special case of similarity in which one-half of an object or scene gives all of the information necessary to construct or visualize the other half. In photographs, symmetry can be a stable and graphically strong compositional strategy.

Synch-cord
A cord used to connect a camera to an electronic strobe to carry the synchronization pulse that will coordinate the peak flash output with the full opening of the shutter.

System ISO
A personalized ISO, developed through testing, that reflects a photographer's individual equipment, techniques, and processes.

Texture
A regular and normally fine pattern of relief on a surface.

Texture gradient
The reduction in size of a texture pattern as it recedes from the viewer or camera. Texture gradient is one of the clues that we use to establish depth in a two-dimensional image.

Threshold level
The minimum level at which change occurs or at which a stimulus is apprehended.

Tonal
In two-dimensional imagery, tonal consists of continuous and subtle alterations of tone and value across the surfaces of a subject.

Tonal modeling
An image rendered in continuous values that yields a sense of space and volume.

Top light
Light coming from above the subject. Top light is moderately contrasty and casts its shadows straight down, rendering the subject in a small but quite deep size. Top light could be considered a form of side light.

Transmission
The ability of a material to pass light. Transmission is never 100 percent, some light is always reflected back and absorbed.

Trompe l'oeil
Literally "to fool the eye." The term is used to describe illusionistic two-dimensional images in perspective rendering that create an impression of reality.

Tungsten
A type of light incorporating a tungsten filament in a glass bulb. Tungsten lights have a nominal color temperature of 3,200°K.

Umbrella
In photography, a reflector, or sometimes a diffuser, shaped like its worldly namesake. Umbrellas are often used as attachments to strobe heads; they spread out and somewhat soften the illumination from the strobe.

Value
The particular brightness of a surface; value is related to reflectivity.

Variable spot/floodlight
A light that can be adjusted to either focus or spread out its illumination. A variable spot/flood will approximate the illumination of a spotlight or a broadlight.

Video back
An attachment available for some view cameras that, when connected to a monitor or VCR, will form a video image of what the lens views.

Video printer
A printer that will grab a freeze-frame from a video transmission and produce a hard copy print of the image.

Visible light
The portion of the energy spectrum to which human vision is sensitive. It is composed of wavelengths from approximately 300 to 700 nanometers.

Visual illusion
A visual perception believed to be accurate that does not conform to reality.

Visual percept
The mental image formed from the integration of visual stimuli into a meaningful whole.

Visual stimulus
An external event that registers a response in the visual system.

Visual system
The complete eye/brain infrastructure that makes visual perception possible.

Volume
Three-dimensional form.

Watt-second
A measure of the power stored and available for use in the capacitors of an electronic strobe system. Because they ignore the efficiency of power usage, watt-seconds are not necessarily a good measure of actual light output.

Wipe
A lateral movement of the camera or subject made visible in a long or multiple exposure.

Zoom
A movement of the camera in distance along the lens-to-subject axis made visible in a long or multiple exposure.

BIBLIOGRAPHY

Visual Perception and Photographic Theory

Barthes, Roland. *Camera Lucida*. New York: Hill and Wang, 1981.

Barthes, Roland. *Image Music Text*. New York: Hill and Wang, 1977.

Berger, John. *Another Way of Telling*. New York: Pantheon Books, 1982.

Capra, Fritjof. *The Tao of Physics*. Revised, 1984. New York: Bantam Books, 1984.

Foster, Hal, ed. *The Anti-Aesthetic*. Seattle: Bay Press, 1983.

Gombrich, E. H. *Art and Illusion*. 2nd ed. Princeton, New Jersey: Princeton University Press, 1961.

Hofstadter, Douglas. *Goedel, Escher, Bach: an Eternal Golden Braid*. New York: Vintage Books, 1979.

Hooper, Judith and Teresi, Dick. *The 3-Pound Universe*. New York: Dell Publishing Co., Inc., 1986.

Sarup, Madan. *Post Structuralism and Postmodernism*. Athens, Georgia: The University of Georgia Press, 1989.

Segal, Marshall H., Campbell, Donald T., and Herskovits, Melville, J. *The Influence of Culture on Visual Perception*. New York: Bobbs-Merrill Co., Inc., 1966.

Sekula, Allan. *Photography Against the Grain*. Halifax, Nova Scotia: The Press of the Nova Scotia College of Art and Design, 1984.

Squiers, Carol, ed. *The Critical Image*. Seattle: Bay Press, 1990.

Stroebel, Leslie, Todd, Hollis, and Zakia, Richard. *Visual Concepts for Photographers*. London: Focal Press, Ltd., 1980.

Webster, Frank. *The New Photography*. New York: Riverrun Press, Inc., 1985.

Zakia, Richard. *Perception and Photography*. Rochester, New York: Light Impressions, 1979.

Basic Photographic Practice

Davis, Phil. *Photography*. 3rd ed. Dubuque, Iowa: William C. Brown Publishers, 1990.

Gassan, Arnold. *Exploring Black and White Photography*. Dubuque, Iowa: Wm. C. Brown Publishers, 1989.

Pittaro, Ernest M., ed. *Photo Lab Index*. Lifetime Edition. Dobbs Ferry, New York: Morgan and Morgan, 1991. Updated annually with inserts available through subscription.

Swedlund, Charles with Yule, Elizabeth. *Photography*. New York: Holt, Rinehart, and Winston, 1981.

Color

Albers, Josef. *The Interaction of Color*. New Haven, Connecticut: Yale University Press, 1963.

Hirsch, Robert. *Exploring Color Photography*. Dubuque, Iowa: William C. Brown Publishers, 1989.

Spencer, D. A. *Colour Photography In Practice*. Revised 1975. London: Focal Press, 1975.

Zakia, Richard, and Todd, Hollis. *Color Primer 1 & 2*. Dobbs Ferry, New York: Morgan and Morgan, 1974.

View Camera

Shaman, Harvey. *The View Camera: Operations and Techniques*. New York: Amphoto, 1977.

Stone, Jim. *A User's Guide to the View Camera*. Boston: Little, Brown and Co., 1987.

Stroebel, Leslie. *View Camera Technique*. New York: Hastings House, 1967.

Photographic Sensitometry/Densitometry

Adams, Ansel. *The Negative*. Basic Photo Series. Boston: New York Graphic Society, 1971.

Sanders, Norman. *Photographic Tone Control*. Dobbs Ferry, New York: Morgan and Morgan, 1977.

Todd, Hollis and Zakia, Richard. *Photographic Sensitometry*. Dobbs Ferry, New York: Morgan and Morgan, 1974.

Photographic Lighting

Bron Elektronik. *Professional Lighting Technique*. Allschwil, Switzerland: Bron Electronik, 1988.

Feininger, Andreas. *Light and Lighting in Photography*. New York: Amphoto, 1976.

Freeman, Michael. *Light*. New York: Amphoto, 1988.

Hunter, Phil and Fuqua, Paul. *Light: Science and Magic*. Boston: Focal Press, 1990.

Kerr, Norman. *Techniques of Photographic Lighting*. Watson Guptil, 1982.

General Studio

Carroll, Don and Marie. *Focus on Special Effects*. Watson Guptil, 1982.

Freeman, Michael. *The Photographer's Studio Manual*. New York: Amphoto, 1984.

Livingston, Kathryn. *Special Effects Photography*. Watson Guptil, 1985.

Perweiler, Gary. *Secrets of Studio Still Life Photography*. New York: Amphoto, 1984.

Reznicki, Jack. *Illustration Photography*. Watson Guptil, 1987.

Time-Life Books. *The Studio*. New York: Time, Inc., 1971.

Set Design and Construction

Buerki, F. A. *Stagecraft for Nonprofessionals*. 3rd ed. Madison, Wisconsin: The University of Wisconsin Press, 1983.

Gillette, A. S. *Stage Scenery: Its Construction and Rigging*. New York: Harper and Row, Publishers, 1972.

Pinnell, William H. *Theatrical Scene Painting*. Carbondale, Illinois: Southern Illinois University Press, 1987.

Wolfe, Welby B. *Materials of the Scene*. New York: Harper and Row, Publishers, 1977.

INDEX